Trade and Transformation in Korea, 1876–1945

Transitions: Asia and Asian America

Series Editor, *Mark Selden*

FORTHCOMING

Trade and Transformation in Korea, 1876–1945

Dennis L. McNamara

WestviewPress

A Division of HarperCollins*Publishers*

Copyright © 1996 by Westview Press, A Division of HarperCollins Publishers, Inc.

Published in 1996 in the United States of America by Westview Press, 5500 Central Avenue, Boulder,
Colorado 80301-2877, and in the United Kingdom by Westview Press, 12 Hid's Copse Road,
Cumnor Hill, Oxford OX2 9JJ

Library of Congress Cataloging-in-Publication Data
McNamara, Dennis L.
  Trade and transformation in Korea, 1876–1945 / by Dennis L.
McNamara.
     p.   cm.
  Includes bibliographical references and index.
  ISBN 0-8133-8994-1 (hc)
  1. Korea—Commerce—History—19th century.   2. Korea—Commerce—
History—20th century.   3. Grain trade—Korea—History.   4. Korea—
Economic conditions.   I. Title.
  HF3830.5.M39   1996
  382'.09519—dc20   96-16626
                                                                                        CIP

The paper used in this publication meets the requirements of the American National Standard for
Permanence of Paper for Printed Library Materials Z39.48-1984.

10   9   8   7   6   5   4   3   2   1

In memory of Bro. Michael Daniels, S.J.,
a scholar and a friend

Contents

Tables

Preface

Eager to dispel differences, we often compare markets and merchants East and West with distinctions between "public" and "private" or "state" and "society." But the mixture of public and private or state and society that confronts us in Asia only fuels trade conflicts, confounds business ties, and bedevils efforts to forge cultural bridges. Apart from concepts, more tangible legal boundaries of nation-states within stable regional systems of trade and polity offer a further basis for distinguishing paths of capitalist development, but shifting sovereignties in Korea's modern history deprive us of this comparative ground as well. The decline of the Chinese Empire in East Asia coincided with the rapid rise of the Japanese colonial empire at the turn of the last century, and led to colonization of the Korean Kingdom after five centuries of independence within the same territory. Core concepts of capitalist society and basic premises of sovereignty and regional stability appear in the modern history of Northeast Asia as little more than targets of conquest and contest.

Contested boundaries of idea and institution distinguished Korea's entry into international market capitalism from the late nineteenth century. Conflicts over sovereignty at court and countryside plagued the monarchy in Seoul from the Treaty of Kanghwa through colonization in 1910, just as contradictory assimilation policies and nationalist sentiment subsequently frustrated cultural and political identification with the Japanese Empire through 1945. Yet neither competing categories nor confusing political chronicles should divert attention from the success and significance of a Korean road to capitalist development. Indeed, it is in the crucible of contested sovereignty and competing expatriate and local business communities following the extension of international markets to the peninsula from 1876 that modern capitalism on the peninsula gains definition. Our story begins not with early capitalist roots in modes of production in the countryside or among merchants at Seoul or rural periodic markets but, rather, with international trade and entry into a world capitalist system of interstate and intermarket ties.

Korea's contested history has spawned contesting histories, with some scholars discovering capitalist sprouts in the Chosŏn Dynasty (1392-1910) and others citing changes from the years of alien rule (1910-1945). Further study of court and countryside in the late Dynasty and of agriculture and industry in the colony promise to bring light to the emotional debate over the origins of Korean capitalism, but the recent literature on development has already greatly enhanced our understanding of colonial legacies for subsequent growth in South Korea. Bruce Cumings captured the essence of the debate with the term "colonial overdevelopment" contrasting the remarkable growth of infrastructures benefitting the Japanese islands with the limited participation of Koreans or "underdevelopment" of local human resources. Following the path of pioneering scholars such as Cho Ki-jun and Koh Seung-je, recent studies of colonial Korea have advanced our understanding of local capitalist development. I extended the thesis of "dependent development" to Korea's leading colonial entrepreneurs in *Colonial Origins of Korean Enterprise*, distinguishing varieties of autonomy, cooperation, and collusion in enterprise and ideas. In *Offspring of Empire,* Carter Eckert pointed to industrialization as tangible evidence of economic moderniza-tion in a case study of the Koch'ang Kim family. The studies of Michael Robinson and of Ken Wells have broadened the focus beyond business to culture and ideas in the colony.

Unlike the major colonial business elite, the vast majority of Korean businessmen in late kingdom and colony lived out their lives in relative obscurity and have captured far less attention. A recent collection of essays by An Pyŏng-jik, Kajimura Hideki, and others breaks new ground with a focus on local market histories. In a similar vein, this study looks to agriculture and trade rather than large-scale industry, to medium and small-scale enterprise rather than major firms, and to ports rather than the capital city. Traditional Korean brokers or *kaekchu* take center stage here as I look to firms, business associations, and semi-official or chartered companies.

I find evidence of ethnic distinction, subordination, and yet cooperation in the "circles of enterprise" constituting the Korean *chaegye* at the ports. Earlier precedents of ethnicity, political authority in the economy, and enterprise and association help account for features of distinction or separation, dependence or subordination to the Japanese *zaikai,* and cooperation or integration into the colonial economy. A colonial program of law and contract, of business-state ties, and of semi-official firms such as the Grain Exchange likewise fostered and sustained such features in the circles of enterprise on the peninsula across the colonial years.

The significance of *chaegye* formation extends beyond market to society and indeed to more profound changes in modern Korean history. The consolidation of a business community at the port with its own patterns of enterprise and association and, more importantly, its own interests and organizations provides evidence of a nascent civil society in the colony. Issues of "public" versus "private" interests, and of "state" and "society" first surfaced in the trade debate in the late nineteenth century between conservatives and Enlightenment advocates. The latter countered the earlier *kunsin* (monarch and minister) model of polity with a new emphasis on *kwanmin* (official and citizen) and popular participation. The debate resurfaced in more tangible issues of local sovereignty and development in the "Native Products Campaign" of the 1920s. A heated controversy over the transfer of the Grain Exchange from Inch'ŏn to Seoul in the same decade brought the debate to still more immediate issues of local versus imperial interests, giving shape to a "public" and "private" interest, and to the roles of state and private sectors in projects critical for the commonweal.

The journey of the port brokers through 1945 tells us as well of a wider historical transition or "transformation" in the interplay of market and society. Karl Polanyi's work on the growing autonomy of market over traditional societal constraints of kinship, tribal loyalties, religious or moral controls gives direction to our chronicle of enterprise at the ports. A transformation in the organization and idea of exchange led to a remaking of market institutions and a rethinking of ideas of enterprise and association, public and private, state and society. But if trade led to greater legitimacy and relative autonomy of the market dynamic of supply and demand, it also spurred new societal constraints on unfettered markets and destructive competition, particularly significant for post-colonial capitalism in South Korea. Legacies of traditional enterprise and guild association marked the early path of brokers in the transformation pressed by trade and traders from 1876, and legacies of colonial association and enterprise, both institutions and ideas, were prominent in the return of the *chaegye* in South Korea's First Republic (1948-1960).

The blend of formal political control and informal economic accommodation adds a Korean chapter to studies of colonialism, while the focus on circles of enterprise tests the comparative significance of the interaction between colonizers and colonized. The Korean experience contributes a new chapter to the growing literature on World System formation, but with more attention to the interplay of core and periphery rather than simply to the extension of core market and state. In the confrontation of early precedents of enterprise and association with a colonial program of law, state oversight of business associations, and chartered firms, the "incorporation" of Korea unfolds as an unequal interaction rather than simply imposition. Of significance for comparative political economy and Asian history alike, the work of Karl Polanyi brings light here to an Asian experience of market and system. Following Korea's transformation through the reembedding of institution and idea in the economy, the study counters the Western division of market and society with the interaction of market and society so familiar in Asian capitalism. Thirdly, recent efforts towards democratization and market liberalization in South Korea have turned attention to the origins of civil society, particularly to the discontinuities between autonomous or independent interests and structural or associational dependence. Of particular significance to students of Korean history and society, our study of the grain brokers assesses the role of market and trade in the formation of "private" interests apart from the state critical for the emergence of civil society.

The passage of the brokers across seven decades of Korea's turbulent modern history has taken me on a journey as well. I was able to weave a profile with various threads of enterprise and association from documents at the Korean National Library and the Korea Research Library in Seoul, and at various archives at Chambers and banks. Materials at the Diet Library in Tokyo and the Library of Congress in Washington added rich detail, and interviews at the Inch'ŏn Chamber of Commerce and Industry, at the Association of Korean Grain Agents, and at the Koryŏ Rice Mill in Inch'ŏn brought color and drama to the story. Research directors and librarians at the Chamber of Commerce and Industry Libraries in Seoul, Inch'ŏn, Tokyo, and Osaka patiently located archival materials adding still further detail to an increasingly complex chronicle, while the advice of eminent colleagues in Korea such as Lew Young-ick, Lee Kwang-rin, and Shin Yong-ha engendered confidence in identifying themes and sorting out the significance of the brokers and their journey. The Fulbright Program under Mr. Fred Carriere in Seoul and the Committee for the Mellon Research Grants at Georgetown University deserve many thanks for making this journey possible. I alone remain responsible for the study, and trust it will shed light on both past and present.

Dennis L. McNamara

Korean Peninsula

Siping
Huadian
Tumen
Vladivostok
Russia
Nakhodka

China
Hurha He
Erdao Jiang
Khasan
Musan
Najin

Badaojiang
Ch'ongjin

Shenyang
Tonghua
Hyesan

Anshan
Ji'an
Manp'o
Kanggye
Kimch'aek

Yalu Jiang
Yalu

Dandong
Sinuiju
Kusong
North

Yongbyon
Hamhung

Sojoson-man
Korea
Tongjoson-man

P'YONGYANG
Wonsan

Korea
Bay

Namp'o

Changyon
Sariwon
P'yonggang

Haeju
Ch'orwon
Demarcation
Line

Paengnyong-do
Ch'unch'on
Kangnung

Sunwi-do
Ongjin
Kaesong
Munsan

Sea of
Japan

Kyonggi-man
Inch'on
SEOUL
Wonju
Ullung-do

China
Suwon
South

Ch'onan
Korea

Kum-gang
Ch'ongju
Andong

Taejon
P'ohang

Kunsan
Chonju
Taegu
Nakdong

Yellow
Sea
Masan
Ulsan

Kwangju
Pusan

Mokp'o
Koje-do
Japan
Hiroshima

Chin-do
Yosu
Tsushima
Korea

Cheju-haehyop
Strait
Fukuoka
Kitakyushu

Cheju
Sasebo

Cheju-do

0   50   100 Kilometers
0   50   100 Miles
Lambert Conformal Conic Projection SP 23N/45N

Boundary representation is
not necessarily authoritative.

802191 (R00141) 7-93

Abbreviations

CGKKY. Tōa Keizai Jihōsha. *Chōsen ginkō kaisha kumiai yōroku* [A list of banks, corporations, and partnerships in Korea]. Edited by Nakamura Sukeryō. Tokyo: Tōa Keizai Jihōsha. Early volumes are titled *Chōsen ginkō kaisha yōroku*, and abbreviated CGKY.

CSTN. Chōsen Sōtokufu. *Chōsen Sōtokufu tōkei nempō* [Statistical annuals of the Chōsen Government-General]. Keijo: Government General, annual.

DKB. Tōyō Keizai Shibosha. *Dairiku kaisha benran* [Handbook of companies on the continent]. Edited by Akihishi Sawano. Tokyo: Tōyō Keizai Shibosha.

HHS. Taehaksa. *Han'guk hyŏndae sup'ilchip charyo ch'ŏngsŏ* [A compendium of materials on modern Korean essays], vol. 1. Seoul: Taehaksa, 1987.

IBA. Inch'ŏn Brokers Association [Inch'ŏn Mulsan Kaekchu Chohap].

KHWM. Koryŏdae Dong'a Munje Yŏn'guso, compil. *Ku Han'guk woegyo munsŏ* [Diplomatic documents of the late Chosŏn Dynasty]. Seoul: Korea University Press, 1965.

TGKY. Teikoku Kōshinjo. *Teikoku ginkō kaisha yōroku* [A list of banks and corporations in the empire], Chōsen and Manchuria Section. Tokyo: Teikoku Kōshinjo.

Trade and Transformation in
Korea, 1876–1945

1

Transitions

Boundaries between the state and the private interests of the market remain the pillars of capitalist society East and West, but with remarkable differences even between major trading partners. The porous borders between Asian state and society which bewilder traders and politicians from the West reflect deep historical legacies. Recent attention to Korea's history of development from the turn of the century has ignited a heated debate over indigenous versus colonial or alien origins on the one hand, and over continuities with the colonial experience versus the discontinuities of division, war, and reconstruction on the other.[1] At the same time a Korean path of capitalist growth has gained notoriety in conceptual debates over prescriptions for third world development.[2] State rather than society has garnered most of the scholarly attention in historical and theoretical debates over Korea's colonial interlude (1910-1945), just as studies of the "developmental" states of post-war Japan and post-1960 South Korea look back more to bureaucratic legacies than to the organized interests of civil society. But if cooperation with private interests rather than simply insulation is one key to an effective state role in transforming markets, we can learn how the state actually becomes embedded in the economy by tracking the origins of a Korean private sector in a business community or *chaegye*.

Attention to long-established societal ties with the polity among Korea's nascent capitalist class forces us beyond the easy dichotomy between "roots" and "revision," the former emphasizing indigenous capitalist "sprouts" and the latter "revisions" highlighting the colonial contribution. Differences in administration and economic policy between the Korean monarchy of the late Chosŏn Dynasty and the subsequent Japanese government-general offer evidence for such a dichotomy, but a competition of precolonial legacies and colonial patterns better explains the reorganization of enterprise and markets in colonial society. Extending the study of colonial business-state ties from industry to agriculture, from manufacture to trade, from leading economic elites to medium and small-scale enterprise, and from the capital city of Seoul to the port cities refocuses the historical debate over legacies and offers a colonial profile of how markets were reinstituted in state and society. If precolonial precedent and colonial pattern define the Korean *chaegye* at Inch'ŏn plying the rice trade, the transformation spurred by trade tells us more broadly of the interests, enterprise, and association of a private sector in Korea's nascent "civil society." Yet the trade opening Korean markets at the turn of the century appears today as little more than a distant memory for an exporting giant like South Korea. This small country with borders closed to commerce until 1876 now ranks as the thirteenth largest trader in the world with annual exports of eighty-two billion dollars.[3]

Many entrepreneurs in the First Republic (1948-1960) were either landlords or millers or traders in agricultural products during the colonial period. Apart from precedents of enterprise and association, the entrepreneurs constitute a critical human link between early trade and later chaebŏl, the industrial and trade combines leading Korean industrialization. Mills appear prominently in the early history of postcolonial business leaders such as Sin Tŏg-gyun, Yang Chŏng-mo, and even Lee Byung-chull. Sin gained prominence in the colony with his T'aep'yŏng Mill in Pusan, and only later organized and chaired a prominent postwar business group, the Dongbang Corporation. Yang Chŏng-mo, founder of the once prosperous Kukje Group, also has roots in the milling industry of the colony where his father owned and operated a rice mill in colonial Pusan.[4] The foremost of Korea's postcolonial entrepreneurs, Lee Byung-chull of the Samsung Group launched his career with a rice mill in the colony.[5] Grains and mills in early Korean business history helped establish patterns of entrepreneurship significant well after liberation.

The Treaty of Friendship with Japan concluded at Kanghwa Island in 1876 opened Korean ports to foreign commerce. Japanese clippers and steamers set off to Korea with farm tools, textiles, oil and matches, and returned laden with rice and soybeans. With trade came Japanese merchants, new ideas and institutions of enterprise and association, and a modern capitalist interstate system of polity and commerce. What the Japanese met at the ports were local brokers hustling to compete with the foreign merchants and straining to span contending worlds of traditional commerce and modern trade on their own territory. It was the brokers who would bridge a Chinese world order with a Japanese interstate system and survive first an embattled monarchy and then an authoritarian colonial state. It was the brokers who would mediate between a Japanese business community at the ports and a local community of landowners, carriers, and merchants. And it was the grain agents and millers among the brokers who held the reins at enterprise and association in the port cities. The introduction of a stable currency, modern banking and insurance systems helped institutionalize exchange and expand commerce, but within and beyond such institutions, the brokering of rice persisted as a critical marketing role in both kingdom and colony. Rice in this agrarian society not only fed the population and set the rhythm of planting and harvesting marking the seasons, it also served as currency and collateral, as the spur to early mechanization in the milling industry, and as a leading export. Together with land and labor, rice remained the most basic form of capital across kingdom and colony.

The grain trade forged patterns of exchange which would dominate market and enterprise at the ports through 1945 and give initial shape to international market capitalism on the peninsula. One key to the extension of market relations is the reconstruction of trust ensuring the confidence necessary to sustain ties between producer and consumer. A transition from status to contract, from custom to legal or "institutional" precedent ensures the reliability of large-scale, impersonal commercial transactions distinguishing modern capitalist trade. The extensive colonial reorganization of exchange has captured the attention of scholars tracing the shift from farming to organized finance associations and agricultural associations in the countryside, from storefront and wharf to registered firm and grain exchange, and from barter and pawn shop to currency, bank, and insurance firm. What is sometimes lost in the rich lode of colonial statistics and official documents on banking and exchange, the land survey, irrigation projects, or the "Senbei taisaku [Korean Rice Policy]," is the fact that the colonists changed little in the actual organization of agricultural production. As newcomers to the peninsula at the very end of the nineteenth century bent on expanding the grain trade to support markets in the home islands, the commercial vanguard from Japan and subsequent colonists settled for reform rather than revolution in the countryside. What did change dramatically were the markets for Korean grains, and the organization of trade commerce at major ports and urban centers.

Karl Polanyi wrote of the "great transformation" from a premarket economy embedded in social relations or "society," to the liberated or relatively "free market" of modern capitalism. No longer constrained by societal norms of kinship or tribal authority or religion, the market dynamic in capitalist society gains its own legitimacy. But his contribution was less the distinction of "market" from "society" than the interpenetration of society and state in modern markets, an insight which continues to inspire scholars hoping to unravel the interplay of market with non-market, often opaque cultural patterns and historical precedents. Ruggie extends the insight to a balance between "authority" and "market" in state-society relations, where the state had now to "institute and safeguard the self-regulating market."[6] Abrupt shifts in Korean markets and society from the late nineteenth century offer a case study of the uneasy blend of kinship, traditional enterprise and association, and other cultural continuities on the one hand, with impersonal market rationality on the other.

We might well frame a study of transformation in late nineteenth century Korea with the contrast between an earlier exchange dominated by society, and the organization and enterprise of merchants in more unfettered markets. Assessing the interplay of status and contract, of *gemeinschaft* and *gesellschaft*, of traditional agents [*kaekchu*] in Korea with modern brokers, and of earlier guilds with modern chambers would provide a language and calculus for assessing change. But economies or markets alone tell only a partial story, just as histories of administrative policy or political hegemony chronicle but a piece of Korea's transition through 1945. Tracing market and society within the history of polities and trading partners extends the analysis to the passage from Korean kingdom to Japanese colony, and from Chinese Empire to Japanese interstate system. And if market, state, and regional ties weave a tale of transformation for relatively sovereign nations, what can be said of change under colonial rule?

What distinguished the transition to modern capitalist forms of exchange on the peninsula were disorienting shifts from local sovereignty to colonial dependence, and from traditional agriculture in the kingdom to colonial agriculture, industry and commerce dominated by foreign interests. Fundamental changes in state and Korea's place in regional markets marked the passage towards a more autonomous market dynamic, and few confronted these simultaneous and at times contradictory trends more directly than the grain brokers at the major seaports. In contrast to a largely rural population, the port brokers stood at the intersection of changes in market, state, and regional system as they struggled to hold their ground in the fast-growing international commerce in Korean rice and soybeans. Intent on little more than family and business, brokers at the raucous, bustling seaports served as unlikely pioneers moving between two widely discrepant worlds of Chinese Empire and colonial system, of kingdom and colony, and of traditional exchange reconstructed within a more independent market.

Portraits of Korean brokers and their Japanese colleagues bring more than just drama to our chronicle. Histories of their enterprise and association suggest legacies from earlier styles of exchange, but also reveal the colonial process of instituting new norms of business-state ties, of new networks within a professional business community, or of contract and entrepreneurship within new forms of enterprise. In an earlier work on the colonial Korean elite I cited levels of related enterprise stretching from family-owned agrarian estates and firms, to the leading semi-official, chartered colonial companies.[7] Intersecting circles of investment revealed patterns of business-state ties, of alliances within the Korean and Japanese business communities, and of family enterprise. As I turn from the exceptions in finance, commerce, and large-scale industry to the norm of smaller-scale local manufacture and commerce in the milling and marketing of rice, I find still other patterns of enterprise and association and discover more of the legacies of Korea's past and lessons of the colonial years. Entrepreneurs both big and small pioneered Korea's transition into a modern capitalist society of international trade.

Market, State, and System

A dialectic of society and market unfolds in the transformation from subsistence production to motives of gain, and from economies enmeshed in social systems of reciprocity and redistribution to self-regulating market economies. The separation of economy and polity in the rise of a self-regulated market suggests one dimension of change, encouraging the profit motive and rooting the self-regulating market in institutions such as grain exchanges.[8] Cumings briefly assessed the transition from subsistence to profit late in the colonial years and concluded that the force of the world market system and the rise of industry sparked the "onset of Korea's capitalist revolution" among the peasant class.[9] Beginning with the chain of events stretching from Kanghwa Treaty of 1876, a chronicle of change in idea and institution brings light to the "relative invisibility" of the process of freeing the economy from earlier constraints of monarchy and society, and then reorganizing the colonial economy to harness market rationality to imperial goals.[10] The Kabo Reforms of 1894-1895 authorized Korean business associations under close government supervision. Circulation of Japanese currency on the peninsula from 1902 at branches of the Daiichi Bank and transportation on the Seoul-Inch'ŏn (1900) and Seoul-Pusan (1905) railroad lines facilitated commerce and extended Japanese influence in the economy. Annexation of Korea in 1910 completed Japanese control of finance and foreign affairs, and permitted further controls on domestic commerce. One could point to the reorganization of the regional agricultural banks into the Chosen Industrial Bank in 1918, or its affiliated network of finance associations as likewise critical for commerce.

We can follow the transition from barter to currency, and from spot transaction to trading in futures through the history of the grain and stock exchanges. Japanese traders at Inch'ŏn gained the support of the Japanese Legation in organizing the Jinsen Grain Exchange already in 1899. Speculation at the exchange aggravated by an economic recession during the first World War forced a suspension of trading in 1919 and a government bailout to ensure the survival of the exchange. A subsequent decade of fierce debate over the future of the Jinsen Exchange ended with a merger into the Chosen Exchange (1932) with stock transactions at the Seoul headquarters and grain sales at the Inch'ŏn branch.[11] The Chosen Grain Market Company replaced grain exchanges in 1939 with a system of wartime controls on food distribution.

One can hardly deny the significance of close merchant ties with the court of the late Chosŏn Dynasty, and then with the colonial state. The rise of the market cannot be viewed in isolation from persisting political controls, for it is the interaction of polity and economy that distinguishes market in kingdom, colony, and Republic. Marketers allied with rulers both local and alien gained greater freedom of enterprise only because of the interdependence of polity and market necessary to sustain a political mandate. The fact that authorities in kingdom and colony helped make and then manage markets, and thus secured a major role for the polity in new economic institutions cannot be overlooked in the rush to highlight trade in Korea's transformation. For instance despite the relatively low status of merchants in the Chosŏn Dynasty, we find Korean commission agents accorded a role in collecting duties from international commerce, implementing embargoes, and monitoring trade. Despite extensive state oversight of colonial enterprise and association, one finds Korean brokers and their Japanese colleagues with a voice in shaping legislation on commerce and trade, if only because of their role in sustaining prosperity and the complexity of market dynamics testing the competence of state bureaucracies.

But we cannot understand the role of polity without a better grasp of societal dynamics in the emerging private sector. A dialectic of organizing principles pitting economic self-regulation against societal self-protection remains central to the literature on "civil society."[12] Keane cited the same dialectic but argued against property-centered interpretations of the term "civil society" that ignore equally important political developments such as intermediate associations beyond simply the market. He emphasized rather the interdependence of state and market, and the dependence of state on market success to sustain legitimacy.[13] Indeed, the effort to untangle polity or "state" from economy or "civil society" may divert attention from mediating patterns of associational life with roots predating both modern state and market economy, and thus from the mixture of traditional and modern patterns basic to historical transformations. Intent on a more inclusive definition, Perez-Diaz referred to "civil society" as the "social institutions such as markets and associations and the public sphere," in contrast to "state institutions proper."[14] The work of Durkheim and de Tocqueville on intermediary associations offers a starting point for assessing the reordering of state and society in Korea at the turn of the century. Durkheim emphasized the independent role of voluntary associations in mediating the growing power of the state in industrializing societies. Tocqueville wrote likewise of associations "for political, commercial, or manufacturing purposes" as "powerful and enlightened members of the community," which "save the common liberties of the country," and concluded that "among democratic nations it is only by association that the resistance of the people to government can ever display itself."[15]

Porous borders between state and society in Korea, Japan, and China have forced refinements in theories of interest group formation. Sorting through constraints on organizations in late nineteenth-century China, William Rowe found a process of continual negotiation between state control and associational autonomy.[16] One could cite even more severe constraints on organizations in Korea at the turn of the century. Yet capitalism did bring market to polity in Korea's new political economy and in the process reshaped both state and society, even though the rapid pace of Japanese penetration limited popular political mobilization. If authoritarian rule constrained the scope of activities and publications among intellectuals and religious groups, neither the speed nor the character of incorporation precluded the consolidation of mercantile interests into a cohesive business community at the major ports.

No longer content to broadly distiguish roles of state and society in capitalist transformation, scholars have returned recently to Polanyi's thesis of embedded ties of state and society in markets.[17] The grain trade brought greater recognition to the expertise of merchants in the late years of Kojong's reign, and even formal government approval for chambers to represent the merchants across trades. Bergere and Fewsmith cited similar developments in early twentieth century China as evidence of intermediate groups bridging the interests of state and society.[18] Fundamental differences between China and Korea are apparent at the turn of the century as the nascent Korean *chaegye* emerged as an unequal partner under the shadow of a more specialized, better funded and organized Japanese business community or "zaikai." Unlike the Chinese, Koreans mobilized their organizations largely without political voice under an alien state. Yet drawing on insights from studies of the Chinese business community, I cite trade associations and approved chambers as evidence of government recognition of commercial groups relatively distinct from the state in Korea as well.[19]

New organizations and ideas marked the shift to more independent status among the brokers in Korea's treaty ports. Kojong's government gave initial legal approval to their organizations, signalling limited recognition of their distinct interests in Korean society. An ideological shift from a hierarchical emphasis on "monarch and minister," to a more egalitarian emphasis on "officials and citizens" gave notice of an initial distinction between state and society.[20] The latter denoted the limited separation between state and market necessary for a capitalist economy, and an ideological basis for a private sector gradually staking their claim for legitimacy in Korean society. The place of private profit would remain problematic in the discussions of capitalism in the 1920s, yet the brokers would at least gain greater respect for their goal of profit, and for organizations to moderate the effects of unregulated competition.

Local intellectuals in the colony disrupted administration efforts to equate the commonweal of the colony with imperial goals. The "Native Products Campaign" gave public voice to aspirations for "national capital," and indirectly, for a national good apart from the commonweal of the empire.[21] This third issue of "common" benefit would prove most difficult under colonial rule where a foreign state ruled over business interests of two nations. Trade advocates and supporters of the precolonial Korean Chamber of Commerce came to rely on business groups as the nation's only hope for eventual commercial sovereignty following the Protectorate Treaty of 1905. Annexation in 1910 dimmed but did not destroy their hopes. Cooperative efforts in the combined chamber between Japanese and Korean mercantile interests from 1916 permitted little opportunity to distinguish local benefit from wider imperial benefit. But despite constraints on independent ideological development after annexation, the Korean business community at the ports did coalesce around more conventional ideas of the role of profit and commerce, the need for organized competition, and the ideal of economic growth.

The ideological journey highlights a further transition in regional orders deeply affecting the interplay of market and society, and more broadly of state and society. Events such as the Kanghwa Treaty of 1876, Japanese victories in the Sino-Japanese War of 1894-1895, and then in the Russo-Japanese War of 1904-1905, and the Anglo-Japanese treaties strengthened Japan's claim to regional hegemony. With the annexation of Taiwan (1895) and Korea (1910), and the establishment of the colony of Manchukuo in Manchuria (1931), Japan drew the boundaries of not only a colonial empire but of a military base for a global war (1941-45). What lends perspective to a picture of change on the peninsula is regional transformation where a shift in world orders drove the task of remaking markets and rethinking exchange. Dominating trade through 1945, grain exports offer a chronicle of Korea's entry into a new regional, capitalist order.

Wallerstein and Martin defined "incorporation" as the integration of "production processes into the interdependent network of production that constitutes the world market."[22] The consolidation reflects the growing influence of core state capital on market dynamics in the periphery and a reorientation of political decision-making towards core state interests. They cited a relentless drive towards the center or core nation which undermines local economic networks impeding capitalist penetration as well as political structures inimical to the expansion of the core power.[23] Cross-national alliances between capital in core and periphery remain the key to effective integration of smaller, precapitalist nations into international capitalist markets, just as a system of international markets makes such alliances both possible and profitable. A directive, authoritarian state can encourage, order and demand links between merchants in core and periphery, but only the merchants themselves can ply the trade. I would emphasize that such alliances may well permit accommodation of traditional patterns of enterprise and association, or at least gradual reform, in order to quickly establish and expand commerce between core and periphery markets.

Complementary processes of "incorporation" and "peripheralization" insure the integration of new areas into a world system. The former refers to the linking of peripheral zones with a world economy and interstate system, and the latter denotes the transformation of structures in the periphery, or "deepening" of capitalist development.[24] Hopkins and Wallerstein wrote more simply of two dynamics in the geographical expansion of the capitalist interstate system: extension of a division of labor, and of an interstate system.[25] Links among local workers and merchants with a wider, regional division of labor would suggest expanding cross-national ties among capital and labor in periphery and core. Penetration of market and political structures in peripheral areas dominated by a regional power extends the interstate system. But does the emphasis on markets come at the cost of ignoring geopolitical factors, or attention to international system at the cost of overlooking local society? Skocpol faulted system theorists for their misplaced emphasis on market over state and their inattention to preexisting institutional patterns of class and state in the local area.[26] Chase-Dunn has countered the former criticism with his thesis of a "single logic in which both political-military power and the appropriation of surplus value through production of commodities for sale on the world market play an integrated role."[27]

World Systems theorists have only begun to address the more telling criticism of attention to system at the expense of local society.[28] Brenner faulted Wallerstein for an overemphasis on a trade-based division of labor in the origins of capitialism, to the detriment of local class relations of production.[29] Critics such as Eric Wolf and Peter Worsley later distinguished between Wallerstein's "capitalist world market" and a capitalist "mode of production," arguing that trade relations alone do not explain changes in modes of production.[30] The cogent criticism has prompted a refocus on articulation or interpenetration of competing modes of production, such as slavery, tenancy, and wage-labor. Foster-Carter concluded that the world system is "constituted perhaps by relations of exchange rather than consisting of a unitary mode of production."[31] Kelly has recently returned to the debate to distinguish overlapping modes of production: "Capitalist production extended wage labor and commodity exchange a predominant features of the economy. However, it also depended, for the realization of profit, on the maintenance of preexisting productive arrangements."[32]   She cites subsistence activities within a wider agrarian economy as an example, and calls for greater attention to the "preexisting modalities of labor organization" in the informal economy.   Shin Gi-wook's thesis of a partial proletarianization among agrarian peasants offers evidence of overlapping modes in colonial agriculture on the Korean peninsula.[33]   By the late nineteenth century Korean grain brokers had largely completed the transition from barter or subsistence to a cash economy with enterprise for profit, but not from guild to more professional organization within chambers.   We step back to the early Korean mills, associations, and exchanges, and find new styles of Japanese enterprise and association superimposed on Korean guild precedents of cooperation and competition.

Chase-Dunn extended the focus on articulation by recalling a distinction of Althusser and Balibar between mode of production and "social formation."   The latter suggests the economic, political, and ideological processes distinguishing a nation's level of development or "social transformation."[34]   Such processes draw attention to "historical events and social institutions which may contain more than one mode of production."[35]   I look to the ideologies and organizations of Korean brokers at the cusp of dramatic political and economic changes on the peninsula.   If we cannot assume either a single mode locally nor a market determinism from abroad, neither can we ignore the role of exchange in shaping emerging Korean markets and marketers at the turn of the century.   The debate underlines the centrality of a collision or compromise of the operating rules of a worldwide organization of production with the preexisting rules of local polity and market.[36]   Our task is to distill significant, enduring patterns from the interplay of international and local dynamics, market and polity, and custom or precedent and more modern bureaucratic practices of enterprise and administration.   Similar efforts are apparent in Alvin So's study of incorporation in early nineteenth century China where the local economy was "restructured to meet the demands and opportunities of the capitalist world-system."[37]   Thomas Hall addressed both external and internal factors with attention to (1) the character of the incorporating state or system, (2) types of incorporated groups and their effect on the process, and (3) the timing and degree of incorporation.[38]   He examined not merely the interaction of core and periphery but the "internal dynamics of both incorporating and incorporated groups."[39]

Peripheral incorporation would signify the "ability of metropolitan capitalists to exert pressure on local production relations to ensure maximum capital accumulation at the core."[40] Such leverage presumes an effective interaction making possible the penetration of core state and capital in the frontier of interest. Colonization of the Korean peninsula suggests more than pressure for this was not a distant colonial enclave with colonists content to draw off raw materials for export to world markets. Unlike most dependencies in the eighteenth and nineteenth centuries, the colony of Korea maintained a negative balance of trade with the metropole throughout the occupation. Yet this colony was very much a Japanese possession with little room for foreigners other than a few missionaries and a very small community of Chinese and European businessmen. Nor did incorporation under Japan, itself only a semi-periphery state, draw Korea into a world of multilateral international trade.[41] Trade with the Japanese islands accounted for better than eighty percent of the colony's exports and imports through 1945, as the Japanese came to the peninsula and established factories, a railroad system, harbors, and energy facilities.[42] Such penetration made the interaction between colonists and colonized all the more important, but a focus solely on the immediate precolonial and colonial interaction would tell us more of the colonists than of the colonized. Centuries of local commerce and limited international trade helped shape the subsequent patterns of commerce and organization among the local brokers in kingdom and colony.

Argument

A passage from relative isolation within the Chinese Empire to the status of agrarian periphery and later industrializing semi-periphery from the 1930s in Japan's colonial empire fostered new forms of exchange on the Korean peninsula. Looking to both the extension of Japanese market networks of capital and organization, and to their effect on the organization and ideas of grain brokers at the seaports, I chronicle the process of incorporation and capitalist deepening from 1876. My subject is neither as broad as "society" itself, nor as narrow as the brokers and their Japanese colleagues, but aligns rather with the embedded "circles of enterprise" encompassing individual firms, association, and the chartered or "semi-official" companies dominating the commerce in grains. The circles tell us much of the brokers themselves, and of patterns of enterprise stretching beyond grains to other areas of medium and small-scale enterprise in Korean society. The circles offer a window on the process of reinstituting exchange and rethinking enterprise in the transformation of state and society on the peninsula. Following the course of market and firm from 1876 we find Japanese networks superimposed on, competing with, and sometimes eliminating existing Korean networks of association and enterprise. The history of this interaction between alien and local merchants in Korea's passage between discrepant regional systems suggests that incorporation in tandem with precolonial precedents of commerce and association shaped the circles of enterprise constituting the Korean *chaegye*.

Polity in kingdom and colony played a major role in determining the course of integration of commerce on the peninsula into market systems beyond Korea. Max Weber's classic definition of *state* denotes a bureaucratic and legal order with control over the means of violence to establish sovereignty within its borders. Such criteria suggest differences between the Korean and Japanese polities on the peninsula, with the fading sovereignty of the monarchy after 1876 contrasting with the authoritarian, comprehensive controls of the Japanese colonial administration through 1945. Despite efforts at centralization in both polities, the monarchy could never establish effective infrastructure and control at the close of the nineteenth century. Both regimes gave high priority to control of grain commerce, but the monarchy struggled to monitor and manage a trade falling into the hands of the Japanese. The government-general of the colony, however, commanded extensive resources for implementing agrarian and trade policies in law and institution.

Political authorities remained prominent in the grain trade in both kingdom and colony, and played a role in shaping the circles of enterprise which spawned new forms of capitalist exchange. The Korean monarchy belatedly encouraged early commercial agencies and trade associations, mandating the organization of Korean chambers of commerce and delegating the brokers with semi-official tasks of duty collections at the ports and compliance with occasional grain embargoes in the interior. Colonial officials assumed a far more aggressive and comprehensive state role in shaping both enterprise and association in the grain trade. Histories of Western colonial policy towards indigenous business networks suggest alternatives of assimilation, accommodation, or elimination. Despite the official declaration of "assimilation," I argue that accommodation with subordination and distinction characterized the colonial policy towards the local business community in the grain trade, and that accommodation in turn deeply affected the circles of enterprise. An interplay of colonial state policy with precolonial roots of agency and association helps explain three features of local enterprise: (1) brokers remained an ethnically and economically distinct group with their own enterprise and associations; (2) brokers developed at best small and medium-scale enterprise in contrast to the larger enterprise of the Japanese, due in large part to lack of access to capital in Osaka and Tokyo enjoyed by their Japanese competitors; (3) and brokers found a place in both binational chambers of commerce and the semi-official companies such as the Grain Exchange dominating the grain trade. The administration superimposed more modern networks on existing patterns of commerce rather than isolating or eliminating local networks. The resulting circles of enterprise with roots in both Korea and in the colonial infrastructures of commerce nonetheless came to define the emerging private sector, a critical step in the capitalist transition from society to market.

Overlapping networks of private firm, business chambers and trade associations, and chartered companies whether banks or exchanges appeared in Korea's passage to a new interstate market system. Changes in both market and polity marked the careers of brokers at the seaports in the transition from the fading sovereignty of the Korean monarchy to the directive rule of the colonial administration. The expanding role and growing leverage of the market spurred developments in civil society readily apparent in the business community, but profoundly significant for the wider society. A shift in ideas was evident already in the trade debate in the closing years of the kingdom as intellectuals broached topics of public versus private, and of individual profit versus the common good. Under the rubric of *kwanmin* (officials and citizens) enlightenment activists countered the earlier emphasis on monarchy and faithful ministers with new themes of distinction between official and non-official spheres critical for a self-regulating market. Contested definitions of the commonweal evident in peasant and labor protest in the colony, or in the "Native Products Campaign" among intellectuals and business elites, and in the Jinto Transfer Controversy were evidence of an emerging "civil society" on the peninsula.

Depicting the fading monarchy as "predatory" and the colonial administration as "developmental," Atul Kohli has credited the latter with the "depersonalization of authority structures, so that public and private interests were first separated and only then reintegrated on a new basis, with public goals mainly in command."[43] The author cited a study of

Carter Eckert and my own work on the business history of major Korean colonial entrepreneurs as evidence of private interests, but devoted his major attention to the economic strategies and authority structures of the state. Kohli extends our comparative understanding of the colonial state without addressing the pressing societal question of consolidation among now private business interests. Moreover the focus on business histories of major entrepreneurs severely limits discussion of state penetration to the small number of leading Korean enterprises. I turn attention to the broader business circles beyond Seoul at the port cities, and beyond the large-scale economic elites to brokers in the grain trade. More complement than counterpoint to Kohli's thesis of distinction and reintegration of public and private spheres, I sift through the consolidation of enterprise, association, and ideas among the *chaegye* to learn more of the transformation spurred by trade.

Society rather than state has dominated the recent work of Hagen Koo on colonial precedents for contemporary tensions between state and society in South Korea. He argued that despite the protest and organization of dissident Korean groups, what impeded the "nascent civil society" of the colonial period was the absence of autonomous associational life.[44] While one cannot overlook constraints on organizations in the colony, the contradiction between independent or contesting ideas yet dependent or collusive organizations does not adequately explain institutional development in the private sector on the peninsula. Moreover, the rapid emergence of political interest groups in the South after 1945, and the quick reorganization of chambers of commerce and industry as reliable fora for the interests of business large and small indicate a preexisting basis for interest formation and organization. Beyond a strong colonial state and often contentious associations among labor and tenant farmers, there is much to be said of market and civil society among the local business community despite reliance on colonial finance and transport and membership in officially sanctioned associations. Yet Koo has correctly refocused our attention to issues of institution formation and their significance for post-colonial rivalries between a "strong state and contentious society."

Korean enterprise and association among the medium and small-scale grain brokers provides evidence of important institutions in the commerce and small-scale industry of the colony. Embedded circles of firm, association, and chartered colonial companies reflected both new forms of exchange and the initial consolidation of a modern Korean business community at the seaports. I develop the broader thesis of trade and inclusion in a new regional interstate order with motifs of both *kwanmin* or the official/private distinction, and business circles to link idea and organization in Korea's transformation. A chapter devoted to legacies of Korean state policy towards trade is followed by two chapters on the *kwanmin* thesis and its foil, the earlier *kunsin* thesis of monarch and minister. I turn to the nascent *chaegye* among the brokers in chapter five looking to cohesion among ethnically distinct enterprise and association as initial evidence of a private sphere. The colonial zaikai of Japanese enterprise and association in chapter six offers a clearer example of the dominant Japanese model of distinction and cooperation between official and private sectors. A counterpoint to both cohesive organization and ideological consensus is offered in chapter seven as competing factions across Inch'ŏn of Japanese and Korean businessmen contest colonial state policy for the Grain Exchange, providing evidence of both dissent and distinction. Theories of incorporation, state and society, and comparative colonialism return to center stage in a concluding chapter.

Notes

1. Atul Kohli, "Where Do High Growth Political Economies Come From? The Japanese Lineage of Korea's 'Developmental State,'" *World Development* vol. 22, no. 9 (September 1994): 1269-1293; Stephen Haggard, Stephan, David Kang, and Chung-in Moon, "Japanese Colonialism and Korean Development: A Critique," Research Report of the Graduate School of International Relations and Pacific Studies, # 95-04, 1995.

2. Robert Wade, *Governing the Market: Economic Theory and the Role of Government in East Asian Industrialization* (Princeton: Princeton University Press, 1990); Stephan Haggard, *Pathways from the Periphery* (Ithaca NY: Cornell University Press, 1990); World Bank, *The East Asian Miracle: Economic Growth and Public Policy* (New York: Oxford University Press, 1993).

3. International Monetary Fund, *Directions of Trade Statistics Yearbook, 1994* (Washington DC: IMF Publications, 1994), Table 542, p. 265; Korean Development Bank, *Korean Industry in the World, 1994* (Seoul: KDB, 1994), p. 1.

4. Ch'oe Hae-gun, *Pusan ŭi maek* [The pulse of Pusan] (Pusan: Donga Chŏnsa Insoesa, 1990), pp. 246-251.

5. Lee Byung-chull, "Yi Pyŏng-ch'ŏl," in Wŏllo Kiŏpin, ed., *Chaegye hoego* [Memories of the business world] (Seoul: Han'guk Ilbosa, 1981), vol.

I, pp. 288-290.

6. John Gerard Ruggie, "International Regimes, Transactions, and Change: Embedded Liberalism in the Postwar Economic Order," *International Organization* 36, 2, (Spring, 1982): 386-387.

7. *Colonial Origins of Koren Enterprise, 1910-1945* (Cambridge: Cambridge University Press, 1990).

8. Karl Polanyi, *The Great Transformation* (Beacon Hill, Boston: Beacon Press, (12944) 1957), 29-30, 70-71; *The Livelihood of Man* (New York: Academic Press, 1977), p. 53.

9. *The Origins of the Korean War: Liberation and the Emergence of Separate Regimes, 1945-1947* (Princeton: Princeton University Press, 1981), p. 48.

10. William James Booth, "On the Idea of the Moral Economy," *American Political Science Review*, vol. 88, no. 3 (Sept. 1994): 654; Terence K. Hopkins, "Sociology and the Substantive View of the Economy," p. 299 in Karl Polanyi, Conrad M. Arensbert, and Harry W. Pearson, eds., *Trade and Market in the Early Empires* (Glencoe, Illinois: The Free Press, 1957); Polanyi, "The Economy as Instituted Process," in Karl Polanyi, Conrad M. Arensbert, and Harry W. Pearson, eds., *Trade and Market in the Early Empires* (Glencoe, Illinois: The Free Press, 1957), p. 250.

11. I cite Japanese organizations according to their Japanese language pronunciations, such as the "Jinsen" Grain Exchange, i.e., a Japanese-dominated organization in the city of "Inch'ŏn." The names of firms in which Japanese nationals held a majority of the shares are cited in Japanese, and in Korean when Korean nationals held the majority of shares. Japanese terms are transliterated according to the modified Hepburn System as used in Koh Masuda, ed., *New Japanese-English Dictionary* (Tokyo: Kenkyusha, 1974), and names according to P. G. O'Neill, *Japanese Names* (New York: Weatherhill, 1972), although I have relied on the annual volummes of *Who's Who in Japan, with Manchoukuo and China* whenever possible. I transliterate Korean terms according to the McCune-Reischauer System, as explained in "Tables of the McCune-Reischauer System for the Romanization of Korean," *Transactions of the Korea Branch of the Royal Asiatic Society* 38 (Oct. 1961), pp. 121-128. Exceptions to both systems were made for place names in common Western usage under different spellings, such as "Tokyo" and "Seoul," "Chosen" and "Keijo."

12. Jean L. Cohen and Andrew Arato, *Civil Society and Political Theory* (Cambridge, MA: The MIT Press, 1992), p. 424.

13. John Keane, "Introduction," in John Keane, ed., *Civil Society and the State -- New European Perspectives* (London: Verso, 1988), pp. 7, 19, and in the same volume, "Despotism and Democracy: The Origins and Development of the Distinction Between Civil Society and the State 1750-1850," pp. 64-65.

14. Victor Perez-Diaz, *The Return of Civil Society: The Emergence of Democratic Spain* (Cambridge MA: Harvard University Press, 1991), p. 56.

15. Alexis De Tocqueville, *Democracy in America* (New York: Vintage Books, 1945), vol. 2, book 4, c. 7, p. 343, c. 6, p. 330.

16. William T. Rowe, "The Problem of 'Civil Society' in Late Imperial China," *Modern China*, vol. 19, no. 2 (April 993): 147-148.

17. Peter Evans, *Embedded Autonomy: States and Industrial Transformation*. (Princeton NJ: Princeton University Press, 1995); Thomas Callaghy, "Toward State Capability and Embedded Liberalism in the Third World: Lessons for Adjustment," pp. 115-38 in Joan Nelson, ed., *Fragile Coalitions: The Politics of Economic Adjustment*, (New Brunswick, NJ: Transaction Books, 1989); Mark Granovetter, "Economic Action and Social Structure: The Problem of Embeddedness," *American Journal of Sociology*, volume 91, no. 3 (Nov. 1985): 481-510; and Ruggie, "International Regimes."

18. Marie-Claire Bergere, *The Golden Age of the Chinese Bourgeoisie, 1911-1937* (Cambridge: Cambridge University Press, 1989); Fewsmith, *Party, State, and Local Elites*.

19. I have examined colonial Korean business organizations in the following articles: "The Keishō and the Korean Business Elite," *Journal of Asian Studies* (Berkeley: University of California Press) 48, no. 2 (May 1989), pp. 310-323; "Toward a Theory of Korean Capitalism: A Study of the Colonial Business Elite," pp. 713-725 in Academy of Korean Studies, ed., *Korean Studies, Its Tasks and Perspectives*, vol. 2 (Seoul: Academy of Korean Studies, 1988).

20. I first identified this issue in a paper titled, "*Kwanmin* in Colony and Republic -- Theme and Variation in Korean Capitalism," presented at a conference on the "Impact of Japanese Colonial Rule on Korean Development" for the Regional Seminar on Korean Studies at the University of California, Berkeley on April 29, 1991.

21. See my discussion of "benign capitalism" in *Colonial Origins*, pp. 19-33.

22. Immanuel Wallerstein and William G. Martin, "Peripheralization of Southern Africa, II: Changes in Household Structure and Labor-Force Formation," *Review* (Fernand Braudel Center) III (1979): 193; Immanuel Wallerstein, "The Rise and Future Demise of the World Capitalist System: Concepts for Comparative Analysis," in *The Capitalist World-Economy* (Cambridge: Cambridge University Press, 1979), pp. 1-36, and "Class-Formation in the Capitalist World-Economy," *Politics and Society* vol. 5, no. 3 (1975): 367-376.

23. Giovanni Arrighi, "Peripheralization of Southern Africa, I: Changes in Production Processes," *Review* (Fernand Braudel Center) III (1981): 163; Joan Sokolovsky, "Logic, Space, and Time: The Boundaries of the Capitalist World-Economy," in Michael Timberlake, ed., *Urbanization in the World-*

Economy (New York: Academic Press, 1985), p. 51.

24. Immanuel Wallerstein, *The Modern World-System III. The Second Era of Great Expansion of the Capitalist World-Economy, 1730-1840s* (New York: Academic Press, 1989), p. 130.

25. Terence K. Hopkins and Immanuel Wallerstein, "Structural Transformations of the World-Economy," in Terence K. Hopkins, Immanuel Wallerstein et al., eds., *World-Systems Analysis: Theory and Methodology* (Beverly Hills: Sage Publications, 1982), p. 128; *The Modern World-System III.* p. 167.

26. Theda Skocpol, "Wallerstein's World Capitalist System: A Theoretical and Historical Critique," *American Journal of Sociology* vol. 82, no. 5 (1977): 1075-1090; Bruce Cumings, "World System and Authoritarian Regimes in Korea, 1848-1984," in Edwin A. Winckler and Susan Greenhalgh, eds., *Contending Approaches to the Political Economy of Taiwan* (Armonk NY: M. E. Sharpe, 1988), pp. 250-251.

27. Christopher Chase-Dunn, *Global Formation: Structures of the World-Economy* (Cambridge MA: Basil Blackwell, 1989), p. 131.

28. Andre Gunder Frank, *Dependent Accumulation and Underdevelopment* (London: Macmillan, 1978), pp. 2-7.

29. Robert Brenner, "The Origins of Capitalist Development: a Critique of Neo-Smithian Marxism," *New Left Review* No. 104 (July-August 1977): 25-93.

30. Eric R. Wolf, *Europe and the People Without History* (Berkeley, CA: University of California Press, 1982), pp. 22-23, 297-298; Peter Worsley, "One World or Three? A Critique of the World-system Theory of Immanuel Wallerstein," in David Held et al., eds. *States and Societies* (New York: New York University Press, 1983), p. 511.

31. "The Modes of Production Controversy," *New Left Review* no. 107 (Jan.-Feb. 1978): 75.

32. Patricia M. Kelly, "Broadening the Scope: Gender and the Study of International Development," p. 163 in A. Douglas Kincaid and Alejandro Portes, eds., *Comparative National Development: Society and Economy in the New Global Order* (Chapel Hill: The University of North Carolina Press, 1994); Immanuel Wallerstein and William G. Martin, "Peripheralization of Southern Africa, II: Changes in Household Structure and Labor-Force Formation," *Review* (Fernand Braudel Center) III (1979): 193-207.

33. Shin Gi-wook, "Social Change and Peasant Protest in Colonial Korea," Ph.D. diss., University of Washington, 1991, p. 66.

34. Etienne Balibar, "The Basic Concepts of Historical Materialism," pp. 199-325 in Louis Althusser and Etienne Balibar, eds., *Reading Capital* (London: NLB, 1970).

35. Chase-Dunn, *Global Formation*, p. 301.

36. The term "operating rules" is drawn from an insightful review by Bruce Andrews, "The Political Economy of World Capitalism: Theory and Practice," *International Organization* 36, 1 (Winter 1982): 153.

37. Alvin Y. So, *The South China Silk District: Local Historical Transformation and World-System Theory* (New York: State University of New York Press, 1986), p. 8; "The Process of Incorporation into the Capitalist World-System: the Case of China in the Nineteenth Century," *Review* vol. 8, no. 1 (Summer 1984): 91-116. Elizabeth Lasek had earlier emphasized the interaction of system, state and class in China's experience of Western imperialism in the late nineteenth century. See her "Imperialism in China: A Methodological Critique," *Bulletin of Concerned Scholars* 15, 1 (1983): 50-64.

38. Thomas D. Hall, *Social Change in the Southwest, 1350-1880* (Lawrence, Kansas: University Press of Kansas, 1989), p. 241.

39. Thomas D. Hall, "Incorporation in the World-System: Toward a Critique, *American Sociological Review*, vol. 51 (June 1986): 398.

40. Sokolovsky, "Logic, Space, and Time," p. 44.

41. For the shift from periphery to semi-periphery status in the Korean colony, see Shin, "Social Change and Peasant Protest in Colonial Korea," p. 240. Regarding Japan as a semi-periphery nation, see Walter L. Goldfrank, "Silk and Steel: Italy and Japan between the Two World Wars," in Richard Tomasson, ed., *Comparative Social Research*, vol. 4 (Greenwich Connecticut: JAI Press, 1981), pp. 297-315.

42. Samuel Ho, "Colonialism and Development: Korea, Taiwan, and Kwantung," in Ramon H. Myers and Mark R. Peattie, eds., *The Japanese Colonial Empire, 1895-1945* (Princeton: Princeton University Press, 1984), pp. 370, 396-397

43. Kohli, "Where Do High Growth Political Economies Come From," p. 1287.

44. "Strong State and Contentious Society," in Hagen Koo, ed., *State and Society in Contemporary Korea* (Ithaca: Cornell University Press, 1993), p. 237.

2

Trade

Trade across borders affects not only local commerce and local rule, but also ties between nations. Trade brought new modes of exchange to the peninsula and attracted foreign merchants who exposed local commerce to market forces beyond the peninsula. Trade can reflect integration or isolation from regional hegemonies, state initiative or insulation from international markets, and the prominence or absence of local merchants in the commerce across borders. Trade statistics through the turn of the century portray an uneven exchange of raw materials and agricultural products for Japanese manufactures, just as a review of grain sales indicates a dramatic reorientation within Korea's agrarian economy to Japanese markets. A history of idea and institution in the grain trade reveals both historical precedents and new patterns of colonial accommodation shaping circles of enterprise among local capital.

Rice remained the leading export across late kingdom and colony, the basic staple of the Korean diet, and the leading sector of the agrarian economy. Some eighty-four percent of households at the turn of the century worked in agriculture, cultivating rice, soybeans and wheat.[1] More than simply a commodity, rice was the lifeblood of the nation and central to the economy: "commercial and credit operations, as well as transportation and other related activities were organized around rice production, and industry was centered in the field of rice-polishing and the production of rice wine."[2] If we compare Korea with other colonies in Asia, we find colonial Indonesia exporting sugar, coffee, and spices, and Taiwan sending out sugar and rice, but Korea relying on grains as its only major cash crop for export. Colonial rule altered that tradition only slightly, drawing off rice from the local market, promoting local consumption of beans and millet, and moving some workers from farm to factory.

The merging of Korea into an interstate system of market relations under Japan forced a realignment of domestic commerce in conformity with markets beyond Korea.[3] But it was not simply economic interest that brought the Japanese to the peninsula, nor solely market demand that hastened the extension of capitalism, for trade highlights the interplay of polity and economy in Korea's initiation into a new interstate system, and recalls precedents for commerce across borders established well before the arrival of the Japanese. Korea's role in a non-capitalist, tribute trade system with China, and informal and formal trade with Tokugawa Japan set the context for realignment within a colonial capitalist system. Indeed, scholars such as Hamashita Takeshi point to a regional tribute trade system as the critical variable spurring the beginnings of "modernization" in nineteenth century Asia.[4]

Korean brokers stood precariously at the forefront of this transformation moving from state-controlled guilds to more independent business associations characteristic of a more "professional" business community. Guild organization and chartered monopoly control of trades receded in the face of powerful foreign consulates and aggressive Japanese enterprise in the port cities. It was the end of an era as the demise of the guilds highlighted the erosion of commercial sovereignty for the Korean monarch, but it was also the dawn of a new era evident in the rise of a local business community at the ports.

Empire

Although the Chosŏn Dynasty (1392-1910) maintained formal links as a tributary state of the Chinese Empire, informal commercial agreements permitted commerce also with Manchuria and Japan. Symbol and custom, rather than international law, defined tributary status in the Chinese Empire with the court at Beijing approving succession at the Korean court and receiving tribute from regular Korean embassies to Beijing. The entourage showed deference through gifts of tribute, use of the Chinese calendar, various prostrations and other formal gestures. Custom rather than international law served as a basis for international relations within the Empire.

In the West, all governments were conceived as resting on law, regardless of the particular form law took in each state; therefore, all sovereigns were equal. Moreover, international relationships and even organizations existed on the basis of, or strove toward the creation of, international law... In traditional East Asia, on the other hand, the international system consisted of ties that were quite distinct from internal political links.[5]

Colonization would foster law and formal contract, but ironically, the treaty of Kanghwa with Japan in 1876 established a new legal framework for Korean sovereignty even as the Japanese imposed inequalities regarding extraterritoriality and other concessions. Entry into a new regional hegemony brought a new emphasis on international law without the premise of equal rights among sovereign states.

Kim Key-hiuk distinguished between political and economic dimensions of the tributary tie. Politically, Korea gained the protection of the powerful Chinese court, particularly evident in the Chinese military alliance to repel the Hideyoshi invasions from Japan in the late sixteenth century. Despite reliance on Chinese power to maintain regional security, the Korean court enjoyed remarkable autonomy in domestic affairs.[6] In contrast, colonial dependence brought a quick end to Korea's contested political autonomy at home. The absence of political voice would distinguish Korean brokers from their counterparts in China's treaty ports at the turn of the century, and pervasive colonial controls on political activity would preclude even the limited political mobilization evident among Chinese brokers dominating trade in Indonesia during the latter years of Dutch rule.

Commerce between China and Korea continued across the years of the Ming (1368-1644) and Qing (1644-1912) Dynasties in Beijing, including gift trade, administered trade, and market trade. Gift trade refers to items of tribute carried by Korean embassies to Beijing and Chinese embassies to Seoul, with nearly seven hundred embassies from Korea to China during the Qing years alone, averaging every fifteen months, and better than 150 embassies from Beijing to Seoul. Embassies would include between 200 and 300 people, with merchants often disguised as official retainers.[7] Koreans brought mainly textile goods such as silk, hemp, ramie, and cotton products, but also hides, tobacco, medicine, rice, and art objects. Following the formal presentation of tribute, the embassy set up shop at its residence in Beijing to barter goods with Chinese merchants, and later would trade along the route home and at the border. Commerce loomed large in these ceremonial visits as an object of formal negotiations and an integral function of the exchange of gifts, but perhaps the more important goal was to moderate border conflicts and provide norms for other forms of trade in the absence of international law.[8]

The monarchy of the later Chosŏn Dynasty also sent twelve formal embassies to Japan during the Tokugawa Period (1603-1867).[9] As was the case with China, the embassies helped stabilize relations between the two nations, including trade through the Japanese island of Tsushima. Toby argued that Japanese efforts evident in diplomatic documents to gain Korean recognition of Japan's equality with China signalled aspirations already in the Tokugawa era to establish a establish a Japan-centered regional order.

> By choosing to have relations only with those countries that would accept ground rules for international discourse determined solely (at least in appearance) by Japan, by structuring those relationships in a protocol hierarchy crowned by the bakufu, by refusing relations with China that might sacrifice that appearance of primacy, by even achieving a hierarchy which appeared to devolve from Japan, to Korea, and thence through Ryukyu and Holland to China, the bakufu had created the environment in which the Japan-centered *k'ai* [maritime] order appeared to exist.[10]

Hamashita argued that Japan's aggressive trade efforts and industrialization program of the late nineteenth century were an effort to relocate the "center of the tribute trade structure in Japan."[11]

Whatever the intentions of the Japanese, the Koreans made clear their equality with Japan, defining their ties as *kyŏrin* or "neighborly relations" in all diplomatic documents and procedures. In contrast, a formula of *sadae* or "serving a superior" conveyed the essence of the tributary relationship with China. The distinction suggests a Japanese exception to Chinese hegemony well-evident in the seventeenth century, and now affecting security and trade on the peninsula. Within the changing context, the Korean monarchy found itself in the odd position of maintaining a tributary, dependent relation with one neighbor, and bilateral, equal relations with another neighbor which itself rejected subservience in the Chinese order. The complexity of such ties was matched by the variety of literati attitudes within Korea toward its neighbors. Literati cherished the culture of earlier Ming China but distanced themselves from the reigning Mongols in the Qing Empire, evidence of a growing cultural or ethnic independence in the later Chosŏn Dynasty. Some Korean scholars cite evidence also of disdain for the Japanese who had separated themselves from the Chinese cultural order of the Ming Empire.[12]   This penchant for identifying with the Chinese of the distant Ming Dynasty, but not with the Mongols of the contemporary Qinq Empire, and for faulting the Japanese as "uncivilized" due to their alienation from the earlier Ming culture persisted among conservative literati in subsequent debates over trade.

We find evidence of "administered trade" with China, with Manchuria prior to their conquest of China and ascendancy in the Qing Empire, and with Tokugawa Japan.   Distinguished by long-term contracts between governments, administered trade helped moderate border disputes and discourage plundering of the coastline by foreign vessels.   Mancall cited a growing volume of exchange between Manchuria and Korea by the sixteenth century formalized in commercial treaties from 1628, and others document trade with Japan.[13] The Korean monarchy issued copper seals to authorize foreign traders from Japan at the beginning of the Chosŏn Dynasty and licensed a specified number of ships annually for trade in the next century, including allotments of grain.   The Japanese island of Tsushima in the straits separating Korea and Japan had long served as a forward base for Japanese trade, and was formally recognized in a treaty of 1443 with the overlord of Tsushima permitted 200 ships annually to Pusan and to ports near today's cities of Chinhae and Ulsan.[14] Koreans sent rice, cotton goods, luxury items, and artwork to Japan, and imported copper, lead, and sulphur from Japan, as well as dyestuffs, spices and medicines all the way from Southeast Asia through the Japanese traders. Given the traditional insulation of the kingdom, one wonders what prompted a reluctant monarchy to agree to trade relations with the Japanese. One motive was control of piracy ravaging the Korean coast since opportunities for a legitimate, regular trade either diverted and domesticated the energies of the pirates, or encouraged the Japanese authorities to better control adventurers from their islands. Concerns for coastal marauders might explain the curious resumption of trade ties so soon after the brutal Hideyoshi invasions at the end of the sixteenth century as the Korean court sanctioned trade through Tsushima as early as 1609.

We read also of "market trade" beyond the tribute missions and the formally authorized commercial trade between Korea and China. Market trade refers to both commerce by individual merchants associated with the embassies in Beijing, and to commerce at authorized ports or border towns. Chun cited commerce as a major topic of negotiation for the embassies, including "trade in Beijing and on the tributary route by Korean embassies, local trade, trade in drugs, and fines accruing from suspending local trade."[15] Tribute trade would thus serve as a sanction not only for administered trade, but also as an opportunity to resolve border disputes arising from the barter trade by local merchants at ports and border towns. Elisonas cited authorization of private trade with Japan by the Korean monarchy already in 1485, a century prior to the Hideyoshi invasions, and well before official trade relations with the Tokugawa.[16] A picture of a constrained foreign trade gradually comes into focus across the five centuries of the Chosŏn Dynasty. Hamashita concluded that competition within a multi-lateral tribute trade system in the region, rather than the threat of Western imperialism prompted modernization in Japan, but in the Korean case we find instead only bilateral trade ties with China and bilateral trade with Japan.[17]

Joining accounts of trade with diplomatic records from the period, we can piece together a rough picture of commerce across borders in the century leading up to the Kanghwa Treaty. Custom and symbol rather than market served as the cement of the Chinese Empire, with trade used to stabilize border ties and prevent conflict. Absence of a common currency, reliable finance or transportation systems for large-scale international commerce, and the prominence of barter would inhibit the extension of markets distinguishing the world capitalist system. Bilateral trade between suzerain and tributary, rather than an integrated system of interstate trade under Chinese hegemony remained the norm through the nineteenth century. Thirdly, we read of Chinese state constraints on foreign travels of local merchants and might assume a similar policy on the peninsula, given the lack of evidence of any concerted Korean advance into markets of neighboring nations.[18] Relative international isolation of the merchants left Korean merchants reliant on border trading posts, or commerce with Japanese traders at Korea's early treaty ports.

A traditional state role of authorizing and managing trade might suggest parallels with a colonial administration, but the mandate of the monarchy can hardly be compared with the comprehensive controls of Japan's government-general on the peninsula through 1945. Palais argued that the monarchy lacked the autonomy necessary for radical reform: "The extraordinary stability of the Yi (i.e., Chosŏn) dynasty polity was the product of a balance of power between centralized monarchy and an aristocratic elite, and that any tendency toward the aggrandizement of power by either the throne or the aristocracy was eventually checked by reaction and counterpressure."[19] Constraints on state power in the later Chosŏn Dynasty would have discouraged any dramatic effort to expand trade since conservative literati often allied with the landed gentry would likely have opposed any aggressive state promotion of international commerce beyond the traditional patterns of exchange with Beijing. Yet close government control of the commerce established an important precedent of merchants cooperating with the monarchy in plying their trades. Domestically, the court was closely involved in managing and monitoring the grain supply to insure domestic stability, and also chartered a limited number of merchants in Seoul to procure local and foreign luxury items for the crown. Finally, we can point to official tolerance of guild organization in the early nineteenth century and their role in managing trade and periodic markets.[20] The record of Korean trade in the years of empire highlights overriding priorities of domestic stability and international security, with international commerce permitted only to discourage piracy and stabilize border relations. The monarchy showed little enthusiasm for promoting trade, whether due to constraints of their status within the Chinese Empire, to a conviction about local self-sufficiency, or perhaps due to anxieties about their borders. Indeed a nation ravaged by the Mongols from the north in the thirteenth century and by the Japanese from the south in the sixteenth century probably took comfort in relative isolation.[21]

Trade from 1876

In line with earlier efforts to eliminate China's regional hegemony, Japan insisted Korea explicitly renounce their "special relationship" with China in the Treaty of Kanghwa (1876). Kojong's government finally relented and agreed to open the port of Pusan, the site of earlier commerce with Tsushima, to international trade. Other ports opened in quick succession, including Wǒnsan near P'yǒngyang in 1881, and Inch'ǒn near Seoul in 1883. Further agreements opened the ports of Mokp'o and Kunsan in 1897 and 1899, allowing more direct access to grain producers in the fertile plains of Chǒlla Province, but Pusan to the south, Kunsan to the west, and Inch'ǒn would remain the major ports through the colonial years. Korean foreign commerce grew steadily with the annual value of trade expanding by more than 300% between 1886 and 1894, and then growing by 400% over the next ten years. By the time of annexation in 1910, the yearly value of trade amounted to about 60 million yen or 30 million U.S. dollars.

Trade opened markets for Korean products abroad and provided access to foreign manufactures at home, as exports of grains and cowhides, ores and metals helped defray the cost of imported textiles and utensils. Rice and soybeans comprised the bulk of grain exports, complemented by sales of gold, silver and coal to China and Japan. Local demand for British and Japanese cottons, farm tools and household utensils fueled a fierce competition with Japan succeeding China as Korea's leading trade partner by the 1890s, absorbing most of Korea's exports and providing most of her imports.[22] An exchange of raw materials for manufactured goods from Japan insured both dependence on foreign suppliers and trade deficits. Agricultural production on the intensely cultivated plains of the Korean peninsula could be expanded only at great expense, whereas Japanese manufactures of textiles and other light industrial goods could be expanded to meet demand with limited investment in machines and labor.

Revenues from the expanding trade initially buttressed the shaky finances of Kojong's government. Total duties from international trade in 1886 amounted to only 160,000 yen, but grew to 740,000 yen in 1895, and a million yen by 1900. Keep in mind that the total outlay of the Korean government in 1905 was only 9.5 million yen, and only 27 million yen in 1910.[23] The Commissioner of Customs collected 2.2 million yen in 1905 or 30% of the total annual income for that year, and 3.4 million yen of duties in 1910.[24] But the trade presented the court and cabinet in Seoul with difficult choices of either radical reform to recover economic sovereignty within its borders, or restraints on the profitable trade. Financial constraints and the absence of a strong consensus for reform deprived the monarchy of the former alternative, just as powerful foreign embassies in Seoul and their consulates at the ports stood ready to scuttle efforts to restrain the trade.

Despite the meddling of foreign powers and inconsistent efforts at local reform, elements of a trade policy were evident in procedures for entry and collection of duties at the trade ports. What distinguished the period of port openings prior to the Kabo Reforms of 1894 was control through authorized guilds. Since predecessors at the throne of the Chosŏn Dynasty had authorized merchants to ply but also control commerce in Seoul and at the borders and embassy routes, it is not surprising that Kojong's government and provincial officials turned to the brokers to control the trade in grains in the late nineteenth century. For instance, the local magistrate of Inch'ŏn designated the guild for collection of all duties in 1884, only to rescind the order after strident Japanese protest from their Embassy in Seoul.[25] The Japanese Consulate in Pusan proved even more vocal in their protest against the guilds.[26] Consular pressure against restraints on free trade would continue and intensify as Japanese merchants moved beyond the ports to other cities and rural areas, but still the local polity did not easily surrender rule in the local market. The Foreign Office of Kojong's government decreed a territorial monopoly system of twenty-five brokers at Inch'ŏn in 1889 selecting from among forty or so brokers at the port on the basis of capital holdings, and formulating plans to extend the system with similar guild selections at Pusan and other ports.[27] A broker mandate to collect the business tax would have monopolized all legal transactions in grains. This remarkable intervention by the Foreign Office between November of 1889 and June of 1890 codified collection procedures, designated areas of jurisdiction, and stipulated cooperation between the brokers and other merchant.[28]

Clearly the government in Seoul was committed to managing international commerce on the peninsula. Their justification and the vehement consular protest in response offer a painful picture of an adjusting polity still caught in earlier habits, and of impatient foreign powers. The Korean Foreign Office argued precedent, local jurisdiction, and procedure: (1) the system was in place well before the ports were opened; (2) the system concerned domestic rather than foreign trade; and (3) the inspection of weights was necessary due to discrepancies between the traditional Korean system and the Western system.[29] The Office insisted that precedent and maintenance of local order be given priority in interpretation of the legal agreement. Asking for patience, they argued that the authorities needed time to adapt procedures such as weights and measures, necessary to maintain local sovereignty and oversight in the trade. Their rationale that chartered guilds would help broker and polity alike to adapt to market changes drew nothing but scorn from irate foreign merchants interested in grains and other local resources. The government soon bowed to foreign pressure and voided the formal system, yet continued informal efforts to collect duties on inland trade bound for the ports.

The strategy of the chartered guild familiar to government and merchant alike excluded the Japanese and other foreign traders. The monarchy planned to use guilds to supervise and control trade just as brokers used the guilds to monopolize markets, insure profits, and cement a base of trust and security among fellow tradesmen. Yet the guild was not simply for the convenience of the Seoul authorities in controlling unruly markets, nor for the profit of brokers fearful of competition. Guild solidarity was rooted in structure as well as sentiment. A system of impersonal law equally applied provides a basis for trust in a market society, but in the absence of a viable domestic system of business law, Koreans reverted to the guild. Ironically, international law in the form of trade agreements with Japan and the West stipulated free trade at the ports, putting a legal writ in the hands of foreign powers for dissolution of the local guild monopolies which brokers found necessary in the absence of a local legal system.

The foreign community dismissed the chartered guild of 25 brokers as an anachronism. Anachronistic indeed, but nonetheless deeply embedded in ties between state and enterprise dating from the later years of the Chosŏn Dynasty. Features of the earlier pattern such as extensive state oversight of commerce through selected agents, reliance on semi-official merchants for state revenue collection, and state chartered monopolies represented a legacy for state and broker alike. An emerging mercantile class in the port of Inch'ŏn would adapt in time from guild to more professional business interest organization, but the legacy would affect the direction and depth of the adaptation. An earlier pattern of state control through chartered brokers proved untenable in the new era of "free trade." A mercantilist strategy might be sustained through other means, as evident among Japanese merchants with their organized markets, but would demand more distinct spheres of "public" and "private," and new ministries and business interest organizations to insure cooperation and direction. And to dispel any thought of reversion to earlier patterns, the diplomatic uproar over the broker system of the Kojong's Foreign Office gave a face and a voice to forces of the interstate system unfamiliar in the hermit kingdom.

A second phase of more professional chambers, again with semi-official tasks, marked the final years of Seoul controls on trade prior to establishment of the Japanese Protectorate on the peninsula in 1905. Legal recognition of an interest group distinct from the state yet crucial for the state's survival represents a critical step in the consolidation of a private sector. Kabo reform legislation finally brought legal status to a trade association organizing an indigenous business community in the port. A Commerce Association Law of 1895 mandated reorganization of brokers' cooperatives across Korea into commerce associations and by decree four years later, into commercial firms. The 1895 legislation provided the stimulus for Inch'ŏn's first peak business interest association for local businessmen, reported in the *Independent*: "The Korean merchants of Chemulp'o have organized a Chamber of Commerce for the purpose of holding public meetings to discuss the best methods of conducting business, etc. They subscribed $900 at the meeting with the intention of fixing up the building and purchasing necessary furniture."[30] Retired Inch'ŏn magistrate Sŏ Sang-jun, and broker Sŏ Sang-bin founded the group in 1897 to conform with the new regulations, but with its own distinctive title, the "Port of Inch'ŏn Merchants [*sinsang*] Association." The latter belied the reluctance to recognize the independence of the business sector, for these "merchants [*sinsang*]" were special. The compound *sinsang* combines the term *chinsin*, referring to government officials with business interests, with *sangmin* or "private merchants."[31] The latter distinction paralleled the emphasis of trade advocates on *kwanmin* [officials and people], though now we find it in the emerging private sector. But the divide between state and society in Western political theory gained little headway in Korea's emerging capitalist society where a private sphere would stake its claim under close supervision of the monarchy and colonial state.

State documents approving the Merchants Association do not provide clear recognition of the distinction between public and private spheres, but offer rather an initial step towards acknowledging a group in society apart from the state. The Chamber Law of 1895 legislated a single chamber for each city with authority to collect dues from all businessmen paying a minimal amount of business tax.[32] Conventional chamber functions of information-gathering regarding commerce in Inch'ŏn, and even joint action on sovereignty issues paralleled the mandate at the more independent Japanese chamber in Inch'ŏn. But unlike the Japanese chamber, the bylaws of the Merchants Association reserved the presidency to former government officials, whereas the vice-presidency and most of the membership would be brokers. Moreover, the government authorized the association only under the banner of the nation's security and profit, not profit for the merchants.[33] Minister of Agriculture, Commerce and Industry Yi Wan-yong urged the group "to work together with the government to maintain fair prices, keep abreast of market changes, and protect the nation from exploitation by foreigners." He then mandated the association to supply goods from abroad to supplement local goods, and to collect duties for the state.[34] The government reasserted the latter function, and closer state control of the association in a document of October, 1899, and also renamed the organization the "Merchants Firm."[35]

Embargoes on the sale and transport of grains for export represented a further effort to reassert government control in the trade and again suggest growing respect for the market role of the grain brokers. Annual rice exports grew from 326,000 koku in 1890 to 419,000 in 1900 and, given little growth in the harvest across these years, diverted supplies from the now less attractive local markets and turned the ideological issue in the diplomatic struggle from simply government cooperation with local brokers to legal constraints on market dynamics to preserve food supplies.[36] Three principles of foreign trade had been established by treaty: (1) free trade at the treaty ports without the intervention of Korean officials,[37] (2) prohibition of all additional duties beyond agreed upon tariffs,[38] and (3) strict guidelines for the temporary interdiction of grain imports in times of scarcity. Although the latter article recognized a government role in monitoring the effects of trade on the local food supply, foreign powers would question the government's authority to embargo trade, the government estimate of local hardship, and the length and extent of the constraints.[39] Multiple embargoes on the transport and/or sale of grains imposed by provincial and central government officials between 1884 and 1901 represented the state's most dramatic yet unsuccessful effort to intervene in commerce on the peninsula and control foreign trade.[40]

An unbalanced exchange of grains for manufactured goods linked local markets to Japanese markets for both exports and imports, leaving the Korean economy vulnerable to factors of supply and demand abroad. Grain embargoes reflect the intricate interplay of economic and political incorporation as the local polity found itself unable to assert local priorities against the mercantile interests of the core state. Fading economic sovereignty coincided with fading political sovereignty on the peninsula, leaving the busy brokers stateless in their own markets. Deprived of the resources and authority of the polity, the brokers found themselves at a disadvantage in competition with the tightly organized Japanese chambers at the treaty ports. Just as brokers started gaining attention at court and cabinet as major players in the new political economy, local political authorities lost ground to the Japanese state in political and economic direction on the peninsula. The circle of mercantile interests at the ports would soon learn to ply their trade not only in close cooperation with foreign merchants but under the guidance of a foreign state.

Colonial Trade

Three phases of administration policy can be distinguished across the years of colonial rule.[41] An initial period (1910-1919) under Generals Terauchi and Hasegawa have been characterized as "military rule (*budan seiji*)," highlighted by the extension of Japanese military and police controls into all areas of civilian life on the peninsula. Authorities developed the peninsula primarily as a source of grains with the rapid expansion of rice and soybean exports to Osaka, Yokohama and Nagasaki, and as a market for light manufactures of textiles and cooking utensils from Japan. Infrastructural efforts included the massive land or "Cadastral Survey" to clarify land ownership on the peninsula, and the "Corporation Law" temporarily prohibiting the legal incorporation of enterprise as tighter reporting procedures were designed. Independence rallies in the spring of 1919, together with the ascendancy of liberal forces in Japanese politics spurred policy adjustments in the next decade under Admiral Saitō Minoru, characterized as the years of "cultural rule (*bunka seiji*)." Japanese military and police activities were curtailed and controls eased on assembly and public expression among the local population. The demand for grains to feed the fast-growing urban population in the home islands dictated colonial economic policy, resulting in strong promotion of rice production for export on the peninsula through the second decade of colonial rule. The bureaucracies of the government-general mobilized resources for irrigation and reclamation projects to increase acreage under cultivation, improve seeds and expand the supply of fertilizers.

Events in Manchuria and elsewhere on the Chinese mainland, and later the Pacific War led to a new phase of policy in the final fourteen years of colonial rule. Efforts toward a limited "assimilation (*Naisen ittai*)" replaced the more relaxed cultural policy, with the colony and its population forced to play a more prominent role in the hard-pressed Japanese empire. The Japanese scholar Yanaihara Tadao[42] questioned the logic of assimilation among a colonial population deprived of even basic political rights: "It would appear, therefore, that the assimilation policy expressed in the form of paternalistic protection in the economic and social spheres of life can be carried out only under the guardianship of an oppressive bureaucracy in control of political and military affairs." Apart from cultural assimilation efforts in education, language, and even religion, paternalism and bureaucratic oppression persisted though with

34

some measure of accommodation for the brokers in the grain trade.

Exports of grains and ores, and imports of manufactures continued in the colony as the trade which had eroded political authority in Kojong's monarchy now enhanced colonial authority under the Japanese. The annual value of trade grew from 60 million yen in 1910 to better than 600 million yen by 1930, or 300 million dollars. By 1939, the value of the trade had again doubled to better than one billion yen.[43] A price deflated index of export volume indicates growth of 400% in the first decade of colonial rule, and a further 150% through 1929. The latter represented growth on a much larger base, amounting to an increase of 150 million yen in the annual volume of trade between 1920 and 1929. The value of trade then more than doubled again to 880 million yen in 1938 with the addition of marine products, ores for industrial production, plus textiles and chemicals.[44] Annual deficits in trade of about 20 million yen in the years of the Protectorate [1905-

TABLE 2.1 Rice Exports from Inch'ŏn, 1896 to 1909 *

Year	Volume	Value	Year	Volume	Value
1896	121.3	853.3	1903	106.4	1,142
1897	287.0	2,297	1904	15.0	194.1
1898	99.9	1,022	1905	4.4	0.61
1899	67.2	510.7	1906	39.2	451.9
1900	185.1	1,432	1907	184.6	2,013
1901	180.5	1,435	1908	59.6	720.5
1902	58.3	618.2	1909	28.2	354.7

*Volume listed as thousands of koku, originally recorded as picul and recalculated as 2.6 picul per one koku. Value listed in hundreds of thousands of yen. E.g., in 1896, an export volume of 121,300 koku at a value of 853,300 yen.

Source: Jinsen Shōkō Kaigisho, *Jinsen Shōkō tōkei menpyō, 1937* [Statistical annual of the Jinsen Chamber of Commerce and Industry, 1937] (Jinsen: Tsukiji Publishing, 1938), Table 62, pp. 10-11.

1910], jumped to 52 million yen by 1920, 140 million yen in 1930, and 380 million yen by 1939.

Grains represented the leading export across the colonial years. Exports of grains and marine products averaged 70% annually of total export value across the first decade of colonial rule, 67% in the second decade, and 55% between 1930 and 1938.[45] Consistent trade expansion in the colony resulted in exports of nearly 2.3 million koku of rice in 1915, 4.6 million by 1925, and 10.9 million koku in 1938.[46] How important was the trade for local production and consumption? Exports amounted to 19% of the rice harvest in 1915, 48% in 1925, and nearly 70% by 1938. Statistics on rice available for local consumption document a decline in the annual volummes from 1925 through 1936, coupled with an increase in the population on the peninsula.[47]

Exports of rice from the port of Inch'ŏn began to prosper soon after the Sino-Japanese War (1894-1895). As evident in Table 2.1, the volume of trade fluctuated between 100,000 and 200,000 koku annually from 1896 through 1903 prior to the Russo-Japanese War (1904-1905) and Protectorate. Table 2.2 traces the trade through the first decade of colonial rule, documenting a dramatic rise in the volume and value of Inch'ŏn rice exports, reaching a height of 453,000 koku in 1919 with a value of 17 million yen.

One trend evident already at the outset of colonial rule is the inconsistency between annual harvest and exports volume as demand in Osaka rather than supply at home determined exports. Table 2.3 follows the now mature grain trade from 1921 through 1930.

Table 2.4 continues the record in the late years of the Grain Exchange. Export volummes now level off between 1.3 and 1.5 million koku but with fluctuating prices. The decline in Inch'ŏn prices of exported rice between 1925 and 1931 prompted calls for merging the Jinsen Grain Exchange with the Stock Exchange at Seoul.

Priorities of macro-economic policy in the colony included mainly agrarian production for the first two decades, and then industrial production from the 1930s to develop the peninsula as a forward base for colonization of Manchukuo. The former strategy of agrarian supplier for core state urban areas paralleled Dutch efforts in Indonesia, the French in Vietnam, or indeed the Japanese in Taiwan, yet in both Taiwan and Korea the fact that rice was produced across much of the peninsula resulted in wider colonial penetration and integration into international markets. Not only were both colonies less compartmentalized into

TABLE 2.2 Rice Exports from Inch'ŏn, 1910 to 1920

Year	Harvest*	Export Volume	Export Value
1910	-	69	745.5
1911	-	55	680.1
1912	8,982.0	81	1,531.4
1913	10,090.0	355.0	2,883.1
1914	12,159.0	177.3	2,665.1
1915	11,373.0	402.7	4,547.3
1916	12,531.0	288.4	3,715.6
1917	12,227.0	272.6	4,759.5
1918	15,394.0	384.8	11,113.2
1919	12,708.0	453.9	17,683.5
1920	14,882.0	344.0	12,407.1

    * Harvest and export volume cited in thousands of koku, and export value in thousands of yen. For example, 81.1 thousand koku were exported at a value of 1.5 million yen from a total harvest of 8.9 million koku in 1912.

    Sources: Figures on the total annual harvest of paddy and upland rice on the peninsula were drawn from CSTN. Other data provided in Jinsen Shōkō Kaigisho, Jinsen Shōkō Kaigisho tōkei nempyō, 1937 [Statistical annual of the Jinsen Chamber of Commerce and Industry, 1937] (Jinsen: Tsukiji Publishing, 1938), Tables 54, 62.

isolated export enclaves, but both retained earlier patterns of ownership and production rather than reorganization into plantations for export.[48] A further feature of Japanese colonization was immigration from the home islands, particularly to Korea. Unlike the case of Western colonial powers in Indonesia and elsewhere in Asia, Japanese colonists flocked to the neighboring Korean peninsula in large numbers. Comparing the number of colonists to total population in Asian colonies, Maddison

TABLE 2.3 Rice Exports from Inch'ŏn, 1921 to 1930 *

Year	Harvest	Export Volume	Export Value	Price/ koku
1921	14,324.3	879.5	24,292.6	27.62
1922	15,014.2	761.3	25,613.1	33.64
1923	15,174,6	895.5	25,463.1	28.43
1924	13,219.3	1,168.5	43,821.2	37.50
1925	14,773.1	1,158.1	47,072.1	40.64
1926	15,297.4	1,232.1	45,003.4	36.52
1927	17,298.8	1,378.0	43,514.0	31.57
1928	13,511.5	1,484.0	40,398.0	27.22
1929	13,701.7	1,165.6	31,122.0	26.69
1930	19,183.1	1,224.7	26,919.0	21.97

*Harvest and export volume cited in thousands of koku; export value cited in thousands of yen. The price per koku was calulated by dividing the total export value by export volume.

Sources: Annual figures for the total harvest of paddy and upland rice on the peninsula are drawn from CSTN. Other data is drawn from Jinsen Shōkō Kaigisho, *Jinsen Shōkō Kaigisho tōkei nempyō, 1937* [Statistical annual of the Jinsen Chamber of Commerce and Industry, 1937] (Jinsen: Tsukiji Publishing, 1938), Tables 54, 62.

estimated the Japanese comprised 2.6% of the entire population in Korea by the early 1930s.[49] In contrast, the Dutch in Indonesia or the British in Burma or Malaya represented between 0.4% and 0.7%. The grain trade drew large numbers of Japanese to the treaty ports and especially to Inch'ŏn, where Korean residents numbered only seven hundred in 1885, 4,700 a decade later, and 10,800 by 1905. The number of Japanese residents kept pace with the Korean population through 1895, and jumped ten years later in the midst of the Russo-Japanese War

TABLE 2.4 Rice Exports from Inch'ŏn, 1931 to 1937

Year	Harvest*	Export Volume	Export Value	Price/ koku
1931	15,827.9	1,897.5	29,637.0	15.61
1932	16,354.8	1,527.5	30,998.0	20.29
1933	18,192.7	1,438.8	28,798.0	20.01
1934	16,717.2	1,899.3	44,398.0	23.37
1935	17,884.6	1,589.5	44,394.0	27.92
1936	19,410.7	1,351.6	40,452.0	29.92
1937	26,796.9	1,373.4	43,202.0	31.45

* Harvest and export volume cited in thousands of koku; export value cited in thousands of yen. The price per koku was calulated by dividing the total export value by export volume.

Sources: Annual figures for the total harvest of paddy and upland rice on the peninsula are drawn from CSTN. Other data is drawn from Jinsen Shōkō Kaigisho, *Jinsen Shōkō Kaigisho tōkei nempyō, 1937* [Statistical annual of the Jinsen Chamber of Commerce and Industry, 1937] (Jinsen: Tsukiji Publishing, 1938), Tables 54, 62.

[1903-1904].[50] By 1910 the city of Inch'ŏn registered 44,000 Koreans and 11,000 Japanese or about one fifth of the port's population. With a stable Japanese population and fast-growing Korean population, the ratio of Japanese fell to 17% of the total Inch'ŏn population of 63,000 by 1930, and to 15% of 80,000 five years later.[51]

Three phases of colonial agrarian policy promoted the commercialization of agriculture in the production, processing, storage, and marketing of rice and soybeans. Upon completion of a comprehensive land or "Cadastral Survey" in 1918 clarifying land ownership and in response to demand for rice in Japanese markets, colonial authorities implemented a "Rice Increase Plan" initiated in 1920 and suspended in 1934.[52] Grajdanzev detailed the means such as use of improved seeds and wider availability of fertilizers, but also infrastructural investment in irrigation and land reclamation. Although the plan never fulfilled its ambitious goals, production of rice did grow from 12.7 million koku in

1920 to 18.1 million koku in 1934, with Korean exports now flooding the Japanese grain markets. Finally, wartime controls from 1939 reorganized marketing and consumption of rice for the years prior to liberation in 1945, and again promoted expanded production.[53] Improvements were usually financed through credit and loans rather than grants, necessitating the investment of scarce resources among the rural population. What the administration did provide was a fairly sophisticated infrastructure of finance, a "key mechanism" in Korea's integration and progression within the colonial world system.[54] For instance, the finance associations [kinyū kumiai] from 1907 were designed to promote rural credit as "people's banks," but also played a role in marketing of grains through consignment purchase and sales, warehousing, and trucking.[55] Reorganization under a system of province federations in the 1920s brought an infusion of government cash and control. Both financing and controls were further strengthened with formation of a national umbrella group, the Chosen Federation of Finance Associations from 1933 with more direct ties to the Bank of Chosen.[56] But links between finance and grains were already well-established, for the Industrial Banks and other semi-official finance institutions under the direction of the Government-General invested initially in granaries at the ports and production areas, which were reorganized and expanded under the Chosen Grain Storage Company from 1930.[57]

The results of such efforts suggest "growth without development," reminiscent of the overdevelopment of infrastructure and underdevelopment of local human resources.[58] Most agree that seeds, fertilizers, and cultivation methods improved productivity in the colonial years, and some such as Ban conclude that "agriculture was transformed from a feudalistic to a capitalistic system."[59] Miyajima Hiroshi argued for at least structural change towards production for a market in his thesis of commercialization of agriculture, but many also cite little improvement in the farmers' lives during the period.[60] Still others emphasize organization and interest formation among the peasants evident in tenant disputes, and suggest initial changes in the mode of production, prompting Shin Gi-wook to write recently of at least partial proletarianization to acknowledge the growth of wage labor.[61] What gains our attention however, are the changes in markets and merchants of the grain trade, and the formation of local mercantile interests at the major export centers.

Although compradors often appear in semi-colonial situations rather than in occupied colonies, the relatively brief tenure of the Japanese colonists in Korea may well have supported a similar role for local brokers. But there was less need for the compradors in Korea, given the proximity to Japan, linguistic similarities, and the large immigration of Japanese settlers and traders.[62] A pattern of accommodation with distinction and subordination joining ethnically distinct firms within larger exchanges and business associations soon became the norm at the treaty ports, with Korean brokers building their enterprise in the shadow of a better funded and organized Japanese business community on the peninsula. The small numbers of Japanese agents in comparison to the size of the market, coupled with the extensive networks of transport, lodging, and consignment of the Korean brokers forced cooperation between colonist and colonized for expansion of the grain trade.

Trade, grains, and guilds offer a glimpse of the business world at Inch'ŏn and Pusan at the turn of the century. Hong Chae-bŏm led the Inch'ŏn Brokers Cooperative, and later operated a rice mill in Inch'ŏn. Among the most prominent of Inch'ŏn's traditional brokers, Hong later served as a councillor of the joint Korean-Japanese Chamber of Commerce at Inch'ŏn in the early colonial years. Chu Myŏng-gi prospered with his Wayang Variety Store and later the Chu Rice Mill in the Yanagi-chō district, listed with a capital of 245,000 yen by 1939.[63] Yu Kun-sŏng operated the Yu Rice Mill in the Hana-chō district of Inch'ŏn, but gained fame more as a broker than an industrialist with sales of lumber for building barges and houses, and with a seat on the prestigious Jinsen Grain Exchange and later, even on the Chosen Exchange.[64] Kim Pyŏng-jo operated the Such'ang Rice Mill in Pusan from 1925,[65] but perhaps the most prominent Korean in Pusan's grain markets was Sin Su-gap who parlayed a successful brokerage into leadership positions at the Pusan Grain Retailers Association, the Fuzan Chamber of Commerce, and even the Fuzan City Council.[66] Brokers were commoners, usually newcomers to the ports who found a place in milling and trade at Inch'ŏn and Pusan alongside the giant Japanese mills of Katō Heitarō and Rikimu Kajirō.

Firms, trade associations, and the Grain Exchange gave shape and texture to a business community in the port cities. On the one hand, ethnically separate organizations helped quickly establish Japanese dominance on the peninsula and integration of Korean markets into the empire, but also encouraged solidarity among the Korean business leaders as a distinct business circle. On the other hand, combined organizations such as grain exchanges or joint chambers of commerce brought Koreans and Japanese together, providing a forum for Koreans to gain the contacts and information necessary for enterprise in an economy directed by the colonial state, and dominated by Japanese businessmen.[67]

Conclusion

The sweep of five hundred years of polity, market, and regional ties reveals significant precedent and provides a context for colonial patterns of enterprise. Autonomy within and constraints beyond national borders permitted a distinctive style of political control on domestic markets and merchants in the Chosŏn Dynasty, and limited, carefully managed exposure to markets of border states. A tradition of guild organization, government authorization and control, particularly of rice markets, and cooperation between government and merchant in border trade guided polity and commerce in the late nineteenth century. Market penetration then challenged deeply rooted precedent as colonial patterns of enterprise and association forced a reinstituting and rethinking of exchange. Beyond simply linkage of production and profit to the markets of the core, incorporation suggests a deepening or extension of capitalist structures. The harnessing of Korean grain production to the priorities and interests of markets and merchants in Osaka and Tokyo spurred the commercialization of agriculture but also the formation of a more distinct and professional business circle or *chaegye* for what crystallized in the crucible of the colonial experience were the institutions and ideas of a modern business community.

In the context of five centuries of state policy and merchant ties, the Kabo reforms at the end of the nineteenth century represent a watershed in the traditional interpenetration of polity and market. The earlier cooperation of designated merchants or mandated guilds with state authorities permitted limited specialization without clear distinction or autonomy. If the complexity of market dynamics and limited bureaucratic resources, together with foreign pressure against earlier modes of state control in the market forced greater distinction between merchant and ruler in the Kabo reforms, the challenges of markets and the improving status of merchants continued in the colony. The extension and sophistication of market dynamics fostered more autonomy among the colonial zaikai, and to a lesser extent among the Korean chaegye, and greater sophistication in state policy. Yet our insight here is not simply market over traditional societal controls, but rather how society becomes embedded in modern markets as precedents of enterprise and association mixed with patterns of colonial penetration in Korea's transformation. It was accommodation of distinct albeit subordinated local brokers, rather than assimilation that distinguished Japanese colonial rule.

The commercialization of agriculture extended and enhanced the market dynamic in the countryside but especially at the grain export gateways of Inch'ŏn, Pusan, and Kunsan. Reorientation away from Seoul and towards Osaka and Tokyo furthered the shift towards grain production for sale and the dominance of grains as the leading sector in the colonial economy. Standing at the center of grain exports on the peninsula, the history of the Jinsen Grain Exchange documents the growth of new institutions and new ideas, and chronicles as well developments in the colonial "civil society" of Japanese zaikai and Korean chaegye.[68] But if market is pivotal, the marketers themselves both Korean and Japanese tell us still more of organization and attitudes. Firms, trade associations, and the Exchange constituted a circle of enterprise structuring markets in the colonial years. The late nineteenth trade debate among Korean intellectuals, the legal structure of enterprise, associations and markets in late kingdom and colony, and the furor over the merger of the Exchanges at Seoul and Inch'ŏn introduce us to ideas of exchange, old and new.

Notes

1. Government General of Chosen, *Annual Report on Reforms and Progress in Korea, 1911-1912* (Keijō: Government General of Chosen, 1912), pp. 63-79; Ramon H. Myers and Yamada Saburō, "Agricultural Development in the Empire," in Ramon H. Myers and Mark R. Peattie, eds., *The Japanese Colonial Empire, 1895-1945* (Princeton: Princeton University Press, 1984), pp. 424, 451-452.

2. Hatada Takeshi, *A History of Korea* (Santa Barbara, CA: ABC-Clio Press, 1969), p. 117.

3. Alvin Y. So, *The South China Silk District: Local Historical Transformation and World-System Theory* (New York: State University of New York Press, 1986), p. 55.

4. Hamashita Takeshi, "Tributary Trade System and Modern Asia," *Memoirs of the Research Department of the Tōyō Bunko* 46 (1988): 9.

5. Mark Mancall, *China at the Center: 300 Years of Foreign Policy* (New York: The Free Press, 1984), p. 35; and "The Ch'ing Tribute System: An Interpretive Essay," in John King Fairbank, ed., *The Chinese World Order:*

Traditional China's Foreign Relations (Cambridge MA: Harvard, 1968), pp. 63-89.

6. "It was neither China's intention nor its normal practice under the tribute system to interfere in or to assume responsibility for Korean affairs, internal or external. Nor was Korea, its ceremonial submission to China notwithstanding, ever willing to accept Chinese interference in its affairs. Korea remained master in its own house, functioning as a fully independent state in fact, if indeed not in name as well." Kim Key-hiuk, *The Last Phase*, p. 9. Mancall cited only domestic autonomy: "Korea functioned internally as a completely independent country, with all the attributes of internal independence that were normally a part of Western concepts of the state, but externally Korea deferred to China in international politics." See *China at the Center*, p. 35.

7. Chun Hae-jong, "An Historical Survey of the Sino-Korean Tributary Relationship," *Journal of Social Sciences and Humanities* (Seoul) vol. 12 (1966): 28, and "Sino-Korean Tributary Relations during the Ch'ing Period," in John K. Fairbank, ed., *The Chinese World Order* (Cambridge: Harvard University Press, 1969), p. 96.

8. Mancall, "The Ch'ing Tribute System," p. 77.

9. Ronald P. Toby, *State and Diplomacy in Early Modern Japan. Asia in the Development of the Tokugawa Bakufu* (Princeton: Princeton University Press, 1984).

10. Toby, *State and Diplomacy*, pp. 229-230.

11. Hamashita, "Tributary Trade," p. 20.

12. Koh Byung-ik, "The Attitudes of Koreans Toward Japan," in Marshall R. Phil, ed., *Listening to Korea* (New York: Praeger, 1973), pp. 43-52; Lee Yong-ha, "The Spiritual Aspect of Korea-Japan Relations: A Historical Review of Complications Arising from the Consciousness of Peripheral Culture," *Social Science Journal* (Seoul) 3 (1975): 20-45.

13. Mancall, "The Ch'ing Tribute System," pp. 85-86; Chun, "An Historical Survey," p. 27.

14. Jurgis Elisonas, "The Inseparable Trinity: Japan's Relations with China and Korea," in John Whitney Hall, ed., *The Cambridge History of Japan* vol. 4, "Early Modern Japan" (Cambridge: Cambridge University Press, 1991), pp. 235-300; Benjamin H. Hazard, "Korea and Japan: Premodern Relations (to 1875)," in Kodansha Publishing, *Kodansha Encyclopedia of Japan* vol. 4 (Tokyo: Kodansha, 1983), pp. 276-279; Kawashima Fujia, "Yi Dynasty," in Kodansha Publishing, *Kodansha Encyclopedia of Japan* vol. 8 (Tokyo: Kodansha, 1983), pp. 324-325; Lee Ki-baik, *A New History of Korea* (Cambridge MA: Harvard University Press, 1984), pp. 191-192.

15. Chun, "An Historical Survey," p. 5.

16. Elisonas, "The Inseparable Trinity," p. 247.

17. Hamashita, "Tributary Trade," p. 13.

18. Mancall, "The Ch'ing Tribute System," p. 81.

19. James B. Palais, *Politics and Policy in Traditional Korea* (Cambridge: Harvard University Press, 1975), p. 272.

20. The largest of the guilds, the peddlers were carefully organized under several levels of administration from the capital down to the local village, and entrusted by the monarchy with local trade and even intelligence-gathering functions. Hwang Sŏn-min, *Pobusang ŭi kyŏngyŏng hwaldong yŏn'gu* [A study of the economic management of the peddlers] (Seoul: Pogyŏng Munhwasa, 1989); Yi Hun-byŏn, *Pobusang kwanggye saryo* [Research materials on the peddlers] (Seoul: Pogyŏng Munhwasa, 1988); Pak Wŏn-Sŏn, *Pobusang* [Peddlers] (Seoul: Han'guk Yŏn'guso, 1965); "Fushō hoshō no enkaku oyobi soshiki [The history and organization of the Peddlers]," *Nikkan Tsūshō Kyōkai Hōkoku* I, no. 1 (September 1895): 114-117.

21. Deuchler wrote of the aftermath of the Hideyoshi invasions: "The rigid lines along which Korean-Japanese relations moved for the next centuries, however, were laid down after the Hideyoshi invasions in the 1590s. These invasions brought disaster to the peninsula and put a halt to trade. They also instilled in the minds of the Koreans a distrust and apprehension toward their insular neighbors. The settlement of 1609 granted the daimyo of Tsushima the monopoly on Korean trade. An elaborate scheme of regulations kept trade under tight control." Martina Deuchler, *Confucian Gentlemen and Barbarian Envoys: The Opening of Korea, 1875-1885* (Seattle: University of Washington Press, 1977), p. 3.

22. Sugihara Kaoru, "Patterns of Inter-Asian Trade, 1898-1913," *Osaka City University Economic Review* no. 16 (1980): 55-76.

23. Chōsen Sōtokufu, *Chōsen Sōtokufu tōkei nempō 1910* [Statistical annual of the Chōsen Government-General, 1910], Table 499, p. 924. This annual publication will be cited as CSTN.

24. Chief Commissioner of Customs, Korea, *Korea: Tables of Foreign Trade and Shipping for the Year 1908* (Seoul: Customs Office, 1908), Table 41, p. 257; Government General of Chosen, *Chosen: Table of Trade and Shipping for 1915* (Keijō: Government General, 1915), Table 60, p. 568. This annual volume was published by the Commissioner of Customs until 1910, and subsequently by the Government-General. The staff of the *Korean Repository* reported projected government revenues for 1896 of $6.19 million, with customs receipts of $429,000. The total revenues included the output of the mint, surplus monies, and even uncollected taxes. Apart from those items, the land tax ($1.47 million), house tax ($221,000), and customs receipts represented the main sources of government income.

25. Hong Sŏn-gwŏn, "Kaehanggi kaekchu," p. 107; Han, *Han'guk kaehanggi*, pp. 182-183.

26. Minister Takahira demanded the abolition of the favored broker system in Pusan already in October of 1885. Koryŏdae Dong'a Munje Yŏn'guso, compil., *Ku Han'guk woegyo munsŏ* [Diplomatic documents of the late Chosŏn Dynasty] (Seoul: Korea University Press, 1965) I, Takahira to Kim Yun-sik, October 16, 1885, doc. 580. This volume will be cited as KHWM, followed by volume and date of correspondence, and document number. An exchange of documents regarding trade in hides at the Tongnae treaty section of Pusan culminated in a note from Hanabusa to Yi Chae-myŏn, July, 1882, KHWM, vol. I, doc. 91. The earlier correspondence between Miyamoto and Kim Sŏn-gŭn at Tongnae can be found in documents 83, and 86-88.

27. Pusan Chikhalsisa P'yŏnch'an Wiwŏnhoe, ed., *Pusansisa* [A history of the city of Pusan] (Pusan: Cheil Printing, 1989), pp. 821-823.

28. The rules for the territorial broker system in Pusan, and the agreement between brokers and other merchants can be found in Han, *Han'guk kaehanggi*, p. 186-187. The Foreign Office [t'ongni amun] of Kojong's government was established in December of 1882, and retitled the Office for the Management of Diplomatic and Commercial Matters [t'ongni kyosŏp t'ongsangsamu amun] the next month. See Deuchler, *Confucian Gentlemen*, p. 153. The new title better reflected the role of trade in Korea's growing international diplomacy.

29. The reply of the Korean Foreign Office can be found in Min Chong-muk to Hillier, April 6, 1890, KHWM II, doc. 690. See also Kim Kyŏng-t'ae, "Kapsin Kabogi ŭi sanggwŏn koebok munje [The problem of the recovery of commercial rights in the Kapsin and Kabo periods [1884-1895]]," *Han'guksa Yŏn'gu* 50-51 (December 1985): 202-204, 212-218. Hillier sent the following reply to Kim Chung-muk of the Korean Foreign Office on April 26, 1890. "In the despatch under acknowledgement Your Excellency observes that the fees in question, would never be levied on native produce bought by foreign merchants, and therefore they are not concerned. It is precisely because these fees are levied on native produce destined for sale to foreign merchants as well as on foreign produce brought by Corean merchants that we have considered it our duty to interfere, and we must beg permission to repeat that we cannot submit to a system which compels Corean merchants to pass goods destined for sale to foreign merchants through a guild, which levies fees thereon, or to subject foreign goods bought by them to the inspection of a corporation which is allowed to tax such goods after inspection." KHWM, vol. 13, doc. 194.

30. *Independent*, January 23, 1897.

31. Yi Chae-ch'im, ed., *Sanggong hoeŭiso paegnyŏnsa* [A one hundred year history of the chambers of commerce and industry] (Seoul: Taehan Sanggong Hoeŭiso, 1984), p. 64; Inch'ŏn Sanggong Hoeŭiso, *Inch'ŏn Sanggong Hoeŭiso kusimnyŏnsa* [A ninety year history of the Inch'ŏn Chamber of Commerce and Industry] (Seoul: Samhwa, 1979.), pp. 153-163. Minister of Agriculture, Commerce, and Industry Yi Wan-yong gave final authorization for

the association in a letter of January, 1897, reprinted in *Kusimnyŏnsa*, pp. 155-156, 161.

32. The Kabo law paralleled the earlier Diet legislation with this principle of mandatory organizations to promote a single, cohesive business voice in each district. But Japanese chambers in the port cities and Seoul, under the jurisdiction of the Japanese Consulates, proved far more formidable competitors for local state attention, and spawned more threatening cooperatives, than any competing Korean association. Annexation would bring more resources to the tri-level support system for the Japanese trader, an awesome advantage for the foreigners even when constrained by a wary local state.

33. Inch'ŏn Sanggong Hoeŭiso, *Inch'ŏn Sanggong Hoeŭiso kusimnyŏnsa* [A ninety year history of the Inch'ŏn Chamber of Commerce and Industry] (Seoul: Samhwa, 1979), p. 161.

34. Yi Wan-yong, "Sinsang Hoesa changjŏng sŏmun [Preface to the bylaws of the Merchants Association]," dated January, 1897, and reprinted in *Kusimny ŏnsa*, pp. 155-156. The legislation placed business associations under the supervision of the newly created Ministry of Agriculture, Commerce and Industry, rather than the Foreign Ministry. W. H. Wilkinson foresaw continued problems with the revenue collection: "the extraction in violation of treaty of inland dues over and above the tariff is a practice as well known as it is difficult to suppress." See his "Report on the Trade of Corea for the Year 1893," in Park Il-Keun. ed., *Anglo-American and Chinese Diplomatic Materials Relating to Korea*, vol. 2, (Seoul: Shin Mun Dang Publishing, 1982), p. 869.

35. The law of May 12, 1899, mandated reorganization of the former business associations [sangmu hoeŭiso] as branch offices of a central business firm [sangmusa] in Seoul. The Peddlers Guild apparently lobbied for the change, hoping to reassert earlier, centralized guild functions under the name of the new organizations. *Kusimnyŏnsa*, pp. 150, 156.

36. Naikaku Tōkei Kyoku (Statistical Office of the Cabinet), *Nihon teikoku tōkei nenkan* [Statistical annual of the Empire of Japan) (Tokyo: Naikaku Tōkei Kyoku, pertinent years). Export volummes are reported in picul which I have converted to koku (Korean: *sŏk*) according to Grajdanzev's calculus of 2.7 piculs for one koku. See his *Modern Korea*, p. 55. See also Chosŏn Ŭnhaeng Chosabu, *Chosŏn kyŏngje yŏnbo 1948* [Korean Economic Annual, 1948] (Seoul: Chosŏn Ŭnhaeng Chosabu, 1948), Section I, p. 237, and Chŏng To-yong, "Korea's Foreign Trade under Japanese Rule," *Journal of Social Sciences and Humanities* no. 27 (December 1967): 29, 43.

37. At each of the ports or places open to foreign trade, British subjects shall be at full liberty to import from any foreign port or from any Corean open port, to sell to or to buy from any Corean subjects or others, and to export to any foreign or Corean open port, all kinds of merchandise not prohibited by this Treaty, on paying the duties of the Tariff annexed thereto. They may freely

transact their business with Corean subjects or others without the intervention of Corean officials or other persons, and they may freely engage in any industrial occupation." See "Treaty of Friendship and Commerce between Great Britain and Corea," Article 5 Section 1.   Reprinted in Tōkanfu [Japanese Residency General in Korea], *Kankoku shūyaku ruisan* [A collection of Korean agreements] (Tokyo: Hideyōsha, 1908), p. 148.

38.   All goods imported into Corea by British subjects, and on which the duty of the Tariff annexed to this Treaty shall have been paid, may be conveyed to any Corean open port free of duty, and, when transported into the interior, shall not be subject to any additional tax, excise, or transit duty whatsoever in any part of the country.   In like manner, full freedom shall be allowed for the transport to the open ports of all Corean commodities intended for exportation, and such commodities shall not, either at the place of production, or when being conveyed from any part of Corea to any of the open ports, be subject to the payment of any tax, excise, or transit duty whatsoever." Article 5, Section 4, in *Kankoku shūyaku ruisan*, p. 148.

39.   Treaty of Friendship and Commerce between Great Britain and Corea," Article V, Section 6, in *Kankoku shūyaku ruisan*, p. 148.   A similar agreement can be found in "Ilbonguk inmin muyŏk kyujik [Trade rules for Japanese nationals]," number 37 in the same volume, p. 99.

40.   A list of the embargoes, including names of province officials and Japanese merchants can be found in Karasawa Takeko, "Bōkoku rei jiken [Grain embargo incidents]," *Chōsen Kenkyūkai Ronbunshū* (June 1969), pp. 72-73.   See also Yoshino Makoto, "Yicho makki ni okeru beikoku yushutsu no hatten to bōkokurei [Rice embargoes and the development of rice exports at the end of the Chosŏn Dynasty]," *Chōsenshi Kenkyūkai Ronbunshū* (March 1973), pp. 101-132.   One government concern at the time was control of inflation.   Kim Chun-po has concluded the embargoes were mainly government efforts to control the price of grains.   See his *Han'guk chabonjuŭisa yŏn'gu* [Studies in the history of Korean capitalism], vol. 3 (Seoul: Ilchogak, 1977), pp. 59-62.

41.   Yamabe Kentarō, *Nihon tōchika no Chōsen* [Korea under Japanese Administration] (Tokyo: Iwanami Shoten, 1971); Suh Sang-chul, *Growth and Structural Changes in the Korean Economy, 1910-1940* (Cambridge: Harvard University Press, 1978); Suzuki Takeo, *Chōsen keizai no shin kōsō* [New ideas in the Korean economy] (Keijō: Taikaido Insatsu Kabushiki Kaisha, 1942), pp. 3-35; Lee Chong-sik, *The Patterns of Korean Nationalism* (Berkeley: University of California Press, 1963); David Brudnoy, "Japan's Experiment in Korea," *Monumenta Nipponica*, 25, 1-2 (1970), pp. 155-195; Military Intelligence Service, War Department General Staff, "Historical Sketch of Japanese Administration in Korea since 1910," Appendix VIII in *Survey of Korea* (Washington D.C.:   War Department, June 15, 1943).

42. "The Problems of Japanese Administration in Korea," *Pacific Affairs* 11, 2 (June 1938), p. 207. However Dong Wonmo concluded that assimilation policy directives regarding Korean names and the Korean language were beginning to affect the wider population by the end of the colonial period. See his dissertation, "Japanese Colonial Policy and Practice in Korea, 1905-1945: A Study in Assimilation," Georgetown University, 1965.

43. Trade figures are drawn from Chōsen Bōeki Kyōkai, *Chōsen Bōeki nempō* [Annual of Korean trade] (Keijo: Chōsen Bōeki Kyōkai, annual), as cited in Han'guk Muyŏk Hyŏphoe, *Han'guk muyŏksa* [A history of trade in Korea] (Seoul: Han'guk Muyŏk Hyŏphoe, 1972), pp. 167, 169, 171. In U.S. dollars at the time, 60 million yen in 1910 amounted to 30 million dollars, and 600 million yen in 1930 amounted to 300 million dollars. Despite an increase to better than one billion yen of exports in 1939, depreciation of the currency outside of the empire left the dollar value at only 250 million dollars. Exchange rates can be found in Nihon Ginkō Tōkei Kyoku, *Meiji ikō hompō shuyō keizai tōkei* [One hundred years of economic statistics beginning with Meiji] (Tokyo: Nihon Ginkō Tōkei Kyoku, 1966), p. 85. The average exchange rate in New York in 1910 and 1930 was about 0.49 yen per U.S. dollar. The yen depreciated vis-a-vis the dollar to 0.25 yen per dollar by 1939.

44. Samuel Ho provides the price deflated index in "Colonialism and Development: Korea, Taiwan, and Kwantung," published in Ramon H. Myers and Mark R. Peattie, eds., *The Japanese Colonial Empire, 1895-1945* (Princeton: Princeton University Press, 1984), pp. 396-397, Table 4, with statistics drawn from Mizoguchi Toshiyuki, "Foreign Trade in Taiwan and Korea under Japanese Rule," *Hitosubashi Journal of Economics* 14 (February 1974): 37-53.

45. Ho, "Colonialism and Development," Table 4, pp. 396-397.

46. Nōrinsho Nōmukyoku [Agricultural Bureau of the Ministry of Agriculture and Forestry] *Kokubutsu yoram 1939* [Grain Annual 1939] (Tokyo: Nōrinsho, 1939), pp. 118-119. The Japanese koku [Korean: sŏk] corresponds to 5.1 U.S. 66 pound bushels.

47. Suh, *Growth and Structural Change*, Table 41. Assuming that calories from rice, barley, and wheat comprised 70% of total caloric intake, he estimated that daily per capita food availability in calories fell from a level of 2,133 calories across the years 1910 to 1914, to a level of 1,924 calories for the years 1925 to 1929. See also Ho, "Colonialism and Development," pp. 379, 398. Grajdanzev cited a 30 percent decline in consumption of rice between 1915 and 1929. See *Modern Korea*, pp. 118-119.

48. Ho, "Colonialism and Development," p. 385.

49. Angus Maddison, "Dutch Colonialism in Indonesia: Comparative Perspective," in Anne Booth, W. J. O'Malley, and Anna Weidemann, eds., *Indonesian Economic History in the Dutch Colonial Era* (New Haven: Yale

University Southeast Asia Studies, 1990), p. 324, Table 14.1. According to statistics provided in CSTN, 1943, p. 2, the Korean population in 1935 numbered 21,891,180, and the Japanese population in the colony numbered 583,428, or .026 of the Korean population.

50. The population in 1930 included 11,238 Japanese, 49,960 Koreans and a small minority of other foreigners, with a total population of 63,658. Jinsen Shōkō Kaigisho, *Jinsen Shōkō Kaigisho tōkei nempyō, 1937* [Statistical annual of the Jinsen Chamber of Commerce and Industry, 1937] (Jinsen: Tsukiji Publishing, 1938), Table 80. See also Inch'ŏnsisa P'yŏnch'an Wiwŏnhoe, ed., *Inch'ŏnsisa* [A history of the city of Inch'ŏn] (Inch'ŏn: Kyŏng'il Publishing, 1973), p. 91; *Kusimnyŏnsa*, p. 84; Chōsen Sōtokufu, *Chōsen ni okeru naichijin* [Japanese nationals in Korea] (Keijo: Chōsen Sōtokufu, 1923), pp. 2-5.

51. CSTN, 1910, 1930.

52. Government General of Chosen, *Annual Report on Reforms and Progress in Korea, 1935-1936* (Keijō: Government General of Chosen, 1936), pp. 115-116. The administration reported results of the Land Improvement Program to increase rice production, initiated in 1920, revised and expanded in 1926 and suspended in 1934.

53. Grajdanzev, *Modern Korea*, pp. 92-94.

54. Woo Jung-en, *Race to the Swift: State and Finance in Korean Industrialization* (New York: Columbia University Press, 1991), p. 30.

55. Hoon K. Lee, *Land Utilization and Rural Economy in Korea* (New York: Greenwood, [1936] 1969), p. 242.

56. Nongŏp Hyŏptong Chohap [National Agricultural Cooperative Federation, NACF], *Nonghyŏp isimnyŏnsa* [A twenty year history of the NACF] (Seoul: NACF, 1982), pp. 56-62; James Frederick McRaith, "The Marketing of Rice in the Republic of Korea," Ph.D. diss., Columbia University, 1960, pp. 36-37.

57. CGKKY 1932, p. 96. Established in May of 1930 with the purpose of securing grains for export, the company was responsible for transport, storage, consignment sales and purchases, and insurance. Major shareholders in the paid-up capital of 250,000 yen included Katō Heitarō, founder of the Jinsen Grain Exchange; the Chosen Industrial Bank; Katō Keizaburō; and the Oriental Development Company.

58. Shin Gi-wook, "Social Change and Peasant Protest," p. 94-95.

59. Moon, Pal Yong, "The Evolution of Rice Policy in Korea," *Food Research Institute Studies* 14, 4 (1975): 385; Ban Sung Hwan, "Agricultural Growth in Korea, 1918-1971," pp. 90-116 in Yujiro Hayami, Vernon W. Ruttan, and Herman M. Southworth, eds., *Agricultural Growth in Japan, Taiwan, Korea, and the Philippines* (Honolulu: University Press of Hawaii, 1979).

60. "Chōsen kango kaikaku igo no shōgyōteki nogyō [Commercial agriculture in Korea after the Kabo Reforms]," *Shirin* 57, 6 (Nov. 1974): 38-77.

61. "Social Change and Peasant Protest in Colonial Korea," p. 66. Shin draws the idea of "semi-proletarianization" from Huang's study, *The Peasant Economy and Social Change in North China* (Stanford: Stanford University Press, 1985). Yoo Se Hee has also written of peasant organization and protest in "The Korean Communist Movement and the Peasantry under Japanese Rule," Ph.D. diss., Columbia University, 1974.

62. Vleming wrote of a similar absence of compradors in the colony of Indonesia under the Dutch. See J. L. Vleming jnr, "The Chinese Business Community in Netherlands India," in M. R. Fernando and David Bulbeck, eds., *Chinese Economic Activity in Netherlands India* (Singapore: ASEAN Economic Research Unit, Institute of Southeast Asian Studies, 1992), pp. 133-134.

63. Keijō Shōkō Kaigijo, *Chōsen kaishahyō 1939* [List of firms in Korea, 1939] (Keijo: Gyōsei Gakkai Insatsujo, 1939), p. 190.

64. Chōsen Torihikijo, *Chōsen Torihikijo nempyō 1936* [Annual of the Chosen Exchange, 1936] (Keijo: Chōsen Torihikijo, 1936), pp. 60-61; Inch'ŏn Chikhalsisa P'yŏnch'an Wiwŏnhoe, *Inch'ŏn kaehang paegnyŏnsa* [A one hundred history from the opening of the port of Inch'ŏn] (Inch'ŏn: Kyŏnggi Ch'ulp'ansa, 1983), p. 222; Sin T'ae-bŏm, *Inch'ŏn hansegi* [One generation in Inch'ŏn] (Inch'ŏn: Hunmi Ch'ulp'ansa, 1983), p. 115.

65. Pusan Sanggong Hoeŭiso, *Pusan sangŭisa* [A business history of Pusan] (Pusan: Pusan Sanggong Hoeŭiso, 1989), p. 214.

66. Note that "Fuzan" is the Japanese colonial term for "Pusan," and used here to denote Japanese dominated organizations. I use the term "Pusan" for organizations dominated by Koreans in the colonial period. Pusan Sanggong Hoŭiso, *Pusan sangŭisa*, p. 255; Pak Wŏn-p'yo, *Kaehang kujunyŏn* [Ninety years from the opening of the port] (Pusan: Taehwa Inswoeso, 1976), p. 262.

67. See my article, "The Keishō and the Korean Business Elite," *Journal of Asian Studies* 48, no. 2 (May 1989): 310-323.

68. Recognizing the frequent use of the term *chaegye* in English, parallel to the use of Japanese term *zaikai*, I will no longer cite the term in italics.

3

Trade Opponents

Confucian norms of empire, polity and market still dominated exchange even as brokers and guilds managed inns and small warehouses, ferried products by cart over country roads and by barge across canals and rivers, and plied their commerce in rice at periodic markets. Joining the bustling local commerce with the closely supervised tribute trade cited above, a picture emerges of markets embedded in social norms and political priorities of court and aristocrat. But if the extension of foreign ties to the peninsula forced a rethinking of Korea's status as a vassal state within the Chinese Empire, it also loosened the moral ties constraining the market dynamic. Heated controversies exposed the trauma of the expanding markets in a society dedicated to the commonweal but confronted with private profit. How could a nation guided by Confucian moral norms permit market interests? How could a hierarchical, carefully stratified society tolerate direction by random forces of supply and demand?

Trade advocates hailed the benefits of exchange as Japan, Russia, Britain, the U.S. and other Western powers pressed for open markets on the peninsula. Commerce promised power and prosperity, a new market for local produce, and access to manufactured textiles and tools. Opening ports to foreign trade would enrich the national treasury and strengthen state efforts to monitor trade and manage change. But the market argument did not persuade opponents who questioned the benefits and necessity of capitalist exchange and indeed countered with frightening images of commodification, of contract destroying morality, and of assimilation under the Japanese.[1] Their protest revealed a profound ideological divide over market and society. Korea was a small country where trade debates at the capitol quickly affected the organization and ideas of the brokers in neighboring Inch'ŏn. But the opponents played a far wider role in framing major issues of the debate such as "nation" versus state, the commonweal and the "people," and of "interest" whether public or private. Trade opponents posed the problem of market in Korean society. Trade advocates were left to resolve the problems of market with new ideas of state and society, and of public and private interest.

An earlier integration of market within society was giving way to more distinct spheres of contract and kinship and new borders between market and morality just as Japan began to penetrate the geographical borders of the hermit kingdom. Erosion of local sovereignty evident at the ports rekindled fear of foreign ties. The depth of opposition among some literati was apparent in the mid-century writings of the eminent Yi Hang-no, and by the flurry of "memorials" to the crown in 1876 vehemently rejecting the Kanghwa Treaty. Persecution of Catholic converts on the peninsula continued from the late eighteenth century through the mid-nineteenth century, spurred by suspected links between converts and French expansionists.[2] The linking of xenophobia with peasant unrest distinguished the trade opposition of the late nineteenth century from the earlier anxieties over foreign penetration.

Historians cite numerous local disturbances in the latter years of the Chosŏn Dynasty, including large-scale uprisings in 1811 and 1862 which the government suppressed without addressing the economic needs of the rural population. The persisting economic plight of the peasants, together with anxiety over foreign penetration later helped fuel the extensive Tonghak rebellion of 1894, pressing administrative and economic reforms, and confronting the government with a cohesive force of angry peasants. Rebel peasants held off the local military but proved no match for a joint Japanese-Korean expeditionary force.[3] And again, military suppression did not resolve peasant discontent with local officials nor anxieties about growing foreign control of the production and commerce of grains.

Trade opponents among the conservative literati would help focus peasant indignation over poverty and corruption on the penetration of foreigner merchants to the countryside. The Kanghwa Treaty of 1876 sparked the ire of conservative literati identified with the "Orthodoxy" School, and two decades later the Kabo reforms drove some from rhetoric to armed rebellion in the countryside. Imposition of the Japanese Protectorate in 1905 finally galvanized peasant discontent and literati opposition into heroic but futile military skirmishes with the well-armed Japanese army. Many rural tenant farmers had suffered in the transition to an international trade in grains, whether from Korean tax officials or rapacious brokers and traders, and the literati had lost political leverage in the Kabo Reforms. Resistance in the Righteous Armies would meld peasant resentment with literati indignation in an uneasy alliance where "Confucian leaders respected the traditional social order and wanted to return to it, whereas peasants wanted reform of that order."[4] Japanese military action rather than ideological differences alone brought an end to the combination of peasant unrest and aristocratic anger, but the conflicting goals of peasant and literati reveal fundamental social changes already in process in minds and well as in markets.

Trade opponents rallied for the public good over private profit, for moral priorities in the face of market attractions, and for a social hierarchy to sustain an earlier order. If private ownership and private profit define capitalism, opponents rejected the very principles of the capitalist market. If unequal commercial ties and subordination defined Korea's entry into international markets, opponents rejected the new regional order. Leadership of a few conservative literati of the Orthodoxy School in the guerilla movement termed the "Righteous Armies," deserves special attention because of their prominence and commitment as trade opponents.[5] In the futile effort of Yi Hang-no, Ch'oe Ik-hyŏn, Yu In-sŏk, and Ki Sam-yŏn to reverse the rise of the market, we find a clear if impractical alternative to the reformist agenda of trade advocates.

Yi Hang-no preferred scholarship to high political office yet found time to direct strident memorials to the crown on behalf of seclusion.[6] His student Ch'oe Ik-hyŏn opted for the active life of politics and government service, but sacrificed all hope of high office with adamant opposition to expanding foreign ties. Frustrated in government service, Ch'oe reemerged as a resistance leader in 1896 and again in 1906, only to be captured and die in prison on Tsushima Island.[7] A reporter offered a sympathetic portrait in 1898: "he enjoys the reputation of being an upright and outspoken scholar, poor and proud."[8] Another disciple, Yu In-sŏk led Righteous Army groups in 1896 before fleeing to the Liaotung Peninsula.[9] The *Independent* described Yu as "the backbone of trouble in several districts of Ch'ungch'ŏng Province," and advertised a $400 government reward for his capture.[10] Among literati prominent in the later resistance, Ki Sam-yŏn led forces in his native Chŏlla Province where he died in action near Kwangju in 1908.

The complaint against trade chronicles a conflict of minds as well as of market organization in Korea's passage to a new interstate regional order. No group better portrayed the chaos wrought by international commerce, nor offered a more poignant challenge to the market-oriented ideas of the new interstate system. A shift in tactics from memorials at court to rebellion in the fields brought this world of ideas to the world of commerce, leaving brokers to parry occasional attacks of angry peasants. What the protest portrays is an earlier ideal of empire, polity, and market which served often as foil and sometimes as father to the ideals of trade advocates. At the same time the Kabo reformers in Seoul legislated a new, more independent role for the brokers, opponents pestered Seoul reformers and hunted down brokers in the countryside. Articulate enemies of trade and traders, they struck an important counterpoint to the emerging model of independent organization and interest among the brokers in the expanding markets.

Empire

The opposition alerts us to the pace and scale of change as their Orthodoxy School countered reform politicians and brokers rushing to secure a place in the new order. One scholar wrote of the School as "a conscious, organized effort of a segment of the elite to perpetuate the Confucian elements of the traditional culture as symbols of the unique character of Korean society."[11] The conventional translation of their banner as "protect orthodoxy and ban heterodoxy" may misrepresent the conservative literati at the turn of the century as simply disgruntled philosophers, for the movement went beyond debate to armed resistance. A mission to "protect good and reject evil" better conveys their profound rejection of trade and what it represented.[12] Indignation and growing resentment was evident as opponents matched the fast pace of incorporation with ever more strident and violent protest.

The progression from 1876 to the reforms two decades later, and then to the Protectorate in 1905 brought anger and despair. An initial campaign against trade ties unfolded in tandem with events in Seoul and the countryside as Yi Hang-no and Ch'oe Ik-hyŏn led the charge against commerce with Japan in the years prior to the Kanghwa Treaty. Such political leadership was not uncommon in a kingdom where literati had played a prominent role at the court during the long reign of the Chosŏn Dynasty monarchs. A censorate with extensive powers of oversight, and a tradition of formal memorials to the crown by concerned scholars had long been part of the Dynasty, prior to the Kabo reforms of 1895 abolishing the censorate and the practice of memorials in favor of representation through a cabinet system within a constitutional monarchy.[13] The legislation may have deprived the literati of formal power in the polity, but the literati with their network of country schools in rural areas remained a formidable force for public opinion. Ch'oe, Yu In-sŏk and Ki Sam-yŏn later helped mobilize peasant resistance to local brokers and Japanese traders ranging across Korea's interior in search of grain. For the literati it was a shocking reversal of status from respected critics at court to rebels in the hinterland. Ch'oe, Yu and Ki reacted to the Kabo reforms with a stream of now "unofficial" memorials and sniper attacks on rice traders and brokers in the interior. For the brokers it was a painful reminder of deeply rooted precedents haunting their passage from guild to chamber.

Proponents of the past often gain a warm welcome in the chaos of the present. An eloquent and nostalgic literati brief for an earlier cultural empire of stability and political autonomy found a sympathetic audience in the countryside. Laying claim to centuries of continuity in political authority and social structure across the Chosŏn Dynasty, they raised a credible complaint against extension of markets linked to the Japanese. Literati had long before defined Korea's regional status in a Chinese cultural and political order, the role of monarchy and aristocracy in directing the state, and the structures of hierarchy within family and workplace. Well-versed in the earlier order, conservative literati now proved formidable critics of new patterns of empire, polity, and market. For instance Yi Hang-no contrasted the "civilized" with the "uncivilized" to distinguish membership in the Chinese world order where Korea had long prided itself as the cultured society on the border of the Chinese Empire.[14] Conservative literati of the late nineteenth century admired the cultural ideals of the earlier Song and Ming Dynasties, but disdained contemporary China under the Manchu barbarians of the Qing Empire (1644-1912).

Respect for the earlier tradition in Ming China conveyed commitment to a cultural world order quite distinct from political and economic ties with the Chinese state of the late nineteenth century. The disjunction between principle on the one hand, and political-economic order or structure on the other plagued debates over trade among advocates and opponents.[15] For instance the premise of an isolated kingdom maintaining the earlier virtues of a Chinese empire hardly described the century preceding the Kanghwa Treaty where we noted above bilateral, cross-border commerce with both Qing China and Tokugawa Japan.

More to the point, diplomatic exchanges with Tokugawa Japan provide evidence of a relationship of equality with Japan quite distinct from, though not necessarily inconsistent with Korea's tributary status within the Chinese Empire. Even if trade opponents would admit the necessity of limited ties and managed trade to sustain the principle of a civilized tributary within the Chinese empire, they did not address the fact that changes in place well before 1876 were now identified with incorporation under the Japanese. Korea's international seclusion as a vassal state under Chinese suzerainty permitted this ideological disjunction between cultural respect and local political autonomy, but a new interstate system in the region would accommodate neither the ideology nor the isolation.[16] Opening of the ports and ties with Japan brought Korea into a new integrated order of both cultural and political/economic ties.

But whatever the inconsistencies, critics such as Yu In-sŏk found an audience with his trenchant criticism of the new interstate system. He rallied peasants in 1895 with the lament that a nation known as a "little China" and proud of its cultural achievements, was fast becoming a "little Japan," as evident in both ideas of the reformers and commerce of the traders.[17] Linking the motto of "enlightenment" to both the breakdown of internal order and erosion of sovereignty, he argued that Korean reformers and their Japanese allies had undermined both family and nation. The suggestion that trade hastened political and economic dependence disturbed even trade advocates who could not ignore the relentless penetration of the Japanese. But it was anger not anxiety that drove the conservative literati to boldly reject Korea's entry into this new order as the "destruction" of the nation and people of Korea. Determined to stem the extension of Korean ties with Japan, opponents turned their anger against the merchants in the grain trade for grains were not only the major export but the lifeblood of this agrarian society. Ch'oe sounded the alarm in 1876 with his theme of grains as the "blood and skin on which our lives depend" to warn against an unbalanced trade of a limited supply of agrarian produce for the unlimited manufactures from Japan.[18] Two decades later Yu In-sŏk linked trade with the fading distinction between civilized and barbarian in the assertion that trade dehumanized Koreans.[19] And by 1906 we find Ki Sam-yŏn echoing the same sentiment to strengthen peasant resolve against the Japanese: "the absence of restraints and prohibitions on the buying and selling of grains is emaciating the people and destroying the nation's thread of life."[20]

Opponents who had initially focused their fury on Western ideas and market ties later turned attention to the power balance in the new regional order. Ch'oe Ik-hyŏn in 1906 lamented the loss of Korea's sovereignty but held out hope for Japan's demise by forces within and beyond the islands. He reasoned that the Japanese populace would be unwilling to bear the costs of expansion and speculated that major powers such as Russia and China, the U.S. and Britain were just waiting for the chance to destroy Japan.[21] Ki Sam-yŏn cited the precedent of Japanese assimilation of the Ryukyu Islands as the death knell for the rest of the region, and then contrasted the division and decline of Asia under Japan with the strength and growing cooperation in the West.[22] The belated turn among these literati to unlikely allies among powerful states in an international system belied the failure of their strategy of personal moral reform without structural change, and of their focus on domestic insulation without regard for a changing regional environment. In contrast, progressive literati such as Pak Ŭn-sik joined enlightenment advocates in shaping reform ideas and gained a place in the expanding field of popular journals and newspapers.

What plagued many trade opponents was a more basic, social and personal issue of dramatic reversal of status among literati formerly prominent as government advisors and officials.[23] Yet despite the dramatic but futile dedication of reactionaries to a cultural world order which had begun to fade well before 1876, one cannot ignore the cogency of their complaint against unbalanced trade with Japan. They promoted an earlier Sino-centric cultural order and a return to economic isolation. They denounced trade as the leading edge of a movement to destroy the earlier monarchy and erode Korea's sovereignty in a new regional system dominated by Japan. They exposed the shift from a system governed by custom and symbol to a colonial empire where contract and market would compete with moral and political norms. And they carefully linked authority and exchange in Korea's incorporation, constantly decrying the interplay of polity and market eroding Korean sovereignty.

Polity

Trade critics hoped to link collapse of the earlier cultural order to foreign penetration rather than to initiatives at Seoul, which explains their rage with the Kabo reforms leading to a constitutional monarchy. Retaining a traditional polity of monarch and government ministers deeply imbued with a Confucian moral ethic would sustain their prominence as well in Korean society. Yi Hang-no presented a Korean Confucian model of authority in an essay titled, "The Destructiveness of the West," where orthodoxy coincided with the way of the "gentleman [*kunja*]" found in the writings of Confucius and Mencius, a way of propriety and moral rectitude.[24] The five relationships of monarch and minister, father and son, husband and wife, older and younger brother, and friend to friend provided a hierarchy of authority, just as the descending ladder of four occupations [i.e., scholar, farmer, artisan and merchant] provided a status hierarchy in the economy.[25] Apart from a moral ideal and norms of personal relations and professions, Yi wrote grandly of authority emanating from the crown. The seminal concept of *kunsin* [monarch and minister] conveyed the central pattern of authority, with the wider populace represented through the scholar-officials serving as the crown's ministers.[26] We find no evidence of the distinction between "state" and "society" later suggested among Korean progressives, nor of the enhanced role of the wider populace or "public" in the nation's direction. But the people were not ignored for indeed government ministers were responsible for the common interest of both monarch and his subjects, and Yi himself devoted attention to the well-being of the "people [*sengmin* or *inmin*]" without distinction between monarch and subject. Whatever their subsequent differences with reformers and their ideas of "state," attention to the well-being of the "people" in earlier Confucian doctrines provided a basis for the interests of "society" popular among Enlightenment advocates.

Themes of crown [*wang*], minister or bureaucrat [*sin*], and nation [*kugga*] gave texture to the model of "monarch and minister" distinguishing authority. They argued forcefully for the institution of the monarchy and rejected reforms diluting the monarch's power. It was not simply the polity that was at stake but rather society since the principle of sovereign over minister served as the key paradigm for other formative relations such as father and son, and husband and wife.[27] What most concerned these critics was the fact that democratic reforms in the polity threatened the hierarchical structure of Korean Confucian culture, not to mention the political leverage of the literati themselves. Trade opponents maintained a respectful loyalty to the monarchy in the fray, but did not hesitate to berate Kojong's ministers for deviations from the norms of Classical Confucianism.[28] Praise of a Confucian past in ancient China and across five centuries of Chosŏn Dynasty Korea, harsh criticism of the present administration, and only occasional reference to Kojong himself came to define their support for the crown. Such restrained loyalty belied a literati group interest in retaining the monarchy to preserve the prominent role of the scholar-official "minister" in the hierarchy, coupled with the long tradition of competition at the court between monarch and minister.

Followers of Yi Hang-no quickly turned their attention to brokers, Japanese traders, and colluding Korean government officials. Ch'oe Ik-hyŏn warned of the destruction of "monarch and minister," and of "the people [paeksŏng]" in a memorial of 1905.[29] He had earlier detailed the virtues of the ancient kings in a memorial of 1866, and struck a theme of a virtuous ruler supported by faithful and public-spirited ministers.[30] Ch'oe addressed the Confucian-educated ministers [yusin] as a peer, identifying himself with the corps of scholar-officials as representatives of the people. He condemned ministers responsible for the Kabo reforms such as Pak Yŏng-hyo or Sŏ Kwang-bŏm, ridiculed their agreements with "barbarians who intend to destroy us," and railed against their failures: the ministers failed to serve the crown, and failed to pursue the common good rather than personal profit.[31] What he promoted instead was an ideal of a Confucian monarch and loyal scholar-officials even in Japan where he condemned their "monarch and ministers" for depriving Korea of sovereignty despite earlier treaty commitments to independence on the peninsula.[32]

Distinct roles of crown, and minister or bureaucrat provided an organizational form to ensure adherence to the principle of "monarch and minister." Ch'oe Ik-hyŏn and Yu In-sŏk looked to crown and minister to reestablish an earlier model of authority on the peninsula, but in contrast to Ch'oe's breadth of topics, much of Yu's complaint concerned the Kabo Reforms of 1895. The familiar refrains of monarch and minister [kunsin], and father and son [puja] continued to distinguish the core of authority in his moral order.[33] Yet it was Ki Sam-yŏn who perhaps best represented the transition from literati indignation to armed revolt. A remarkable personal transition was evident in his own writing where he introduced himself as minister for the crown in a memorial of 1896, but then as a righteous resistance general in a memorial of 1907. The principle of monarch and minister drew his attention in an earlier memorial, as did the virtuous government minister "serving the crown."[34] But if Yu In-sŏk had vented his rage on the Kabo reformers, Ki turned his anger on both merchants and Korean cabinet members colluding with the Japanese: "kill those colluding with the Japs (waeno), revealing state secrets: let there be no pardon."[35] The juxtaposition of government minister and merchant was evidence of the growing importance of the grain brokers in the eyes of the trade opponents.

Rallying against both trade and political reform, Ch'oe, Yu, and Ki carefully chronicled the demise of their earlier order of monarch and minister. Disdaining Korean brokers, Japanese traders, and colluding Korean government officials alike, they saved their animus for the latter. Yet both Ch'oe and Yu sought alliance with government literati, insisting that ministers and rebels shared a common heritage: the Classical Confucian tradition in the *Spring and Autumn Annals*, and respect for Chinese culture. Yu pointedly reminded the ministers of their responsibility to preserve the way of Confucius and Mencius, and avenge its enemies.[36] The continuity between reformers and rebels highlighted a basic institutional dilemma within the Korean state where appointment to the bureaucracy was based on achievement in the civil service examinations, written in Chinese and based on Confucian ideas of government.[37] Training in other foreign languages was not yet widely available, nor were the bureaucrats well-versed in the administrative changes proposed by the Kabo reformers. Such structural problems partially explain the quick reversal of many of the Kabo administrative reforms by 1896 and return to the earlier form of the monarchical rule.

And finally, both Ch'oe and Ki Sam-yŏn highlighted the Japanese role in Korea's demise. Ki spiced the literati writings with a still more negative theme, matching loss of a cultural and material heritage with a traditional enemy, the Japanese, who would destroy the cultural legacy and exploit Korea's natural resources. He boldly joined heritage and foe in a "Manifesto" of 1907: "the Japanese dared to change how our people are governed and developed methods to destroy our people's spirit."[38] This seasoned critic pressed the distinction between people and government to a frightening conclusion where state became the foe and opposition to "state" now defined "nation." Any merchants or politicians who hoped to bridge alien state and indigenous people in the Protectorate would risk attack by the Righteous Armies.

The anti-trade protest served as a painful chronicle of the demise of an earlier model of authority evident in the rapid decline of the Korean crown at the turn of the century. Although advocates of the "protect orthodoxy, ban heterodoxy" school found Kojong's administration far from ideal, they still looked to the institution of the monarchy as the centerpiece of a hierarchical order of monarch and minister. If the Kabo effort to establish a constitutional monarchy shook the foundations of an earlier order, the Japanese Protectorate brought the curtain down on monarch and minister. Expanding trade and foreign ties forced a shift among opponents from an initial appeal to a common cultural heritage to a final call for reprisals against barbarian enemies. The ideological shift was apparent also in changing images of nation. What began with patriotic appeals to grand symbols of monarchy, royal tombs, the land and its people, concluded with laments over a nation besieged by enemies within, collaborators, and enemies without, the Japanese. The initial effort to return the Korean polity to its Confucian roots ended with hostilities to destroy a "barbarian" alien state.

Michael Mann's distinction between despotic and authoritarian states has been cited to distinguish polity in kingdom and colony.[39] The organizational capacities of the authoritarian colonial state permitted more extensive penetration of both rural and urban society, and more comprehensive enforcement of state direction in the economy. Contrasts have been drawn between the limited capacity of the court and the penetrating, extensive capacities of the bureaucracies of the government-general. What deserves equal attention are the organizational resources and functions of semi-official or affiliated organizations such as the Chosen Industrial Bank, the Oriental Development Company, and also the Chosen Exchange which played a major role in bridging private enterprise and state bureaucracy in the colony. A further contrast has been cited between the domestic autonomy of the hermit kingdom in the Chinese Empire and the dependence of the colony of Korea integrated into a regional interstate system dominated by Japan. But what tarnished the eloquence of the literati complaint against the new order of dependence was the long historical precedent of Chinese dominance in Korea's foreign affairs, a dynamic quite distinct from simply benign cultural respect. Rather than boasting of "independence" as an earlier precedent, trade opponents cited only a cultural or racial solidarity akin to the concept of "nation," and gave little attention to the autonomy of court or bureaucracy which would align more with the concept of "state." The contrast between a nation shaped by a common history, ethnicity, geography, and language, and a constrained or alien state offered a path for Korean survival in both kingdom and colony.

Market

A market ideology would suggest the moral neutrality and material benefit of products exchanged in trade. Utter rejection of the free market tenet of benign trade was perhaps nowhere more apparent than in the premise of the immorality of foreign manufactures in agrarian Korean society. Trade would erode both moral structure, such as the four occupations, and the moral fiber of a people that looked to community before self-interest.[40] Opponents equated heresy with immorality - the uncivilized West did not respect their monarch nor the primacy of public over private interest.[41] The distinction between state and society, and the role of the market implicit in Yi Hang-no's image of Western capitalism would undermine both authority and exchange in the Confucian order of Chosŏn Korea.

A Chinese cultural order defined by "civilized" versus "uncivilized" (*hwa/i*), monarch and minister (*kun/sin*), and an organic model of society provided a counterpoint to the new interstate order. A polity of monarch and minister could not accommodate the growing leverage of the merchants with their distinctive interests and organization. An earlier cultural world order which tolerated commerce only for subsistence had no place for the profit and property of the merchants in the grain trade. Trade opponents looked more to a return to an earlier order than reform of the present order, and offered no constructive alternative for the merchants scrambling to survive in the face of foreign competition at the ports.

Yi Hang-no linked morality and market in two important essays published to dissuade the crown from foreign commercial ties permitting penetration of heterodoxy.[42] He raised the banner of *t'onghwa t'ongsaek* [exchange of commodities, exchange of immorality] which would remain the dominant motif in literati opposition to trade through the turn of the century: the circulation of commodities would lead to the penetration of the immorality and promiscuity of the West.[43] Yi himself offered a bleak scenario of commercial relations: "Within a few years our people will exchange manufactures with them (i.e., the foreign barbarians), and then ways of behavior will be shared. Since the exchange of manufactures brings with it an exchange of behavior, then even one far distant is like a neighbor."[44] International trade would permit foreign, especially Western influence on Korean culture, diluting the cultural sovereignty of seclusion. And the problem lay not only with the West and their manufactures as such, but also with fellow Koreans in government and commerce who would belittle such dangers. Yi faulted Korean reformers for their fascination with Western thought and loss of all moral direction.[45] His warning about the demise of the Confucian way brought principle and protest to a sobering conclusion: "barbarians and animals are taking over, and the Way of China is fading."[46]

The very term *kugga* or "nation" [literally, "country and family"] suggested an organic, familial analogy of polity, reinforced with parallels between sovereign/subject and father/son. Yi's disciple Ch'oe Ik-hyŏn and his colleagues frequently sounded the theme of "nation" as (1) the focus of Korean tradition, (2) the goal of government service, and (3) the victim of exploitation by foreign powers. They portrayed Queen Min as the nation's mother and cited symbols such as land, the people, tombs of earlier kings, virtue and a "moral essence" as elements of "our nation." Yu In-sŏk echoed the theme with juxtaposition of nation and family, monarch and minister, and father and son. The five hundred year tradition of the Chosŏn Dynasty was a legacy of nation and family which would be lost in the impending destruction brought on by the Kabo reforms.[47] Trade opponents rallied for a hierarchical society based on the five relationships and ladder of occupations. What prompted their protest was the fear that their ladder had been reversed with the government ministers taking a back seat to the merchants.

The press of events in Seoul and the countryside shifted attention among trade opponents from culture to market and Japanese economic penetration. Ch'oe Ik-hyŏn documented Japan's crimes against Korean sovereignty in his "Letter to the Japanese Government" of 1906, listing three indignities in a chronicle of Japanese trade and Korean dependence.[48] Comparing the commercial treaty of Kanghwa in 1876 with the Protectorate Agreement of 1905, Ch'oe branded earlier Japanese promotion of Korean sovereignty against Chinese domination as a pretext for colonization. Japanese foreign investment amounted to little more than purchase or outright seizure of Korean property and resources. Japanese-led financial reforms on the peninsula such as the minting of a new currency contributed to further usury and larger Japanese profits. Extensive Japanese immigration to the peninsula threatened the racial destruction of the indigenous population. Although some might argue these crimes represented an amoral failure of means or methods, Ch'oe denied the tenet of moral neutrality in economic development. If capitalism was neither morally neutral nor benign, neither were trade, traders and reformers.

Ki Sam-yŏn published his inflammatory "Notice" soon after Ch'oe's letter.[49] Again we find material and moral arguments conjoined to condemn Japanese economic penetration, but now with attention to the actual process of penetration spawning material disorder and moral decline. Ki argued that more powerful nations forced the commercial treaties on Korea in the first place, and then bought off Korean ministers and merchants to gain further access to agricultural goods and natural resources. Later they flooded the local economy with manufactures from abroad eroding social morality and structure, and fostering a commerce which became the "origin of our calamity and endless destruction." Ki went on to dismiss the market dynamic of trade as nothing but cunning and treachery, arguing that the absence of restraints and embargoes on commerce in grains was "emaciating the people and destroying the nation's thread of life." The simple rural population, "who forget a great evil when they see a small profit," were deceived by brokers and traders with their easy credit: "Cunning and treacherous merchants were leading the people astray." The clarity of the analysis of capitalist penetration was matched only by the directness of Ki's solution: killing the merchants and their families. The solution added a tragic, ironic twist to the familial solidarity of nation.

Trade opponents merged themes of material disadvantage, cultural penetration, and xenophobia to counter market expansion. An unequal exchange of limited grains for unlimited manufactures fulfilled the worst fears of Kanghwa Treaty opponents: penetration of Japanese traders and settlers on Korean territory. Erosion of economic sovereignty at the turn of the century recalled earlier warnings of material disadvantage for a weaker nation in international trade. Early opponents also anticipated cultural penetration and decline of an earlier Confucian order in tandem with expanding trade. Thirdly, they raised racial fears of Japanese penetration with their own brand of xenophobia, carefully linked to loss of constitutive national symbols such as land, people, and products. They rejected the inequities of international trade, condemned the immorality of manufactures, and advocated a return to the morality of an agrarian economy.

Insights from the study of moral economy shed light on opposition to growing market autonomy from literati losing both moral and political leverage in the new order, but offer less direction in untangling the persistent role of kinship, polity and public morality in the markets of late kingdom and colony. Kinship remained a prominent model of enterprise, particularly among small and mid-size brokers in need of familial continuity and commitment to gain the trust of their customers. Kinship in turn generated the trust behind contracts in countryside and city. Although kinship faded as the dominant image of polity, brokers in kingdom and colony could prosper only within state-monitored and often mandated associations, and build private enterprise only in line with wider state priorities of the commonweal. Trade opponents and advocates alike grappled with the role of private profit in a communitarian society. The common good itself became problematic in the colony as evident in the distinction between Korean nation or ethnic group, and the empire.

Conclusion

Conservative literati rejected international trade in hopes of retaining at least domestic sovereignty, if not a return to an earlier social order. Seclusion within the region permitted domestic autonomy, the long tenure of crown and bureaucratic elite in the Chosŏn Dynasty, and relative insulation from foreign military and commercial affairs. Commercial ties with Japan and the West quickly wrenched Korea unprepared into a nominal order of sovereign states and a real order of regional imperial control under Japan. In the four decades separating Kanghwa from Protectorate, the grain trade promoted an economic integration into a regional market system which preceded military and formal political integration. Trade opponents had warned that incorporation into a regional system would destroy an earlier order of domestic sovereignty, and indeed market penetration evident in grains coincided with erosion of local state control. A commerce in grains and foreign manufactures brought capitalist ideas of amoral markets and commodities, and self-interest inimical to the earlier Confucian order of authority and exchange.

The literati and their complaint would fade in the turmoil and reorganization of annexation, but questions of market and morality, private and public interest, nation and state would persist in colonial and post-colonial Korea. Trade critics managed to establish the lines of debate persisting across the uneasy passage from empire to system without proffering feasible solutions. No one could ignore their cogent brief against the new regional system or on behalf of a common national interest. It is significant that through their trenchant criticism of market, literati critics made their own contribution to the development of capitalist ideas. Their criticism brought home the fact that despite the dreams of Enlightenment activists, foreign powers such as the Japanese would not permit a self-regulating market to simply stand alone on the peninsula. New types of authority would be necessary to institute, safeguard, but also embed the market in shifting social and political priorities. Literati critics stretched the debate beyond simply market to new forms of authority. Moreover, their strident opposition gave notice of changes in society and polity accompanying the growing autonomy of the market. The new prominence of brokers and traders evident in the grain trade and the grain embargoes threatened an earlier harmony and hierarchy of occupational status. Specialization based on market rather than morality posed a challenge not only to principles such as the ladder of occupations, and also to the power of literati critics in polity and economy.

And apart from foil to the advocates, the complaint of the trade opponents also fathered new ideas. Despite the apparent cohesion of the literati model of monarch and minister, their own protest suggested a distinction between "state" and "nation" which persisted among intellectuals and brokers in the colonial years of alien state rule. Division between government ministers in Seoul without integrity and literati rebels in the countryside with integrity was early evidence of an implicit distinction between government or "state" on the one hand, and a wider cultural and historical solidarity of "nation" on the other. A further step of a "public" or "national" interest distinct from both official and private sectors, would be left to the trade supporters.

The clamor against trade among rebel literati was moral, radical or extreme, and nationalistic to the point of xenophobia. They aimed at personal moral renovation among the ministers as the solution to the nation's eroding sovereignty, rather than institutional controls on trade or traders. The clarity of their moral principles led to a radical critique and rejection of market dynamics in economy and society. Foreign manufactures were immoral, the foreign traders cunning and dishonest, the local brokers treasonous and selfish. There was no middle ground, no viable compromise for controlling the market dynamic in the nation's favor. Always taking the high ground of morality and denying a middle ground of compromise, the opposition was nationalistic, often xenophobic, and deeply committed to a Korean cultural identity apart from Qing China, or the uncultured in Japan and the West.

Notes

1. Hopkins and Wallerstein discuss both processes in "Capitalism and the Incorporation of New Zones," p. 774.

2.   Lee Ki-baik, *A New History of Korea* (Cambridge MA: Harvard University Press, 1984), pp. 234, 240, 257, 263.

3.   Susan Shin, "The Tonghak Movement: From Enlightenment to Revolution," *Korean Studies Forum* 5 (Winter-spring 1979): 1-79; "Tonghak Thought: the Roots of Revolution." *Korea Journal* 19, 9 (Sept. 1979): 11-20. See also Benjamin Weems, *Reform, Rebellion and the Heavenly Way* (Tucson: University of Arizona Press, 1964).

4.   Kim Ŭi-hwan, "Hanmal ŭibyong undong ŭi punsok: Yi Kang-nyŏn ŭibyong pudae rŭl chungsim ŭro [An analysis of the late Chosŏn Dynasty Righteous Army movement: the Righteous Army unit of Yi Kwang-nyŏn] in his *Han'guk kŭndaesa yŏn'gu nonjip* [A collection of studies on modern Korean history] (Seoul: Sŏngjin Munhwasa, 1972), pp. 598-599.

5.   Editors of the *Independent* translated the term as "Righteous Army," although "righteous armies" or "righteous volunteers" better denotes the loose organization and voluntary nature of their service.   The newspaper identified them as "insurgents," a term also found in documents of the residency-general. See Kim Ŭi-hwan, *Ŭibyŏng undongsa* [A history of the campaigns of the Righteous Armies] (Seoul: Pagyŏngsa, 1974), p. 8.   Initial resistance in 1895 and 1896 included small-scale skirmishes involving 300 to 1,000 volunteers at most, in Kangwŏn, Ch'ungch'ŏng and Chŏlla provinces.   See Kang Chae-ŏn, *Chōsen kindaishi kenkyū* [Studies of modern Korean history] (Tokyo: Hyōronsha, 1970), pp. 205-239.   Resistance later spread across the peninsula. Japanese observers listed 323 skirmishes with some 44,000 insurgents in 1907, over 1400 engagements in 1908 with 69,000 rebels, and nearly 900 engagements in 1909 involving 25,000 insurgents.   Kang Chae-ŏn, *Chōsen no jōi to kaika* [Expulsion of foreigners and enlightenment in Korea] (Tokyo: Heibonsha, 1977), p. 286.

6.   A biography of Yi Hang-no, pen name Hwasŏ (1791-1868), can be found in *Hwasŏjip* [Collected works of Hwasŏ Yi Hang-no] (Seoul: Taeyang Sŏjŏk, 1973), edited by Kim Chu-hi, pp. 5-19.   For a review of his ideas, see Yi I-hwa, "Ch'ŏksa wijŏng ŭi pipanjŏk komt'o: Hwasŏ Yi Hang-no ŭi soron ŭl chungsimŭro [A critical study of the 'ban heterodoxy, protect orthodoxy' argument: the ideas of Hwasŏ Yi Hang-no]," *Han'guksa Yŏn'gu* 18 (Oct. 1977): 111-140.

7.   Brief biographies of Ch'oe, pen name Myŏnam (1832-1906), can be found in Kim, *Ŭibyŏng undongsa*, and in Kang, *Chōsen kindaishi*.   The term **literati** [*yusaeng yangban*] denotes the Confucian elites educated for moral and political leadership.   Apart from Ch'oe and a few others, the majority of Confucian leaders active in the early Righteous Armies had never won higher appointment in the bureaucracy.   Mainly scholars [*hakcha yusaeng*] rather than bureaucrats [*kwallyo yusaeng*], they supported themselves by lecturing at regional centers, or even by teaching in small rural schools.   Pak Sŏng-su provides brief biographies of Ch'oe, Yu In-sŏk (pen name Ŭiam, 1842-1915),

and Ki Sam-yŏn (pen name Sŏngjae) in *Tongnip undongsa yŏn'gu* (Studies of the history of the independence movement) (Seoul: Ch'angjak gwa Pip'yŏngsa, 1980).

8. *Independent*, December 15, 1898.

9. Writing in exile on the Liaotung Peninsula, Yu warned the Chinese of the dangers of westernization in a treatise of 1914 titled, "Uju mundap [Discussions of the universe]," republished in his *Ŭiam munjip* [Anthology of Ŭiam Yu In-sŏk], vol. 51, second part. Excerpts from the treatise can be found in Kim To-hyŏng, "Ŭiam Yu In-sŏk ŭi chŏngch'i sasang yŏn'gu [A study of the political thought of Ŭiam Yu In-sŏk], *Han'guksa Yŏn'gu* 25 (Aug. 1979): 105-145.

10. *Independent*, July 25, 1896.

11. Chung Chai-sik, "In Defense of the Traditional Order: *ch'ŏksa wijŏng* [Ban Heterodoxy, Protect Orthodoxy]," *Philosophy East and West* 30 (July 1980): 355. See also his "Christianity as Heterodoxy: An Aspect of General Cultural Orientation in Traditional Korea," in Jo Yung-hwan, ed., *Korea's Response to the West* (Kalamazoo: Korea Research Publications, 1971), pp. 57-86. Scholars refer to the school by their banner or motto of *wijŏng ch'ŏksa* [protect orthodoxy and reject heterodoxy]. I refer to this group of literati more simply as the Orthodoxy School. A review of the early years of the school can be found in Martina Deuchler, "Reject the False and Uphold the Straight: Attitudes Toward Heterodox Thought in Early Yi Korea," pp. 375-410 in Wm. Theodore de Bary and JaHyun Kim Haboush, eds., *The Rise of Neo-Confucianism in Korea* (New York: Columbia University Press, 1985). For an overview of Confucian thought, see Michael Robinson, "Perceptions of Confucianism in Twentieth-Century Korea," pp. 204-225 in Gilbert Rozman, ed., *The East Asian Region: Confucian Heritage and Its Modern Adaptation* (Princeton: Princeton University Press, 1991). And for a study of the influence of Confucianism on Korean society, see JaHyun Kim Haboush, "The Confucianization of Korean Society," pp. 84-110 in the same volume.

12. Yun Pyŏng-sŏl provides an overview of the movement and its relation to the Righteous Armies in his "Hang-il ŭibyŏng (Anti-Japanese resistance of the Righteous Armies)," in Kuksa P'yŏnch'an Wiwŏnhoe, ed., *Han'guksa* (A history of Korea), vol. 19 (Seoul: T'amgudang, 1978), pp. 341-460.

13. Palais described the "censorate" as a powerful tool for aristocratic control of the monarchy: "the censorate, which was an institution borrowed from the Chinese for the exercise of both surveillance and remonstrance functions, became in the hands of the Koreans a powerful check on royal authority.... The yangban bureaucrats even turned the normative standards of Confucian thought against the throne. By insisting that the king conform to moral and ethical standards that transcended his right to the arbitrary exercise of power, by setting themselves up as arbiters of those standards by virtue of their knowledge of Confucian texts, and by insisting on their right to

remonstrate and the king's obligation to tolerate remonstrance, yangban bureaucrats and literati sought to reduce kings to puppets of their own desires and interests." *Politics and Policy*, p. 11.

14. The Chinese character *hwa* can be translated as either "Chinese" or "civilized," and *i* as "uncivilized" or "barbarian."

15. Deuchler highlighted the mixture of local priorities of social status and descent lines in the "Confucian transformation" of Korean society across the first three centuries of the Choson Dynasty. A similar dynamic of adjusting Confucian ideology with local priorities was evident now as Korean Confucianists extolled the virtues of mainly an indigenized Confucianism, and took as their model Ming rather than Ch'ing China. See *The Confucian Transformation of Korea: A Study of Society and Ideology* (Cambridge: Council on East Asian Studies, Harvard University Press, 1992).

16. "The fact that Sino-Korean relations during the Ch'ing [Qing] period consisted chiefly of ceremonial exchanges and symbolic observances suggests that, while China's titular superiority and authority as suzerain were absolute in theory, in practice its suzerainty over Korea seldom extended beyond the realm of ceremonial diplomacy. For all practical intents and purposes, Korea was completely independent in the management of its own affairs." Kim Key-hiuk, *The Last Phase of the East Asian World Order* (Berkeley: University of California Press, 1980), p. 8.

17. Yu, "Kyŏngmun p'aldo yŏlmyŏn [An urgent plea to every corner of the eight provinces]," pp. 27-31 in Yu, *Hang'il sŏnŏn*, pp. 27-31.

18. Ch'oe, "Jibu buggwŏl ch'ŏkhwa ronso [A memorial before the palace with ax in hand on banishing Western thought], in *Myŏnamjip* [Anthology of Myŏnam Ch'oe Ik-hyŏn], tr. by Kim Ju-hi, volume I, letters (Seoul: Minjok Munhwa Ch'ujinhoe, 1977), pp. 124-134, 33-38, and reprinted in Ch'oe Ch'ang-gyu, ed., *Hanmal aeguk myŏngsangso munjip* [Anthology of patriotic memorials at the close of the Chosŏn Dynasty] (Seoul: Sŏmundang, 1975), pp. 11-22.

19. Yu,"T'owoeso [Memorial on banishing the barbarians]," printed in Tongnip Undongsa P'yŏnch'an Wiwŏnhoe, ed. *Tongnip undongsa charyojip* [Materials on the history of the Independence Movement] vol. 1, *Ŭibyŏng hangjengsa charyojip* [History of ŭibyong resistance] (Seoul: Tongnip Undongsa P'yŏnch'an Wiwŏnhoe, 1970), pp. 661-663, 130-137, and reprinted in Ch'oe, "Hanmal," pp. 60-70.

20. "Kwanggomun," in Yu, *Hang'il sŏnŏn*, pp. 77, 80.

21. Ch'oe, "Yusŏ [Final testament]," in *Myŏnamjip*, vol. I, pp. 238-239, 78; also in Ch'oe Ch'ang-gyu, ed., *Hanmal aeguk myŏngsangso munjip* [Anthology of patriotic memorials at the close of the Chosŏn Dynasty] (Seoul: Sŏmundang, 1975), pp. 193-196.

22. Ki, "Kyŏksŏmun [Manifesto], in Yu, *Hang'il sŏnŏn*, pp. 84-88.

23. Chung Chai-sik, *A Korean Confucian Encounter with the Modern World: Yi Hang-no and the West* (Berkeley: Institute of East Asian Studies, University of California, Berkeley, 1995), pp. 19-20.

24. "Yanghwa," in his *Hwasŏjip*, pp. 383-399.

25. *Hwasŏjip*, p. 387, 385.

26. *Hwasŏjip*, pp. 392, 396, 398.

27. Yu In-sŏk in Tongnip Undongsa P'yŏnch'an Wiwŏnhoe, ed., *Ŭibyŏng hangjengsa charyojip* [History of the Ŭibyong resistance], volume one of the *Tongnip undongsa charyojip* [Materials on the history of the Independence Movement] (Seoul: Tongnip Undongsa P'yŏnch'an Wiwŏnhoe, 1970), pp. 148-149, 667-668.

28. For a study of Yu's attitude toward the state, see Pak Sung-un, "Kuhanmal ŭibyong chŏnjaeng gwa Yugyojŏk aeguk sasang [The Righteous Army struggle and Confucian ideas of patriotism in the late Chosŏn Dynasty]," *Taedong Munhwa Yŏn'gu* 6-7 (Dec. 1970): 163-196.

29. *Myŏnamjip*, I, pp. 234, 77.

30. *Myŏnamjip*, I, pp. 82-83, 17-18.

31. *Myŏnamjip*, I, pp. 82, 18; 144-150.

32. "Killbon chŏngbu [To the Japanese Government]." *Myŏnamjip*, II, pp. 223-231, 79-81.

33. *Ŭibyong hangjengsa charyojip*, pp. 641, 87; 642, 89; 663.

34. Ch'oe, *Hanmal aeguk myŏngsangso*, pp. 81-91. "Serving the crown" is a translation of *kŭnwang*.

35. *Ŭibyŏng hangjengsa charyojip*, 621-622, 940; Yu, *Hang'il sŏnŏn*, pp. 77-79.

36. *Ŭibyŏng hangjengsa charyojip*, pp. 130-137, 661-663.

37. Kŭm Jang-t'ae described the Confucian ideal of the government minister in his "Cho Chŏng-am gwa Chosŏn ŭi sŏnbi chŏngsim [Cho Chŏng-am and the spirit of the Confucian scholar in the Chosŏn Dynasty]," *Han'guk Hakpo* 10 (1978): 180-194; also Lee Yoon Ki, "The Sŏnbi Spirit and its Manifestation in the Political Domain," *Korea Journal* (Apr. 1989): 12-17.

38. "Kyŏksŏmun," in Yu, *Hang'il sŏnŏn*, pp. 84-88. "People's spirit" is a translation of *insim*.

39. Michael Mann, "The Autonomous Power of the State: Its Origins, Mechanisms and Results," *The European Journal of Sociology* 25,

40. *Hwasŏjip*, pp. 385, 388, 389, 463.

41. *Hwasŏjip*, pp. 388, 389, 463.

42. "The Destruction of the West [*Yanghwa*]," and "Heresy [*Idan*]" can be found in *Hwasŏjip*, p. 398.

43. *Hwasŏjip*, pp. 383, 384, 386.

44. *Hwasŏjip*, p. 398.

45. *Hwasŏjip*, p. 385.

46. *Hwasŏjip*, p. 398.

47. *Ŭibyŏng hangjengsa charyojip*, pp. 86, 641.

48. "Killbon chŏngbu [To the Japanese Government]," in *Myŏnamjip*, II, pp. 223-231, 79-81.

49. "Kwanggomun," in Yu, *Hang'il sŏnŏn*, pp. 77-80.

4

Trade Advocates

Critics traded barbs over commerce as a parade of governments struggled to salvage control at the capital and brokers scrambled at the ports, but brokers, bureaucrats, and intellectuals sometimes found common cause. A commerce which only slowly gained the respect of the state quickly captured the hearts of Enlightenment activists. Intellectuals latched on to the brokers and other entrepreneurs as the nation's only hope of survival in competitive, international markets, a dramatic and no doubt puzzling reversal for the brokers only recently condemned by trade critics for the nation's demise. A contrast between trade opposition and advocacy provides entree to a political debate which would shape guilds and chambers through the colonial years. Directives from the monarchy and subsequent legislation on business organization helped link this world of ideas to the world of commerce.

A common goal of cultural, economic, and political sovereignty inspired trade opponents and advocates alike, reinforced by a common threat of Japanese expansion. Both camps found themselves adjusting to a similar progression of incorporation from Kanghwa Treaty in 1876, through the Kabo reforms of 1894, and on to the Protectorate of 1905. Even a trade advocate like Yun Ch'i-ho was lamenting Japanese expansion by 1897: "Corea is the land where children have no toys; women, no flowers; men, no independence."[1] The two camps offered radically opposed resolutions to similar challenges with a common hope of stemming the erosion of local sovereignty. But whatever their hopes, conflicting views of regional order, polity and society dimmed hopes for ideological compromise or collective action. Critics scorned "enlightenment" thought as uncivilized and found nothing to admire in Japan or the West. Trade advocates faulted their Confucian opponents for nostalgia and anachronisms, and dismissed the resistance leaders as criminals:

"the insurgents are not after [righteous] revenge, but loot."[2] Neither trade critics nor advocates could halt Japan's relentless extension onto the peninsula, but both would affect the ideas and organization of the emerging local business community at the ports which would survive incorporation.

Three issues divided critics and supporters. The former rallied for the distinction between civilized and uncivilized, and led the struggle to recover Korea's customs and long traditions of respect for the ancestors and the crown. Meanwhile, trade supporters advocated adjustment in polity and economy under the banner of "enlightenment."[3] The role of the state sparked further division. Trade critics promoted the earlier model of monarchy and faithful minister (*kunsin*), but trade supporters countered with a new model of government official and citizen (*kwanmin*) with a wider role for intellectuals, educators, and business interests. Markets likewise divided the two camps. Critics dismissed the market dynamic as malign, but advocates judged supply and demand benign. As trade critics rallied for morality over market, advocates looked to markets as a path to prosperity and national survival.

The debate spawned ideas of a new interstate system, more modern state, and market relations necessary for the changing ideology and organization of the brokers by the time of annexation in 1910. Although initial colonial rule brought a quick end to the free-wheeling discussion, colonial administrators of the 1920s permitted a new debate, now between liberals and socialists, and even tolerated the famous "native products" campaign which gave a boost to Korean millers, but the basic lines of ideology and organization had already been drawn. Trade advocates gave far greater recognition than opponents to the individual, particularly the merchants, and to their efforts to gain profit. Advocates chided the wider population for an absence of the very quality they admired in the business community: an enterprising spirit. The legitimacy of profit-seeking, and indeed, the public contribution of private entrepreneurship here gained recognition and support. Trade advocates championed nascent economic and political groups which could represent the populace apart from the state, and denounced state-chartered monopolies which would constrain more independent groups within the market.

Four leading enlightenment activists helped promote new ideas of market and society. An advocate such as Yu Kil-chun was active in the Kapsin Emute of 1884, a violent effort to force liberal reforms. Other leaders of the abortive coup escaped to Japan, but Yu remained in Seoul under house arrest where he wrote of trade and political reform, and a decade later reemerged as an architect of the Kabo reforms.[4] Like-minded, Western educated reformers such as Sŏ Chae-p'il and Yun Ch'i-ho took their campaign to the public with the Independence Club and its newspaper, the *Tongnip Sinmun*, from 1896.[5] Sŏ returned permanently to the U.S. after the government ordered dissolution of the Club and suspension of the publication in 1898.[6] Yun accepted appointment to a magistrate in distant Wŏnsan, and later worked for educational reform during Japanese rule.[7] Unlike the cosmopolitan Sŏ and Yun, Pak Ŭn-sik was born to an indigent family in the north, but did gain an education in Confucianism from disciples of Yi Hang-no.[8] Already eminent among Confucian scholars in his province of Hwanghae by 1889, Pak turned to progressive schools of thought and quickly became active in enlightenment associations. He gained prominence as an editor at the *Hwangsŏng* newspaper and other publications of the Self-strengthening Movement in the years of the Protectorate [1905-1910], prior to self-imposed exile in China.[9]

Opposing camps of conservative literati and progressive reformers jostled for power in Seoul at the same time leading foreign powers in the capital pressed the government for concessions. Divided within by the debate and constrained without by meddling foreign powers, the local state offered little guidance in the debate but did implement Kabo economic reforms reorganizing the business community at the ports. Brokers muddled through the political uncertainties of court and colony to establish a new business ideology and professional associations. Trade advocates contributed mightily to survival and reorganization among the brokers by offering guidelines for a distinct group interest consistent with the wider commonweal.

Regional Order

If trade critics opted for moral covenant over market contract in a return to a Chinese cultural empire, trade advocates argued for market and a new morality of interest in Korea's entry to a new interstate system of unequal states. To the critics' claim that only seclusion or limited trade would permit survival of Korean culture, advocates countered with national survival only through access to the methods and technologies of the West. Both camps also looked outward whether to Classical China as a cultural model, or to Japan as an example of successful survival and modernization in the new interstate system. Themes of "Protect Orthodoxy, Ban Heterodoxy" gave continuity to the arguments of trade advocates, just as rational adaptation or "enlightenment" ideas provided a common ground for the trade advocates. For instance, Yu Kil-chun described "substantial enlightenment" as "probing the root and principle of things to understand and to find ways of adapting these to the situation of one's nation."[10] Practical rationality would drive enlightened nations to understand, select and adapt, and move individuals from fear or envy of the powerful nations past subservience to self-confident cooperation, preserving their own heritage while adjusting to the best of other cultures.

Editors of the *Independent* echoed the latter theme: "Let us encourage the inflow of foreign capital and aid foreign enterprise for the development of our latent resources, for the greater and more numerous interests involved, the more sure and enduring will be our standing as an independent state."[11] Still later, Pak Ŭn-sik and others in the Self-strengthening Movement under the Protectorate turned the focus from rationality or "enlightenment " to the more immediate issue of adaptation for survival. Pak complemented the emphasis on commerce for power and prosperity among his predecessors with his own emphasis on industry. Here Pak argued that only the nations with wisdom and technology would survive the struggle for existence in international markets [12] and concluded that education would promote industrial production to ensure Korean survival as an autonomous economic power.[13]

Matching opponents in the tenor of their complaint, trade advocates took aim at government corruption but also at attitudes among the people impeding change. Even if rational adaptation provided a way or principle of survival in the new world order, advocates agreed Korea was far behind in the new hierarchy of adapting states. Yu argued that the persistence of social constraints such as the status hierarchy of occupations left Korea among the semi-enlightened nations.[14] Drawing a contrast between Korea's status in earlier empire and contemporary interstate systems, Sŏ and Yun observed in the *Independent* that "China told Korea she was not independent, but acted as if she were. Japan told Korea she was independent, but acted as if she were not."[15] Pak Ŭn-sik portrayed Korea as economically backward in a struggle for survival among richer and more powerful nations, arguing that Korea had become "enslaved," a sacrifice for stronger nations.[16]

Trade advocates from the 1890s coupled lament over Korea's place in the new order with anger over the process of Japanese expansion on the peninsula. What drew their ire was the integration of Korea as periphery economy to the core interests of the Japanese islands, or the process of "peripheralization."[17] Editors of the *Independent* demanded state action to stem the tide of Japanese migration: "until the government and the people become strong and intelligent enough to take care of their own interests, Korea should be protected from the unrestrained influx of its neighbors."[18] A comment from Tokyo in the *Japan Times* that Korea was "incapable of standing on its own legs" drew an angry retort from the *Independent*: "every time she has attempted to do so, her feet have been knocked out from under her."[19] Yet the same editors who deeply longed for Korean political and economic sovereignty were willing to endure temporary dependence in the grain trade for the long-range goal of international competitiveness.

> We believe the time will come when this important and rapidly increasing branch of trade will be transferred to Korean hands where it rightly belongs. Not that we discourage Japanese trade. We believe in fair competition and if the Korean finds it hard to compete with the more thrifty Japanese, let him go to the wall.[20]

When Protectorate controls from 1905 curbed criticism of Japanese expansion, trade advocates turned their attention inward. They faulted Korea's vulnerability in the process of incorporation, citing both poor education and weak economic growth. Pak Ŭn-sik linked the latter with national survival in international affairs: "production of material things is a basis of human existence, and if a nation's production is abundant, the people's life is secure."[21] With the focus shifted from foreign aggression to local survival, intellectuals intent on self-strengthening gave center stage to the brokers and merchants.

Immigration, Japanese purchase of productive paddy land, and growing controls over grain production extended the infrastructure of foreign capitalism on the peninsula. Having dismissed the premise of trade as inimical to the cultural and moral identity of the nation, trade advocates now found themselves uneasy with the status of periphery to Japanese core. Hopes of national wealth and power proved as illusory as the dreams of trade opponents for seclusion. Trade boomed but autonomy faded in the transition from tributary to colonial periphery. Given the constraints on autonomous structural change in the last years of the monarchy, it is not surprising to find advocates pressing for "enlightenment" or intellectual renovation. Education was feasible where revolution was not. Unlike opponents, trade advocates combined ideas with structural efforts to build a more competitive polity and society in the new interstate system prior to annexation, but neither advocates nor opponents could thwart the combination of market and security interests pressing the Japanese through wars with China and Russia to establish hegemony and colonial dominance. The transition from kingdom to colony would bring capitalist organization to larger numbers of the peasants only with intensive industrialization in the last decade of colonial rule,[22] but the brokers had to reorganize to survive already at the turn of the century.

State

Nowhere was the democratic ideal of trade advocates more evident than in the principle of "official and citizen (*kwanmin*)," as opposed to the critics' ideal of "monarch and minister (*kunsin*)." Advocates promoted a public sphere of "citizens," even as they encouraged formation of public opinion in their writings and newspapers. Yu Kil-chun was among the first to promote enlightenment across society, rather than as the aspiration of any single leadership group: "a nation is enlightened if there are many enlightened people among its citizens."[23] Delimiting the state role to domestic order, international security, and welfare programs, Yu left a wide berth for the exercise of individual initiative and responsibility.[24] Even within the economy Yu envisioned solely a supportive role for the state to ensure transportation and stable financial networks, and to maintain a legal structure for the pursuit of private enterprise.[25] Yu himself pointed to the need for state legal protection of commerce among local grain merchants,[26] and even distinguished between the "government" and the "people."[27] The *Independent* gave closer attention to issues of state and society, but Yu had laid the foundation for the new distinction radically different from the earlier model of monarch and minister.

Sŏ and Yun edged cautiously away from absolute monarch and faithful ministers towards a constitutional monarchy with popular participation, all the while maintaining deep respect for the Korean monarchy. Here they distanced themselves from their literati opponents as evident in Yun Ch'i-ho's biting criticism of the Righteous Armies: "Loyalty does not mean to flatter our superiors or to memorialize the

Throne or to kill those who committed crimes years ago."[28] They missed no opportunity to criticize the government, but wrote also of the responsibility of the people. The beginnings of a shift from filial subject to active citizen was evident in their agenda of duties for the people: (a) "love the emperor and help him acquire the highest position in the world; (b) give him comfort; (c) help him eliminate the difficulties which may shake the foundations of the country; (d) promote a better understanding between the people and the emperor."[29] The latter belied their hopes for wider popular participation.

The *Independent* campaigned for a new concept of citizenship and individual rights.[30] Editors argued that state oppression had dulled all sensitivity to individual rights:

> The first indication of progress in a nation is the knowledge of asserting individual rights. The Korean people have been, for centuries, living under the heavy yoke of oppression from their own officials, so that they have practically forgotten the words 'personal rights.'[31]

Apart from the state, they also faulted the population for political inaction, estimating that "80% of Koreans are indifferent to affairs of government,"[32] and pleaded for "a greater sense of equality and birth-rights as citizens of the commonwealth."[33] Trade supporters then shifted from advocacy to action. The "Assembly of Officials and the People" under Independence Club leadership in late October of 1898 remains one of the most remarkable events of the period.[34] Yun Ch'i-ho himself presided over the gathering of private associations and government officials, which resulted in a joint resolution for a representative council quickly accepted by Kojong. The fact that the "Privy Council" idea never went much further concerns us less than the public effort for recognition of the legitimacy of interest groups and their place in direction of society.

A distinction between *kwanmin* and *kunsin* was not the only division in the debate over state or nation. Indeed, the very content of a national identity further distinguished trade opponents from supporters. The former looked to symbols of monarchy, royal tombs, the mountains and rivers, and a moral identity. Among trade advocates, Yu offered an intellectual bridge between empire and system with his "enlightenment of behavior" based on the five relationships emanating from the hierarchy of monarch and minister, but he argued rather that the strength of the Korean legacy lay in a tradition of practical rationality quite evident in earlier technological achievements.[35]   Sŏ and Yun looked more to national character than "nation" as such, and called for an enterprising spirit.   Editors denounced vices of laziness and slavish devotion to custom,[36] and advocated structural changes such as expansion of opportunities for enterprise through port openings, and legal protection to promote a spirit of enterprise.[37] But enterprise alone would not unite the nation for it was apathy that set the nation adrift:

> What makes Korea so weak as a nation is that the people are not united
> in their sentiments, ... they do not appreciate the common fate in which
> they are bound together.[38]

They later quoted an editorial from a missionary newsletter to foster a new consciousness of "nation:" "it is the people who are the nation, the people who make the country what it is."[39]

In a sharp break from the primacy of custom in the empire, impersonal law and equitable procedure would now ensure cooperation between an active citizenry and a delimited state.   Contract rather than simply moral covenant would give texture and direction to a society where impersonal, universalistic norms would distinguish between private and public affairs.[40]   Legal enlightenment would ensure equality and protection from injustice: "the basis for enlightened law is respect for and protection of human rights."[41] Yu went on to enumerate rights such as religion, expression and assembly, but also rights to private property, including freedom to own, dispose of and manage property.   Yet with concerns for individualism reminiscent of the trade critics, Yu proposed law as a means to balance the demands of individual with the public good: law was needed to restrain individuals from unbounded pursuit of self-interests.[42]   To underscore his point, he insisted that the state in an enlightened society cannot tolerate pursuit of private profit if it threatens the government or the public good.[43]

The *Independent* echoed Yu's premise of impersonal, universalistic law, but in a far more practical vein.   Commenting on the revision of criminal law, the editors urged the separation of executive and judicial authority: "Even after laws are revised, if the Executive officers continue to ignore them, it will be a waste of time and labor to endeavor to reconstruct the entire system."[44] Editors complained that laws that should have regulated the relationship between state and society, had been used instead to support official corruption and manipulation particularly rampant in taxation and grain collection.   Such harsh criticism reflected a strong commitment to law as a principle of authority, evident in their ideal of law and liberty: "Korea will never be free till she has good laws, laws that open up the way for every citizen to most readily earn his bread, educate himself... The full definition then, must be that liberty is perfect obedience to perfect law, perfectly administered."[45]

Nonetheless trade advocates among enlightenment activists accorded the state a major role in directing Korea's entry into the new international system, and both Yu and the editors of the *Independent* found fault with the Korean state in the process of Japanese extension onto the peninsula. They looked to the state to help compensate for a weak competitive position in the international economy. For instance, Yu Kil-chun candidly admitted: "We could not compete at first ... there was not profit for us at first in competition with other nations." The problem then was internal rather than external, an issue of domestic attitudes and structures ill-suited for competitive international markets, such as negative state attitudes towards merchants. Admitting that "commerce is what we might call war for normal times," Yu proposed government protection of commercial contract, transport, and local market conditions as necessary conditions for profitable commerce,[46] and cited fraud in the sale of rice to the Chinese as evidence of weak state enforcement of necessary laws.[47] Editors of the *Independent* focused on the latter problem of either incompetence or corruption in regulation of the grain trade as a leading example of maladministration. They reported extortion of local officials against grain merchants[48] and derided the inconsistency and irrationality of government embargoes on the trade.[49] Editors faulted the government for discouraging honest commerce: "Even the Koreans are beginning to possess the spirit of enterprise, but the only subject which makes us despair is the politics of the country."[50] Clearly they saw a necessary role for the state in establishing laws and procedures for commerce, and at times shielding local merchants from exploitation by foreign mercantile interests, but found little praiseworthy in the economic policies of the post-Kabo cabinets.

Trade opponents and advocates alike joined in criticism of state administration in the fading years of the monarchy. The call of trade critics for moral reform among the literati ministers hardly addressed the basic issue of structural reform in state economic policy. Advocates countered with support of reforms towards a constitutional monarchy with aggressive support of trade and private enterprise. Neither moral nor structural reforms proved adequate to stem the Japanese advance, but the ideas of the advocates and their initial structural reforms helped shape enterprise for the local brokers in the colonial years. One legacy was the emphasis on law and contract, but a more profound legacy was the appeal to a public sphere where the interests and opinions of the whole could be heard apart from both state and the private sector. Mary Rankin drew a profile of a "public" sphere from documents of the late Qing: "'public' retains a considerable communal element but refers more specifically to the institutionalized, extrabureaucratic management of matters considered important by both the community and the state."[51] Despite the failure of early efforts such as the Assembly of October 1898 and the *Independent* itself to institutionalize such a sphere in the late kingdom, the concept of a civil society structured by law and institution had found a place in Korean society. A third legacy was the distinction between state and nation suggested by the conservative literati following imposition of the Protectorate in 1905. Enlightenment advocates affirmed not only nation apart from state, but also a public sphere of citizens apart from the "official" sector of the monarchy and his ministers, and a legitimate place as well for the private interests of entrepreneurs.

Market

A principle of legitimate self-interest had found shelter but not yet a home on the peninsula in the transition from kingdom to colony. What most divided trade opponents from supporters was neither regional system nor local rule, but rather market and its role in society. The legitimacy of profit or interest so fundamental to capitalism had been condemned by critics as selfish. Advocacy of such an immoral interest as private profit proved the most disturbing plank in the platform of trade supporters. The trade debate raised fundamental issues for the shape of modern society on the peninsula, with opponents scorning private interest and rejecting capitalism, and trade supporters applauding private interest and embracing capitalism.

In a bold retort to the charge of immoral commerce, Yu Kil-chun argued that an international commerce in ideas contributed to enlightenment, and that material trade like agriculture could be at the heart of the nation. Drawing on Confucian themes, he then countered his literati critics with the assertion that international commerce establishes the "great Way [*taedo*]" among nations, and brings to perfection the "great righteousness [*taeŭi*]."[52] What we find at the heart of his argument was nothing less than assertion of the legitimacy of interest or profit. Countering literati condemnation of individual profit, Yu argued: "it is not whether the human activity itself [i.e., of profit-seeking] is noble or mean, but whether the way of gaining profit is noble or mean."[53] Certainly Yu opposed unconstrained greed in pursuit of individual profit, yet the problem was not profit-oriented behavior as such, but rather exaggerated, divisive self-seeking leading to social chaos. In a revealing blend of categories of official, public, and private, Yu concluded that adequate laws maintained by the state would ensure competition and public benefit from private enterprise.[54]

Editors of the *Independent* elaborated a principle of "benign" interest or profit by linking the legitimacy of individual interest to markets. "Every individual desires to get on, to improve his material position and comfort,"[55] and unfettered markets would promote such desires. An exchange of foreign manufactures for Korean grains provided a model of supply and demand which served the interests of the common people.

> Commerce is the most democratic thing in the world... The supply adapts itself to the demand whoever it is that demands... What is the bulk of Korean imports? Cotton goods. Who uses them? The common people. What is the bulk of Korea's exports? Rice, beans, and hides. Who raises them? The common people.[56]

This democratizing dynamic of impersonal, morally neutral supply and demand serves the individual interests of commoners and aristocrats alike. Editors even called for wider international ties to make more foreign goods available: "Commerce follows the laws of supply and demand, of buying in the cheapest market and selling in the dearest. It is not a problem of demand [in Korea], but of competition to supply."[57]

Yu, Sŏ and Yun raised hopes for a bridging of public and private interest on the premise of cohesion and mutual recognition between a sovereign local state and enlightened citizens. The Protectorate from 1905 dashed hopes of political sovereignty and turned attention towards racial and cultural survival under Japanese rule. Editorials in progressive newspapers associated with the Self-strengthening Movement focused on the role of merchants in sustaining both public and private interest, praising modern chamber organization in Seoul, Inch'ŏn and elsewhere on the peninsula. For instance an editorial in the *Hwangsŏng Sinmun* reported the composition and contribution of the Korean chambers,[58] applauding formation of a common front of designated merchants, brokers, bankers and others in the business community to mobilize their resources against monopolies of foreign merchants. But the purpose of the chambers was still national interest rather than individual profit.

An editorial in the *Taehan Maeil Sinbo* closely linked commercial and national sovereignty. Again we find reference to a discrete, national or ethnic group of Korean businessmen, but still recognized only for their role in recovery of sovereignty, rather than for earning profits.[59] Impending annexation in 1910 again brought attention to the chambers. Finally, an editorial writers in the *Taehan Maeil Sinbo* candidly affirmed profit as the goal of business, but given the dominance of Japanese capital and infrastructure in the Korean economy, they broached the question of benefit and asked, "profits for whom?"[60] The *Hwangsŏng* newspaper repeated the question and offered their own response, proposing a national grain firm to expand Korean soybean exports to Manchuria and insure profits for local farmers.[61] Formal annexation in 1910 muted this linking of economic to nationalist goals, but the principle of private interest had begun to take root.

Markets can foster reorganization and extension of private interests in harness with national interests. Yu Kil-chun applauded an exchange of goods and ideas among states as an international framework for growth and prosperity. He found a parallel on the local level where society needs markets to balance supply and demand, but here the division between trade critics and advocates became painfully clear in their reaction to the leading marketers on the peninsula, the grain brokers. At the same time literati in the Righteous Armies prodded their troops to seek out and kill the brokers, Yu saw the need for brokers to match producers with consumers and concluded, "it is only just that they gain a profit through a charge for their services." Nor was Yu content just to promote markets and marketers, but rather pressed his argument decrying government constraints on competitive dynamics of supply and demand: "It is not right that a government decree condone one person's monopoly of the profits of many people."[62]

The *Independent* repeated the latter complaint in their vigorous opposition to monopolies of the peddlers or the proposed "Central Chamber of Commerce." They applauded orders from the Home Ministry and Ministry of Agriculture and Commerce "to stop the peddlers of the country from forming any guild according to the old custom for the purpose of monopolizing the trade and to collect illegal taxes from the farming classes."[63] The newly organized Central

Chamber of Commerce under the former head of the Council of State, Cho Pyŏng-sik, likewise felt the wrath of the *Independent*. Editors enumerated the functions of Cho's Central Chamber: (1) to establish trade boundaries in Seoul's commercial districts to exclude foreigners; (2) to retain exclusive charge of revenue stamps to replace taxes collected at fairs and ports; (3) to regulate the price of commodities; (4) and to exclude any non-members from mercantile business. Nothing could be more dramatically opposed to the ideal of free trade espoused by trade advocates. Anger at early guilds and other monopolies was consistent with the commitment of trade advocates to the principles of a market economy and law in Korea. Nor did the newspaper accept either the government's rationale or methods of grain embargoes.[64] On the other hand, they applauded growing trade at the ports and penetration of commerce to the interior: "the trade conditions of the different ports for the last two months is more encouraging than it ever has been.... We are told that many new lines of imports find markets in the interior and the Korean are beginning to raise many articles for export purposes... Even the Koreans have begun to possess the spirit of enterprise."[65]

Trade advocates at the turn of the century grew impatient with the slow process of change in society. What they envisioned was economic growth, political reform and survival, spurred by markets and a competitive spirit. What they found was apathy, fading sovereignty, and Japanese dominance in trade and major local development projects such as the railroads and telegraph system. Apathy in polity and economy gained the attention of Sŏ and Yun in the *Independent*, but also of "Self-strengthening" advocates such as Pak Ŭn-sik in the Protectorate years. The *Independent* faulted government corruption for discouraging initiative among the tax-paying public: "For the last one hundred years the corruption of the official has reached such a degree that it has simply killed the enterprising spirit of the whole nation."[66] The newspaper made every effort to spur ambition: "We want to make our readers discontented with their present way of idling away their lives."[67] And finally, the newspaper looked to education to dispel apathy, arguing that "education is the most pertinent lever for reform and progress."[68] Pak Ŭn-sik echoed the latter sentiments in the following decade with his plea for educational reform, arguing that "power comes from knowledge, and knowledge from scholarship."[69] He candidly expressed his own admiration for Japan's efforts to emulate the Western model of education with a system of primary schools, teacher training colleges, and universities.[70] His most practical insight into the process of change brought him back to his own Confucian roots, when Pak challenged the literati and their network of village schools to develop both natural science and a more contemporary moral education.[71]

A call for educational reform represents a basic difference between the enlightenment advocates and their orthodoxy counterparts in the Righteous Armies. Both recognized problems of foreign penetration and a weak local polity, but whereas the former took up the pen, the latter reached for pen and sword. The former advocated a more egalitarian order based on distinction between state and society, whereas the latter promoted an earlier, hierarchical order based on the model of monarch and minister. The former applauded trade, the latter condemned it. Unlike opponents, advocates looked to trade and commerce with a distinction between state and society, supporting state oversight but also the legitimate role of private enterprise and profit. Both trade opponents and advocates shared anxieties about the emerging regional order under Japanese hegemony, but as enlightenment activists looked forward to a new international order of sovereign states, the Orthodoxy adherents looked back to an earlier cultural order of local autonomy and limited foreign ties.

Conclusion

Enlightenment activists welcomed international trade in hopes of reform leading to national wealth and power where trade would promote a new order of popular participation and contractual ties or law. The inaugural issue of the *Independent* left no doubt about enlightenment priorities: "Korea for Koreans, clean politics, and the cementing of foreign friendships."[72] But there were seams in their well-woven garment of system, state, and market as advocates praised entry into international markets despite ominous signs of Korea's dependency. Hopes for new forms of Korean authority to insure the relative autonomy of a self-regulating market met the harsh reality of Japanese political and economic penetration. Growing disillusionment with Japan is apparent as we move from Yu Kil-chun through the Kabo Reforms and Independence Movement to the Protectorate Period and Pak Ŭn-sik. Late nineteenth reformers had no answer to the erosion of cultural and political sovereignty, but no interest in a return to seclusion. Yun and others were not blind to the fact of fading local control, but saw no other choice than competitive, open markets to force change.

Their theme of delimited state and responsible citizens became the motto for popular sovereignty without a clear conception of necessary changes in the state. They lavished attention on the role of citizens in a democracy but offered far less detail on the role of a democratic state. Chandra found a "statist" conception of a new political order evident in the *Independent*: "popular rights and popular participation in government would lead to solidarity between government and people and thus strengthen the state."[73] Capitalism was seen as a means to wealth and power rather than the basis for democratic rule. The failure of constitutional reforms in Seoul limited the *kwanmin* ideology to a populist ideal rather than a program for restructuring state and society. Coupled with this statist and idealistic concept of popular sovereignty was a shift from the traditional focus on nation or race to national character. Trade supporters looked less to customs and symbols of nation and more to modern virtues. Their emphasis on rational, efficient adaptation to the new regional order for national survival, and on an enterprising spirit both supported stronger international commerce.

If the clamor against trade was moral, extreme, and nationalistic, the campaign for trade was secular, but in its own way also radical and nationalistic. Trade advocates distinguished the moral neutrality of the market dynamic from the morality of individuals in the market, whether merchants or officials. Yu, the *Independent* editors, and Pak Ŭn-sik proved more pragmatic than trade opponents, and at times ranged close to individualism in promoting a spirit of enterprise and identification of individual interest, but they ultimately failed to resolve issues of private interest and public interests, private profit and the common good. Trade supporters also called for radical reform of Korean society, whether promoting popular political participation, or acknowledging the legitimacy of private profit. Nor does one find moderation in their rejection of trade opponents. Yu Kil-chun and Pak Ŭn-sik appeared less enamored of Christianity and more sympathetic to Confucian ideals than the *Independent* editors, but Yu's enthusiastic portrayal of Western institutions would have infuriated trade opponents in the Righteous Armies. The contrast between modern legal contract and earlier moral covenant opened an intellectual and emotional chasm between trade supporters in the Enlightenment Movement, and trade opponents in the Orthodoxy School.

The debate contributed more to division than national consensus in the short-term, but the implications stretched well beyond factional struggles at the turn of the century. Reformers had introduced basic principles of capitalist society such as the distinction among official, public, and private sectors. Reformers had broached the separation of state and civil society, and promoted formation of an extrabureaucratic public opinion. The latter appeared intertwined with respect and support of the monarchy in the kingdom, and then closely tied to survival of the nation in the Protectorate years, 1905 to 1910. Reformers appeared committed to law rather than custom as a basic principle of direction in society, whether to protect access to the market or shield citizens from rapacious officials. Advocates at once lauded private profit yet criticized any gain which might erode the common good. Moderate nationalists in the 1920s would return to the same issues, as would local business interests, large and small, trying to explain and justify their own enterprise within a colonial setting.[74]

If private interest had gained initial acceptance, trade advocates offered few guidelines for resolving conflicts between public and private interest. The principle of legitimate interest in open markets suggested by Yu, Sŏ, and Yun provided a rationale for trade and capitalist growth on the peninsula. Contract rather than moral covenant would be the engine for the market dynamics of supply and demand. Advocates dismissed extensive state intervention as inefficient and corrupt, and gave wide berth to the individual entrepreneur within a market society. This was a curious adoption of Western market ideology with enterprise serving now common ends rather than individual goals, but it coincided with the traditional function of law in the Chosŏn Dynasty of preserving social order rather than protecting individual rights. As one scholar observed, "it was the business of the ruling class to govern and the duty of the citizens to be loyal and obedient to the state, in contrast to Western notions of government and individual rights."[75] A passage from guild to chamber would blend covenants of family ties or of trust gained from long-term business relationships with the legal framework of association, enterprise, and semi-official firms such as the Grain Exchange. A new model of private enterprise would come to the fore on the basis of private property and profit, but without the political voice accorded "citizens" in the private sphere.

Notes

1. Yun Ch'i-ho, *Yun Ch'i-ho ilki* [The diary of Yun Ch'i-ho] (Seoul: Kuksa P'yŏnch'an Wiwŏnhoe, 1976), vol 5, p. 29, entry for February 18, 1897.

2. *Independent*, May 23, 1896.

3. I translate the Korean terms *kaehwa* and *kaemong* as "enlightenment."

4. Yu Kil-chun (1856-1914) represented an interesting blend of Confucian sensibilities and enlightenment ideas. A native of Seoul, he studied the Confucian Classics with his father and grandfather, and later the ideas of the School of Practical Learning under the auspices of Pak Kyu-su. Yu joined a group of prominent Koreans in 1881 to tour Japan and observe her modernization efforts, remaining in Japan until late 1882 at Fukuzawa Yukichi's Keio University. He later studied briefly in the U.S. and toured Europe, before returning to Korea in 1885 after the abortive Kapsin Coup. Yu was confined under house arrest for the next seven year because of close ties with enlightenment activists, during which he wrote his influential *Sŏyu kyŏnmun* [Observations on the West], published in Japan in 1895. See Kim Young-ho, "Yu Kil Chun's Idea of Enlightenment," *Journal of Social Sciences and Humanities* 33 (Dec. 1979): 37-60; Kim Hyung-chan, "Yu Kil-Chun: A Korean Crusader for Reform," *Korea Journal* 12 (Dec. 1972): 36-42; and Kim Pyŏng-ha, "Economic thought of Yu Kil-jun," *Korea Journal* 18 (July 1978): 30-48, (Aug. 1978): 42-51.

5. The English language section of the *Tongnip Sinmun*, titled the *Independent*, was distributed with the vernacular edition from April of 1896 through December of 1897. Separate editions were then published until the paper was discontinued in 1899. See Shin Yong-ha, *Tongnip hyŏphoe yŏn'gu: Tongnip Sinmun* [Studies of the Independence Club: the Independent] (Seoul Ilchogak, 1976); also Clarence N. Weems, "Reformist Thought of the Independence Program (1896-1898)," in Jo Yung-hwan, ed., *Korea's Response to the West* (Kalamazoo, Michigan: The Korean Research and Publications, Inc, 1971), pp. 163-218.

6. Born of a prominent aristocratic family, Sŏ Chae-p'il (1863-1951) left Korea after the Kapsin coup to spend nearly a decade abroad absorbing Western and Asian strategies for reform. Joining Kim Ok-kyun in the Kapsin effort, Sŏ later escaped to Japan and finally to the U.S., where he studied Western socio-political thought, natural science, and Christianity. Joining the Presbyterian Church, he married an American and anglicized his own name to Philip Jaisohn. He returned to Korea in 1895 at the request of Premier Pak Chŏng-yang, and served as an advisor on the Privy Council until December of 1897. Sŏ won government financial support for established a newspaper in April of 1896, the *Tongnip Sinmun* [Independent], which he edited until his departure from Korea under government pressure in May of 1898. He was also instrumental in founding the Independence Club of enlightenment activists and publicizing their activities and opinions. See Pak Sŏng-su, *Tongnip undongsa yŏn'gu* [Studies of the history of the Independence Movement] (Seoul: Ch'angjak gwa Pipy'ŏngsa, 1980); Lee Kwang-rin, "The Enlightenment Thinking of Sŏ Chae-p'il," *Social Science Journal* (Unesco, Korea) vol. 7 (1980): 48-91; S. E. Oh, "Dr. Philip

Jaisohn's Reform Movement 1896-1898: A Critical Appraisal of the Independence Club," Ph.D. diss., The American University, 1971.

7. Yun Ch'i-ho (1864-1945) was the son of Yun Ung-yŏl, a prominent military official. Sympathetic with the Kapsin coup leadership, Yun left Seoul in early 1885 for nine years of study and teaching in China and the U.S. Returning to his homeland in 1895, he served briefly as vice-minister of education before travelling to the coronation of Czar Nicholas II of Russia as secretary for the Korean delegation. He joined the Independence Club in 1897, serving as club president during the critical period of mass political action the next year, and finally succeeded Sŏ as editor of the newspaper. With the government-ordered dissolution of the club in that December, Yun accepted appointment as a provincial magistrate. Yun also served as vice-minister of foreign affairs during the succession of agreements with Japan culminating in the Protectorate Agreement of November 17, 1905. He later devoted himself to education during the Protectorate and early colonial period. See Kenneth Wells, *New God, New Nation: Protestants and Self-Reconstruction Nationalism in Korea, 1896-1937* (Honolulu: University of Hawaii Press, 1990), and "Yun Ch'i-ho and the Quest for National Integrity: the Formation of a Christian Approach to Korean Nationalism at the End of the Chosŏn Dynasty," *Korea Journal* vol. 22, no. 1 (Jan. 1982): 42-59; Donald C. Clark, "Yun Ch'i-ho (1864-1945): Portrait of a Korean Intellectual in an Era of Transition," in James B. Palais and Margery D. Lang, eds., *Occasional Papers on Korea, No. 4* (Seattle: Joint Committee on Korean Studies of the American Council of Learned Societies and the Social Science Research Council, 1975), pp. 36-76; Kim Hyung-chan, *Letters in Exile: The Life and Times of Yun Ch'i-ho* (Covington, Georgia: Rhoades Printing, 1980).

8. Pak Ŭn-sik (1859-1926) wrote for the *Hwangsŏng* Newspaper from 1898 through 1905, and joined the staff of the *Taehan Maeil Sinbo* the next year. He was active also in the Taehan Chaganghoe [Korean Society for Self-Strengthening], and other nationalist associations such as the Sŏu Hakhoe and its successor, the Sŏbuk Hakhoe. He spent his final fifteen years in China writing on Korean history. Among the most prominent publications of the latter years were the *Han'guk T'ongsa* [Korea's painful history], and *Han'guk Tongnip undong ŭi hyŏlsa* [The violent history of Korea's Independence Movement]. See Shin Yong-ha, "The Life and Thought of Pan Ŭn-sik," *Korea Journal* 21, 3 (March 1981): 21-30; Lee Kwang-rin, "Korea's Responses to Social Darwinism," *Korea Journal* vol. 18 (1978), part I in no. 4: 36-47, and part II in no. 5: 42-49.

9. For an introduction to the "Self-strengthening Movement," see Shin Yong-ha, "Hanmal ŭi aeguk kaemong undong [The Patriotic Enlightenment campaign in the late Chosŏn Dynasty]," pp. 79-100 in his *Han'guk kŭndaesa gwa sahoe pyŏndong* [Modern Korean history and social change] (Seoul: Munhwa gwa chisŏngsa, 1980).

10. *Sŏyu kyŏnmun* [Observations on the West], translated by Kim T'ae-Chun (Seoul: Pagyŏngsa, 1976), chapter 14, sec. 381, p. 117. The original text of Han'gŭl and Hanmun has been reprinted in Taehaksa, *Han'guk hyŏndae sup'ilchip charyo ch'ongsŏ* [A compendium of materials on modern Korean essays], vol. 1 (Seoul: Taehaksa, 1987), which will be cited as HHS. The reference from the text can be found on page 380 of HHS. I will first refer to this original text, and then to chapter, section, and page number in the more accessible and readily available Kim T'ae-chun edition.

11. *Independent*, June 18, 1898.

12. Pak Ŭn-sik, "Kyoyugi pulhŭngimyŏn sengjŏn ŭl puldŭk [No survival without education]," *Sŏu Hakhoe* (Dec. 1906); reprinted in *Chŏnsŏ* [Complete works of Pak Ŭn-sik] (1975), vol. 3, pp. 86-88. One can also find a selection of Pak's works in *Pak Ŭn-sik* [Pak Ŭn-sik], edited by Yi Man-yŏl (Seoul: Han'gilsa, 1980).

13. Pak Ŭn-sik, "Taehan chŏngsin [Korean spirit]," *Sŏbuk Hakhoe Wŏlbo*, no. 3, 1 September 1909; *Chŏnsŏ*, vol. 3, pp. 67-68.

14. *Sŏyu kyŏnmun*, Book 14, Sec. 377, p. 113-114.

15. *Independent*, 26 March 1898.

16. See "Kyoyugi pulhŭngimyŏn sengjŏn ŭl puldŭk [No survival without education]," *Sŏu Hakhoe* (Dec. 1906); reprinted in *Chŏnsŏ* [Complete works of Pak Ŭn-sik] (1975), vol. 3, pp. 86-88.

17. Christopher Chase-Dunn, "The Korean Trajectory in the World-System," in Kim Kyong-dong, ed., *Dependency Issues in Korean Development* (Seoul: Seoul National University Press, 1987), p. 279.

18. *Tongnip Sinmun*, June 7, 1898; April 18, 1896.

19. *Independent*, September 30, 1897.

20. *Independent*, September 5,1896.

21. "Muljil keryangron [Improvement of quality]," *Sŏbuk Hakhoe Wŏlbo*, no. 8 (1909); *Chŏnsŏ*, vol. 3, pp. 37-39.

22. "In the decade preceding liberation, the peasant class lost upwards of 10 percent of its members, mostly to industry; and many more than this had been touched by the force of the world market system. It was the simultaneity of the coming of the market and the rise of industry that was so critical to shaping the fate of Korea under the Japanese and thereafter." Bruce Cumings, *The Origins of the Korean War* (Princeton: Princeton University Press, 1981), p. 48.

23. HHS, p. 377; *Sŏyu kyŏnmun*, c. 14, sec. 378, p. 115.

24. HHS, p. 205; *Sŏyu kyŏnmun*, c. 8, sec. 205, p. 217.

25. HHS, pp. 121, 362; *Sŏyu kyŏnmun*, c. 4, sec. 122, p. 133; c. 14, sec. 361, p. 100.

26. HHS, p. 362; *Sŏyu kyŏnmun*, c. 14, sect. 362, p. 100.

27. HHS, p. 376; *Sŏyu kyŏnmun*, c. 14. I translate *chŏngbu* as "government," and *paeksŏng* as "people."

28. *Independent*, August 26, 1897.

29. *Independent*, August 22, 1897.

30. The idea of a more egalitarian cooperation between "officials and the people" was explained in a series of editorials of November, 1898, in the vernacular *Tongnip Sinmun*. See editions for November 3, 4, 18, 19, and 20. Advertisements for the Independence Club published in the *Tongnip Sinmun* highlighted the idea of "unanimity and joint effort of officials and the people [*kwanmin tongsim hamnyŏk*]." See editions for December 12, 1898, and December 16, 1898. Editorials in the same newspaper at other times would emphasize a similar distinction between "government" [*chŏngbu*] and "people" [*paeksŏng*].

31. *Independent*, March 9, 1897.

32. *Independent*, March 3, 1898.

33. *Independent*, December 5, 1896.

34. For a study of the Assembly of Officials and Citizens [*Kwanmin kongdonghoe*], see Vipan Chandra, *Imperialism, Resistance, and Reform in late Nineteenth-Century Korea* (Berkeley: Center for Korean Studies, Institute of East Asian Studies, University of California Berkeley, 1988), pp. 195-200, and my review of the study in *Korean Studies* no. 14 (1990), pp. 195-197. See also Lee Kwang-rin, *Han'guksa kangchwa: kŭndae p'yŏn* [Lectures on Korean history: modern period] (Seoul: Ilchogak, 1981), pp. 445 ff.

35. HHS, pp. 375, 384; *Sŏyu kyŏnmun*, c. 14, sec. 376, 384, pp. 112, 121.

36. *Independent*, June 30, 1896; July 18, 1896; April 8, 1897; December 10, 1896; December 12, 1896.

37. *Independent*, February 9, 1897; March 5, 1898; April 30, 1898; June 7, 1898.

38. *Independent*, September 3, 1896.

39. *Independent*, April 8, 1897; *Tongnip Sinmun* December 1, and December 7, 1898.

40. HHS, p. 111; *Sŏyu kyŏnmun*, c. 4, sec. 112, p. 121.

41. HHS, p. 376; *Sŏyu kyŏnmun*, c. 14, Sec. 375, p. 113.

42. HHS, pp. 120-121; *Sŏyu kyŏnmun*, c. 4, sec. 120, p. 132.

43. HHS, p. 131; *Sŏyu kyŏnmun*, c. 4, sec. 131, p. 144.

44. *Independent*, March 30, 1897.

45. *Independent*, October 7, 1897.

46. HHS, p. 364; *Sŏyu kyŏnmun*, c. 14, sec. 364, p. 103.

47. *Sŏyu kyŏnmun*, c. 14, sec. 370, p. 109.

48. *Independent*, February 11, 1897; March 30, 1897; November 20, 1897; December 2, 1897; April 5, 1898; *Tongnip Sinmun* October 4, 1898.

49. *Independent*, December 2, 1897; April 9, 1898, August 9, 1898.

50. *Independent*, March 5, 1898.

51. "Public management by elites thus contrasted with official administration (*guan*), and with private (*si*) activities of individuals, families, religions, businesses, and organizations that were not identified with the whole community." Mary Backus Rankin, *Elite Activism and Political Transformation in China* (Stanford: Stanford University Press, 1986), p. 15; "Some Observations on a Chinese Public Sphere," *Modern China*, vol. 19, no. 2 (April 1993): 158-182.

52. HHS, p. 361; *Observations*, c. 14, sec. 362, p. 101.

53. HHS, p.360; *Observations*, c. 14, sec. 360, p. 98.

54. HHS, 361; *Observations*, c. 14, sec. 361, pp. 100-101.

55. *Independent*, October 4, 1897; April 19, 1898.

56. *Independent*, June 16, 1896.

57. *Independent*, February 10, 1898.

58. *Hwangsŏng Sinmun*, August 9, 1905, p. 2. Excerpted in *Kusimnyŏnsa*, pp. 188-189. I translate *sangŏpgye* and *chaegye* as "business community."

59. *Taehan Maeil Shinbo*, October 31, 1905. The editorial is excerpted in *Kusimnyŏnsa*, pp. 189-190. See also a similar editorial in *Hwangsŏng Sinmun*, November 7, 1905, p. 2. I translate *sangŏpga* as "businessmen."

60. *Taehan Mail Sinpo*, January 15, 1910. The editorial is excerpted in *Kusimnyŏnsa*, p. 195. See also a similar editorial in the *Hwangsŏng Sinmun* of January 16, 1910, p. 2.

61. *Hwangsŏng Sinmun*, February 19, 1910, p. 2, and February 23, 1910, p. 2. They also encouraged commercial education to insure the growth and competence of a business community.

62. *Sŏyu kyŏnmun*, c. 14, sec. 362, p. 100.

63. *Independent*, September 25, 1897; September 28, 1897; also February 3, 1898.

64. *Independent*, December 15, 1896; November 27, 1897; December 2, 1897; April 9, 1898.

65. *Independent*, March 5, 1898.

66. *Independent*, December 12, 1896; March 9, 1897.

67. *Independent*, April 10, 1897.

68. *Independent*, August 6, 1896.

69. "Kyoyugi pulhŭng."

70. "Hakkyo jisei [A school system]," *Sŏu Hakhoe Wŏlbo* no. 1 (1906); *Chŏnsŏ*, vol. 3, pp. 117-118.

71. "Yugyo kunsinron [Reform of Confucianism], *Sŏu Hakhoe Wŏlbo*, no. 10 (March 1909); *Chŏnsŏ*, vol. 3, pp. 44-48. A translation of this essay can be found in *Korea Journal* vol. 21, no. 3 (March 1981), pp. 31-34. See also his "Kusŭp keryangron [Reform of anachronistic practices]," *Sŏu Hakhoe Wŏlbo* no. 2 (1907); *Chŏnsŏ*, vol. 3, pp. 8-11.

72. *Independent*, April 7, 1896.

73. *Imperialism*, p. 216. Chandra had earlier highlighted the possible tension between popular sovereignty and the monarchy. "While the idea of popular sovereignty needed to be introduced to Koreans so that they could begin to stand up for their rights, it need not mean instantly transforming Korea in a republic.... Monarchy was perfectly compatible with the idea of popular sovereignty as long as the concept of social contract and the limited nature of the monarch's position were understood." "The Concept of Popular Sovereignty: The Case of Sŏ Chae-p'il and Yun Ch'i-ho," *Korea Journal* vol. 21, no. 4 (April 1981): 11.

74. Wells, *New God, New Nation*, pp. 138-161; Michael Robinson, *Cultural Nationalism in Colonial Korea, 1920-1925* (Seattle: University of Washington Press, 1988), pp. 78-106.

75. Chung Young-Iob, "The Traditional Economy of Korea," *The Journal of Modern Korean Studies*, vol. 1 (April 1984): 22.

5

Chaegye

The Korean business community stood at the center of a transition in mind and market. Brokers tell us of trade, and their enterprise, associations, and the Grain Exchange offer a chronicle of system, state, and market. Themes of distinction, dependence, and integration give texture to a history of accommodation among local grain brokers in both late kingdom and colony. Korean precedents of enterprise and association, as well as new colonial patterns merge in the chaegye to establish enduring capitalist legacies. If Korea's entry into an international capitalist system forced a reconstruction of ideas of authority and exchange, new capitalist and then imperial goals spurred a reorganization of enterprise, association and even markets.

What links might we expect between the trade debate among intellectuals and the trade practices and practical ideologies of the mid-size and smaller merchants? Trade associations and the larger chambers may in time develop ideas in concert or opposition to intellectuals and politicians, but merchants themselves are often too busy with markets and money to follow the controversies. The broader debates over trade and commerce, and indeed the shape of capitalism more commonly affect mainly the policy-makers. State policies often result in laws which frame a model for competition and cooperation within markets, and in turn are reflected in the constitution of enterprise and association, in commercial contract, and in the procedures of supporting institutions. Rather than a unilinear direction from debate to policy to law and finally to practice, some interplay of ideas, policy and practice appears more likely and alerts us to the significance of legislation, formal business policy at the associations, and the practical business ideology of people in the market. As apart from state economic policy, a "business" ideology can be gleaned from two different sources of the period: advertisements for individual firms, and policies of the trade associations.

Joining ideology to social structure, Robert Wuthnow highlighted the legitimating function of the former without specifying causes. He pointed rather to a "fit" between ideology and structure, explaining that "the two intermingle" and that the key question is how such an interaction develops.[1] Structure or institution draws our attention not solely to understand ideas, but also to assess the scale and direction of the market dynamic through its reinstitutionalization in new organizations. Implicit in the brief of trade advocacy for both state direction and free markets was a blend of competition and cooperation encouraging individual enterprise without mutually destructive competition. The shift in forms of exchange from kingdom to colony was not simply the liberation of the market dynamic, but rather a reembedding of market under new patterns of authority and relations among capital, both Japanese and Korean, particularly evident in efforts of state and capital to address dilemmas of collective action.

Three levels of institutions and ideas gave shape to the Korean business community at the ports led by the brokers. Individual enterprise reflects the practical business ideology of businessmen trying to assure customers of their trustworthiness and professional expertise. We look here to the type and scale of enterprise among Korean brokers, and their expansion from consignment sales to milling, and from storefronts to firms. Businessmen's organizations represent a separate level whether among grain brokers or in peak organizations such as the chambers of commerce at the port. Associations can foster professionalism, provide fora among the chaegye for gaining information on markets and government policy, and facilitate links among state, Korean business community and the Japanese zaikai. In their promotion of business priorities, associations provide a public record of issues familiar in the earlier trade debate regarding public and private profit or interest, definition of the commonweal, and the role of state versus the business community. A subsequent chapter on the Grain Exchange will examine yet a third level of chartered or semi-official joint-stock firms to complete the circle of enterprise.

Incorporation into a interstate system of markets draws us back to the formation of a distinct chaegye at the ports, to their ideas, interests, and institutions. Brokers draw us away from the fractious trade controversy to the frenzy of grain contracting, din of harbor mills, bustling government offices, and the raucous halls of the trade associations.

What we meet in the mills and minds of brokers and their associations is nothing less than the interests and organization of an emerging private sector evident in the port chaegye.

Mills and Merchants

If capital, labor, and technology provide the bases for enterprise, private property begins with ownership. Koreans were able to carve out a place for themselves in the milling industry between 1915 and 1928.[2] They owned 70 of the 170 granaries operating in the colony in 1915, and thirteen years later twelve hundred or 70% of all rice mills, but their scale never matched their Japanese competitors. Local mills in 1915 registered an average capital investment of 1,800 yen and eight workers per mill, as against 265,000 yen and 57 workers at Japanese mills. Annual value of production at a Korean mill averaged 30,000 yen in 1915, but 190,000 yen at Japanese mills. Differences narrowed by 1928 when Koreans averaged a capital investment of 6,500 yen and eight workers per mill, as against Japanese competitors with 30,000 yen and 19 workers per mill. Annual value of production at the Korean mills in 1928 had grown to 50,000 yen, still only about a quarter of the annual value at Japanese plants. Grain mills offered two exceptions to investment patterns in the colony. Koreans registered a mere 6% of total investment in commerce and industry but a remarkable 33% of total investment in rice milling.[3] Secondly, joint Korean-Japanese enterprises represented 34% of total investment in the colony, but none of the investment in rice milling. Koreans invested in Korean mills. The Japanese invested in Japanese mills but employed Korean workers, with ethnic Japanese accounting for 10% of all employment at their mills in 1915, but only 4% in 1928. We might assume the Japanese were employed as engineers initially, but were gradually replaced with locals. At the same time Korean mills employed Koreans almost exclusively. Korean mills procured Ninomiya, Chūō, and Engle milling machines through Japanese trading houses, but did not employ Japanese technicians.[4]

Complementing individual enterprise, associations among trades further contribute to the definition and distinction of private enterprise. Among elder statesmen of the *kaekchugye* or "broker community" still active in the 1920s were Sŏ Sang-bin, Chŏng Ch'i-guk, Chang Sŏk-u, and Hong Chae-bŏm. Sŏ had pioneered brokers' associations such as the Inch'ŏn Merchants Association in 1897,[5] and the Sinsang Hoesa in 1908,[6] and later served as a Councillor on the Board of the Inch'ŏn Brokers Association.[7] He founded the Inch'ŏn Trust Association in 1913 as a finance operation, and registered a capital of 50,000 yen by 1928.[8] Chŏng Ch'i-guk was also active in both trade associations and finance. A Pusan broker, Chŏng first came to Inch'ŏn in 1895 with a financial venture which soon failed.[9] He found his way back to Pusan and established a steamship firm, only to return to Inch'ŏn as general manager of the government's Taehan Hapdong Mail Steamer Firm.[10] An ambitious venture of the Korean government, the transport firm represented the local state's most extensive infrastructural effort which Chŏng managed to operate for a time with only three steamers, but finally surrendered to creditors in 1905. He did succeed in founding the Inch'ŏn Korean Chamber of Commerce and later served as the first Korean vice-president of the joint Korean-Japanese chamber from 1916 to 1921. He assumed leadership of the Industrial Promotion Company [Kwŏnŏpsa] in Inch'ŏn in 1906,[11] which he led through the early 1920s.[12] Apart from leadership in trade associations, Chŏng was also active on the board of directors at the Jinsen Grain Exchange.[13]

Chang Sŏk-u was yet another broker eminent in association and enterprise. Chang gained a place with the major Japanese millers and grain traders in an early finance operation titled the Chosen Trust Company.[14] He was a major shareholder in the Chosen Mutual Loan Company based in Inch'ŏn, where Chang had teamed up in 1922 with Karai Eitarō, Noguchi Bun'ichi and others,[15] and continued with the firm later under the leadership of Imai Kakujirō, who himself had been a broker on the Jinsen Grain Exchange.[16] Chang served as president of the Inch'ŏn Brokers Association in 1921 and 1922 and later as a Councillor,[17] and joined Karai Eitarō in leading the opposition to the proposed transfer of the Jinsen Grain Exchange to Seoul. We read of Hong Chae-bŏm in the early and later history of the Brokers' Association with published reports of his presidency in 1926 and then again in 1937.[18]

Prominent later in both enterprise and association were the Chu and Sim families, Yu Kun-sŏng and others listed in Table 5.1. Prominent among a younger generation of entrepreneurs, Chu Myŏng-sŏng opened the Sŏhungpong dry goods store in Inch'ŏn in 1905, and appears on the roster of the joint chamber from 1916 to 1923.[19] Following their father's lead, Chu Myŏng-gi and Pong-gi expanded into the Wayang dry goods store, and the Chu Myŏng-gi Rice Mill.[20] The combination of enterprise in both textiles and rice milling reflected continuity in consignment and merchandising, but diversity in moving between sales and industrial processing. The long-tenured president of the Rice Sales Association among Korean brokers, Chu Myŏng-gi also served two terms as vice-president at the joint chamber. Chu had succeeded to the vice-presidency following the tenure of Sim Nŭng-dŏk the pioneer of the Sim family. Founder of both a leading local dry goods store and a grain consignment operation in Inch'ŏn, Sim was also president of the Inch'ŏn Commerce Company, a short-lived commercial venture of the Inch'ŏn brokers.[21] His son Sim Ŭi-sŏk continued the consignment sales with both grains and marine products, and later turned to finance with his Taedong Sangsa, and was active in the combined chamber from 1927 to 1931.[22] A third diversified broker distinguished himself in two quite distinct trades of grains and lumber, and later on the prestigious Chosen Exchange. Yu Kun-sŏng gained fame and fortune first in lumber sales, and only later as a broker and miller in the Hana-chō Section of Inch'ŏn among the huge Japanese granaries, and finally as a licensed broker on the Chosen Exchange.[23]

TABLE 5.1 Korean Brokers [kaekchu] at Inch'ŏn

Broker	Enterprise	Association
Chu Myŏng-gi	Wayang Dry Goods Chu Rice Mill	Jinsen Chamber, IBA*, Rice Sales, Jinsen Grain Assoc.
Kim Kyu-myŏn	Kwangsŏngt'ae	IBA
Sim Nŭng-dŏk	Sim Dry Goods Inch'ŏn Commerce	Jinsen Chamber, IBA
Sim Ŭi-suk	Sŏgyŏng Rice Mill Taedong Sales	Jinsen Chamber, IBA
Yi Hŭng-sŏn	Yi Hŭng Rice Mill	IBA, Jinsen Grain Assoc.
Yu Kun-sŏng	Yu Lumber Yu Rice Mill	Jinsen Chamber, IBA

* IBA = Inch'ŏn Brokers [kaekchu] Association.

Still other brokers concentrated on consignment sales and trade in grains, with allied milling operations. Yi Hŭng-sŏn operated a store from the turn of the century, and later established the Yi Hŭng Rice Mill in the Yanagi-chō Section of largely Korean residents, next to the mill of Chu Myŏng-gi.[24] Also mainly in grain sales, Kim Kyu-myŏn was a councillor at the combined chamber, and also at the Korean Brokers Association, and active in the opposition to the transfer of the Jinsen Grain Exchange to Seoul.[25] He operated the Kwangsŏngt'ae brokerage for trade in grains and consignment sales. Established in 1914, the same firm was listed in 1935 with an authorized capital of 100,000 yen and a paid-in capital of 25,000 Yen. Although Kim Kyu-myŏn was no longer active in the firm, the company had diversified into consignment sales of grains, marine products, fertilizers, liquor and fruits, as well as dry goods, and even finance.[26]

Entrepreneurs need capital, plant, and markets, and capital was the first hurdle facing Korean brokers interested in milling. Raising capital within a family of merchants was possible if the family was successful, as evident above with the Chu and Sim families. Chu Myŏng-gi was able to quickly establish a dry goods store, the Wayang [East and West]" for imports of tobacco, textiles and utensils from Britain and Japan.[27] Tax records for 1921 indicate strong tobacco sales, and the most extensive sales of dry goods among Korean stores in the port,[28] before his brother, Chu Pong-gi expanded the business with specially tailored vests.[29] The store generated revenue for reinvestment in expanding consignment sales and milling, and with Pong-gi minding the store, Myŏng-gi was free for both industrial and civic duties. Chu registered his mill in the Yanagi-chō district with a paid-in capital of 50,000 yen in 1928, well above the national average of 6,500 yen per mill.[30] Chu incorporated as an unlimited partnership in December 1929 for milling and trading in rice, straw bags, and money-lending, and registered an authorized and paid-up capital of 100,000 yen.[31] A decade later, the same firm registered a paid-up capital of 245,000 yen.[32]

Also long active in consignment sales and manual rice milling in Yanagi-chō, Yi Hŭng-sŏn finally registered a mill in 1924, and listed a paid-in capital of 50,000 yen four years later. We have no record of how he put together the necessary investment capital, but the long years of brokering would have permitted some capital accumulation. A third broker investing in milling was Yu Kun-sŏng. Probably the most prominent Inch'ŏn broker, Yu began with consignment sales of timber for boats, barges, stores and homes, and turned to rice milling and brokerage prior to annexation. Two decades later, he stood proudly among the very few Koreans with positions on the Jinsen Grain Exchange. A profitable timber brokerage provided the capital necessary for a smaller milling operation, though he reported a paid-in capital of only 10,000 yen at his mill in the Hana-chō section in 1928.[33]

Turning from capital to plant, we find Chu and Yi with the largest locally owned mills in Inch'ŏn, and Yu not far behind. Chu Myŏng-gi operated both gas and electric powered hulling machines with seventy machinists and laborers, far above the national average of 8 employees. The mill could hull 300 koku of of rice daily, and polish 100 koku.[34] Yi Hŭng-sŏn has established a similar operation in 1921, and later listed seventy employees.[35] He reported a daily milling capacity of 125 koku, and polishing of 110 koku.[36] We find the mill of Yu Kun-sŏng in a different neighborhood, and a bit smaller than those of Chu and Yi. Yu had established a mill and consignment brokerage operation in the Hana-chō section of the port near larger Japanese mills already in 1908.[37] He later reported machinery and a labor force quite similar to that of Chu and Yi, and by 1931, his Hana-chō mill could mill 110 koku of rice daily, and polish a further 100 koku.[38] A lumber mill in the largely Japanese section of Hana-chō was established in May of 1928, and a decade later included four warehouses with a total of 660 square meters of storage space.[39] The profile of capital and plant indicates independent ownership, procurement and operation of milling equipment by the three brokers.

Markets no doubt forced the brokers to move towards large-scale milling. Brokers hoping to maintain a reliable supply of rice needed to secure rice cleaning facilities to insure reliable and timely processing. In-house milling facilities helped them maintain delivery schedules and avoid the expense of contracting out to other mills. Good transport and finance networks could bring rice from the countryside to the port, but storage and cleaning facilities were necessary to transfer rice from port to the Japanese shippers. As consignment agents, brokers supervised an exchange stretching from paddy to oceanfront. Small-scale milling plants could clean rice in sufficient volummes for the local market, but expanding foreign demand could be served more efficiently with larger milling operations. Once Japanese firms began churning out huge volummes of milled rice for export, the Korean mills had no choice but to expand to maintain economies of scale. The Japanese brought new market possibilities and new market problems for the Korean millers. Availability of technology from manufacturers or trading houses made mechanized refining possible, and local accumulation of commercial and agrarian capital made the investment feasible, but it was a market for rice exports that made enterprise attractive. A growing demand abroad for Korean rice prompted port brokers like Chu, Yi, and Yu to move their capital from commerce to industry.

A network of mills rather than any markedly nationalist business ideology provided the basis for a distinct, ethnic business community. Ideas among entrepreneurs and their associations indicate rather the growing autonomy of market from traditional ideas of profit and the commonweal. A survey of practical business ideology of the day tells us of distinct interests, and of professional channels for pursing those interests. Chu Myŏng-gi and Yu Kun-sŏng advertised in vernacular business handbooks in 1915 and 1928, with Yi Hŭng-sŏn contributing to the later volume as well.[40] For instance the young Chu placed an ad for his Wayang Variety Store in 1915 emphasizing training and family far more than enterprise or experience.[41] The ad highlights family, ties with leading merchants, and also education as evidence of reliability. In contrast, an ad for Yu Kun-sŏng's lumber shop in the same handbook cites only experience and investment.[42] Chu drew attention to his practical training with leading commercial agents in Seoul and Inch'ŏn, whereas Yu cited his own experience as a merchant. Chu emphasized a family commitment at the variety store, but Yu highlighted his personal investment of capital in the lumber business. Trust between supplier and customer was critical in a society where law and contract did not yet provide adequate safeguards to insure honesty in commercial exchange.

A similar volume thirteen years later documents change in both enterprise and ideology among the Korean chaegye. Associations and enterprise rather than family gave credibility to Chu's Yanagi-chō mill by 1928.[43] A record of enterprise at the Wayang Variety Store preceded rice mill and brokerage, but there were other accomplishments at the Jinsen City Council, School Board, Jinsen Chamber of Commerce, and Rice Sales Association [Misang Chohap]. Paralleling enterprise with civic achievement both Chu and Yu identified themselves as "entrepreneurs" rather than as brokers, millers, or simply citizens.[44] Yu listed positions on two different local school boards, and cited his pioneering lumber business in the ad for his rice mill and consignment operation.[45] The premise of commerce as a sound basis for industry was important for brokers trying to operate mills. Yet a third broker, Yi Hŭng-sŏn stands apart from both Chu and Yu in his exclusive emphasis on twenty years of experience as a rice broker. He sounded a common motif of "knowledge and experience," but could only cite satisfied customers from "here and abroad," and from Seoul and the countryside who did not hesitate to entrust him with their goods.[46] All three ads highlighted either enterprise, association, or both as the bases for trust in impersonal commercial exchanges, and giving definition to the emerging private sector.

Beyond personal careers, the handbook of 1928 opened with a formula for succeeding in business and closed with lessons in bookkeeping. Success depended first on dedication to the pursuit of profit and economic independence, but also on unity within the firm, and a reputation of trust beyond the firm. Unity in firm and business community would moderate selfishness and exaggerated materialism. Safeguards for solidarity in the community included exchange of information, open market competition, and the ethical pursuit of profit. The editor wrote of "profit as the goal of enterprise," but cautioned that selfishness and excessive profits could upset the common pursuit of profit within the business community. "Suitable profits," he argued, accrue when an entrepreneur makes money without overburdening other competitors in the community. In sum, the emerging Korean business community was being urged to unabashedly declare profit as their goal, but brokers would not find here a final resolution to the debate for the profits were immediately tied to the well-being of the business community. Secondly, cohesion in firm and community implied extension of solidarity in enterprise to solidarity in association. Emphases on the exchange of information, "suitable profits," and on open markets raised problems of interdependence within a community of entrepreneurs effectively addressed only within business associations.

Ads for the mills in 1928 highlight both contract and personal relations as a basis for credibility between miller and customer, whereas family and personal contacts provided a basis in 1915. Ads in 1928 convey more general or impersonal criteria such as prominence in business associations, civic service, and particularly service on educational boards. The interplay of idea, enterprise, and association was clear. Successful enterprise and effective association, both commercial and civic, paved the way for the rise of Chu Myŏng-gi in the joint Chamber of Commerce, or of Yu Kun-sŏng at the Grain Exchange. Society was more complex in 1928. Brokers cultivated institutional ties to supplement personal relationships as a basis for trust between contractor and client. Business men had more opportunities for recognition beyond their enterprise, and this recognition could in turn strengthen their business reputation.

Korean Chamber

Guilds, commercial associations, and chambers shed light on the organization and priorities of an emerging chaegye. International market ties eroded the foundations of local state authority and market controls sustaining the guild organization. A contractual, legally defined relationship with the state, organized competition within open markets, and cooperation with government offices, but separation from government bureaucracies would distinguish chambers of commerce or trade associations in the colony. The process of self-definition among Korean business associations took an odd turn in 1905 with establishment of a Japanese Residency-General on the peninsula. The Japanese assumed power on the peninsula just as the brokers were gaining limited recognition as an interest group distinct from the monarchy and their Japanese competitors. Yet rather than reversing the trend, colonization would help institutionalize the distinction from both state and zaikai, with the colonial state overseeing two business communities on the peninsula. Ethnically separate Korean chambers of commerce were established in fourteen cities across the peninsula between 1906 and 1911. The Tongnae Chamber of Commerce was founded in Pusan in 1908 by An Sun-guk and Kim Yŏng-gyu.[47] Broker Chŏng Ch'i-guk also gained the support of the local magistrate, Kim Yun-p'um, for the Inch'ŏn chamber in the same year.[48] The group soon moved into an impressive two story wooden building in the Sinch'ŏn section of Inch'ŏn, where they proclaimed goals of public service, promotion of commerce, and of mutual benefit of society and merchant in the trade competition.

Juxtaposition of public service with promotion of commerce conveyed a new self-confidence in capitalist ideals familiar among earlier trade advocates. The Korean chamber at Inch'ŏn assumed conventional tasks of providing a common voice for business in public affairs, lobbying the government on business issues, gathering information on commerce, encouraging adherence to trade law, and mediating commercial disputes.[49] Their annual average budget of one thousand yen between 1910 and 1912, or the Pusan (Tongnae) Chamber budget of fifteen hundred yen indicated commitment among the chaegye, but little competition with the Japanese Chamber in Inch'ŏn and their average annual budget across the same years of seven thousand yen.[50] Korean chambers may have been separate from their Japanese counterparts at the ports, but they were certainly not equal.[51]

The Korean Chamber at Inch'ŏn published their own ad in the 1915 business handbook.[52] They boldly identified the prosperity of their members and development of commerce with the good of society and portrayed themselves as soldiers at the front line fighting for the commonweal in a world-wide commercial war. This societal mandate linked their success in the marketplace with the common good rather than selfish profit, yet they candidly admitted their goal of promoting profits in commerce and industry, and even singled out strategies for expansion of profits as their special responsibility. Cooperation among the chaegye was also linked to the common good as Chamber members proclaimed their commitment to one another and to the nation. Unity among its members in times of prosperity or recession was necessary for commercial success, just as a unified association of the port's businessmen was necessary for commercial development. Functions included surveys and statistics on commerce, prices, and producing areas, and general information on the financial health and plans of member firms.

Entrusted by the government with the task of informing and advising, the Chamber provided the appropriate ministries with the information gathered from member firms, but their basic function and overriding purpose was more to persuade than simply inform. The Chamber kept the government abreast of a chaegye position on pertinent laws and statutes, advised on macroeconomic policy, and mediated disputes in the Korean business community. The ad drew an impressive picture of chamber solidarity, activity, and government recognition, but a small membership and meager budget would hardly support such an ambitious program. There is no evidence that the Japanese administrators in the port city paid much attention to the group, yet the aspirations, organization, and experience of the Chamber in trying to mediate disputes, gather information, and affect government policy suggest a major step towards a more professional business lobby. The organization was dissolved with the Chamber decree of 1915 mandating joint Japanese-Korean chambers in the colony, yet the seven year span of the Korean chambers at Pusan and Inch'ŏn permitted further consolidation of a chaegye at the ports.[53]

Association

Nowhere is a Korean effort to shape an ethnic trade community at the port more evident than in the persistence of the brokers from 1897, as evident in Table 5.2. The rapid succession of organizations from the Port of Inch'ŏn Merchants Association of 1897, to the Merchants Firm of 1899 and its reorganization under solely broker leadership from 1905, then to the Brokers' Union of 1911, and finally to the Inch'ŏn Brokers Association in 1917 suggests both the difficulty and urgency of their adjustment.[54]   Editors of the *Donga Ilbo* reported anxieties at the Association about their future late in the colonial period, given transport difficulties, tight credit, and the trend towards marketing by local agricultural cooperatives.[55] But through December of 1937 members of the Brokers Association had processed nearly 480,000 koku of grains in the past twelve months, maintaining their traditional share of the colonial trade.[56] Whatever their subsequent fate in the Pacific War, their colonial survival and indeed prominence was the clearest evidence of a distinct chaegye at the port.

TABLE 5.2 Associations of Inch'ŏn brokers [*kaekchu*]

Organization	Est.	Leadership
Port of Inch'ŏn Merchants Assoc. [Inch'ŏnhang Sinsang Hyŏphoe]	1897	Sŏ Sang-bin
Merchants Firm [Sinsang Hoesa]	1899	Sŏ Sang-bin
(Kaekchu) Merchants Firm [Sinsang Hoesa]	1905	Chŏng Yŏng-hwa
Brokers Union [Inch'ŏn Kaekchu Tanhap]	1911	Hong Chae-bŏm
Inch'ŏn Brokers Association [Inch'ŏn Mulsan Kaekchu Chohap]	1917	Chang Sŏk-u, Hong Chae-bŏm

Sources: Jinsenfu, *Jinsenfushi* [A history of the city of Inch'ŏn] (Keijō: Chikazawa Shōten, 1933), pp. 158-159; Jinsen Shōkō Kaigisho, Jinsenkō [The port of Inch'ŏn] (Jinsen: Jinsen Shōkō Kaigisho, 1931), pp. 64-65.

Newspaper reports of their annual general assemblies at their headquarters in Minato-chō, complete with elections of officers, review of the annual audit and subsequent budget, and awards for highest sales offers a continuing chronicle of an *ilban chaegye*, the ordinary or wider business community.[57] Inch'ŏn's brokers remained the core interest group within the chaegye at the port throughout the colonial years. Pressed for better organization within trades due to expanding exports and competition with Japanese trade associations, brokers maintained their own associations among grain merchants. Following dissolution of the Inch'ŏn Merchants firm in 1905, Sŏ Sang-bin and Chŏng Yŏng-hwa had spun off an affiliated group of brokers and smaller businessmen with the same title.[58] Serving as district chief [*myŏnjang*] for the Korean area of the port, Sŏ Sang-bin provided the Korean magistrate of Inch'ŏn with an official list of trade associations in 1910. The list included the Merchants Firm [Sinsang Hoesa] with president Chŏng Yŏng-hwa, approved by the Korean Government in February of 1908, and two groups headed by Chŏng Ch'i-guk, the Industrial Promotion Firm [Kwŏnŏpsa] and the Inch'ŏn Korean Chamber of Commerce.[59] Legislation of August 1915 mandated reorganization of the Merchants' Firm as a trade association or "mandatory" association with authority for cooperative purchase and consignment sales, permitting a legal writ for consolidating their market niche without the earlier monopoly rights.[60]

A journey from guilds with parapolitical roles, to chambers with more directly political roles marked the transition among brokers in neighboring China. Combined chambers in the Korean port cities and capital would assume a carefully bounded political role of advising the colony on economic policy, but most trade associations would find little place for political participation under colonial rule. As evident above, the decree mandated the close supervision of the Government-General in the affairs of the association. The colonial government officially approved the charter of the organization in 1916 for the purpose of promoting consignment sales with information exchange and surveys. Brokers had gained distinction as a business interest group in local markets, but could only survive in the shadow of a far stronger Japanese zaikai. Legal recognition came with no guarantee of a market role.

One example of professionalism at the Association was their role in grain inspections. The Japanese Grain Association at the port had gained the mandate to standardize commercial practices, promote sales, prevent destructive competition, and eliminate speculation in the grain trade.[61] Since the functions coincide with criteria for a more professional trade, one can only conclude that only professionals would be entrusted with the inspection duties. In November of 1916, Chŏng Yŏng-hwa of the Inch'ŏn Brokers Association signed an agreement with Okuda Teijirō of the Jinsen Grain Association for joint responsibilities in grain inspection.[62] Inspectors were mandated with regular inspection tasks, as well as collection of inspection fees. The Jinshō appointed the head inspector, a Japanese national, but left the remainder of the appointments to be divided equally among Japanese and Koreans. The Inch'ŏn Brokers would appoint one half of the inspectors, and the Grain Association the remainder.[63] The agreement appears at first sight to signify nothing more than a shift from competition between separate national groups, to the limited cooperation necessary for the Japanese traders and Korean brokers in the process of economic incorporation. But the agreement also recognized the Brokers' Association and the legitimacy of its role in the grain trade. When the Government-General recognized the agreement in the decree mandating inspection duties to the Association of 1917, the brokers had won recognition in the trade not solely as individuals, but with their own organization.

The Inch'ŏn Brokers' Association campaigned for the "common profit" of Korean merchants, in tandem with the Jinsen Grain Association under Okuda and later Katō Heitarō, and combined Chamber of Commerce under Yoshida Hidejirō.[64] The Association pursued an ambitious program of consolidation among local trade associations, strong ties with the wider business community through the Jinshō, and institutional cooperation to insure its place in the grain trade. Limiting membership to consignment brokers, President Hong Chae-bŏm presided over seventy members by 1928.[65] They actively promoted consignment sales with surveys, information and other efforts, and rallied to maintain rice prices at Inch'ŏn. Provincial governments had long since assumed the duties of grain inspection at the Inch'ŏn Inspection Station and elsewhere, but the Korean Brokers Association continued to prosper. One road to greater power and expanded expertise in the trade was absorption of smaller, allied organizations. President Hong was able to bring the Inch'ŏn Rice Sales Association led by Chu Myŏng-gi, and the Inch'ŏn Grain Association under the aegis of the Brokers, and even add a grain commerce labor association.[66] Expansion also included a new grain survey office to maintain reliable information on sales and methods.

What defines a more specialized, distinctive "profession" are features such as (1) a contractual, legally defined relationship as an interest group apart from the state, organized into cohesive business interest associations; (2) structured, regular opportunities for interest representation with the state; and (3) a legal framework supporting market-oriented business practices. The Inch'ŏn Brokers Association offers some evidence for all three features as a specialized trade association, although under constraints vis-à-vis both the colonial state and the Japanese zaikai at the ports. Yet there was a clear shift from their status as a monopoly guild in the kingdom to a more professional business association in the colony with legal recognition. Businessmen's associations represent an institutional shift from custom to contract and the reembedding of market in new legal and commercial structures permitting greater self-definition for the chaegye.

Conclusion

The early decades of commerce associations through 1905, and then of indigenous chambers through 1916 brought a conclusion to the transition spurred by the influx of foreign traders to the treaty ports. A fledgling business community of brokers scrambled to organize a small, poorly funded group of businessmen with neither strong state encouragement nor state resources. Korean chambers in Inch'ŏn and Pusan evolved from guilds of brokers and remained largely chambers of brokers and small-scale merchants. Yet the early chambers provided the precedent for at least semi-professional organization of the business community as a whole, and greater distinction from the state without isolation from the interstate system. Korean chambers also permitted an experience of a separate business community laboring in the shadow of wealthier and better supported Japanese organizations, where incorporation of the chaegye led to distinction and subordination. Local brokers responded to Japanese penetration with their own chamber and trade associations, a critical step in the formation of an ethnically distinct chaegye.

The pace and scale of integration under Japanese regional hegemony strongly affected the process of incorporation for both core and periphery. In the span of one brief decade (1894-1904), Japan decisively defeated China and Russia in separate wars, and forged an alliance with Great Britain insuring insulation from Western interference. Japan quickly filled the ensuing power vacuum by occupying the Korean peninsula to establish a forward defensive position against Chinese or

Russian expansion, and a forward base for launching its own subsequent expansion into Manchuria.   But the abrupt collapse of regional competitors permitted a very rapid expansion for the relatively small Japanese nation, annexing the islands of Taiwan to the south already in 1895 and Korea by 1910. The relentless penetration of the Japanese state and zaikai on the Korean peninsula after 1895 helps account in part for the rapid reorganization of the brokers. Brokers and the authorities at court scrambled to survive in competition with well-organized Japanese mercantile interests closely allied with their expanding state.

But if Japanese expansion was extensive, it was not comprehensive. Upon arrival colonizers confronted a well-connected if relatively unprofessional network of brokers at ports and rural markets. Japanese did not come to the peninsula in sufficient numbers or with the necessary competence nor interest in local market dynamics to largely displace networks of local brokers. The failure of early colonial plans for large-scale immigration to the peninsula left most Japanese traders with no alternative but at least limited cooperation with the local brokers.[67] Meanwhile, the opportunities for commerce in the growing grain export trade stimulated organizational efforts to establish more effective cooperation among an ethnically distinct Korean business community. The process of incorporation encouraged Korean activities in associations which in turn bring to light three features of this early business community: ethnic identity, subordination to state authority despite growing distinction from the state, and commitment to cooperative efforts to sustain market share. The three features represent deep historical precedents which would help sustain a community of Korean brokers across the decades of colonial rule.

Identity, subordination, and cooperation shed light on the usually opaque interpenetration of official and non-official sectors in the market economy of the colony. A contrast with the more clearly defined blend of distinction and cooperation among the Japanese zaikai at the port adds further insight to both Korean subordination and constraints on cooperation. A chronicle of controversy at the Jinsen Grain Exchange highlights dissent among a surprisingly recalcitrant business community at the port of Inch'ŏn. But Korean mills, merchants, and chamber indicate that the process of separation and distinction between state and society heralded in the kwanmin theme of trade advocates had begun in Korean capital and port cities prior to annexation in 1910. An ideology, a material base and an organizational structure set the stage for not only survival in the grain trade, but for distinction and reintegration under a colonial regime.

Notes

1. Robert Wuthnow, *Communities of Discourse: Ideology and Social Structure in the Reformation, the Enlightenment, and European Socialism* (Cambridge: Harvard University Press. 1989), p. 17.

2. The Government-General began reporting Korean and Japanese ownership of mills in 1913. Ownership statistics were continued after 1928, but with no distinction between Korean and Japanese ownership. See the *Chōsen Sōtokufu tōkei nempo* [CSTN], pertinent years. A discussion of Korean capital in the colony can be found in various issues of the *Shokugin Chōsa Geppo*, a publication of the Chosen Industrial Bank. See the following: "Chōsen no kōgyō go kōjō [The industries and plants of Korea]," *Shokugin Chōsa Geppo* no. 58 (Dec. 1939): 53-94; "Chōsen tōka naichi shihon go kore ni yoru jigyō [The enterprise of Japanese capital invested in Korea]," *Shokugin Chōsa Geppo* no. 65 (June 1940): pp. 12-43; "Chōsen shikin mondai no shin dankai [A new phase in the problem of Korean capital]," *Shokugin Chōsa Geppo* no. 76 (May 1941): 35-43; "Chōsen ni okeru dochaku shihon no kenkyū [A study of indigenous capital in Korea]," *Shokugin Chōsa Geppo* no. 59 (1943): 1-9.

3. Statistics on total investment of Japanese, Koreans, and joint Japanese/Korean enterprises can be found in CSTN, pertinent years. One finds some change in the percentages of each group in authorized capital for investment across the two decades, which I refer to here. But there is little overall change in statistics on paid-in capital among the groups between 1910 and 1930. Koreans registered a mere 6% of paid-in capital in both periods. Japanese registered 54% of total paid-in investment in 1910, and 62% in 1930, while joint investment fell from 39% in 1910 to 30% in 1930.

4. *Jinsenfushi*, p. 1098.

5. Inch'ŏnsisa P'yŏnch'an Wiwŏnhoe, ed., *Inch'ŏnsisa* [A history of the city of Inch'ŏn] (Inch'ŏn: Kyŏngil Publishing, 1973), p. 370.

6. Jinsenfu, *Jinsenfushi* [A history of the city of Inch'ŏn] (Keijo: Chikazawa Shōten, 1933), p. 463; Yi Pyŏng-ch'ŏn, "Kaehanggi woeguk sangin ŭi ch'imip gwa Han'guk sangin ŭi taeŭng [Penetration of foreign traders and the response of Korean merchants in the treaty port era]," Ph. D. diss., Seoul National University, 1985, p. 85.

7. *Donga Ilbo* June 22, 1922, p. 4.

8. Information on the Inch'ŏn Sinyung Chohap can be found in Chang Che-hŭp, *Chōsenjin shakai daishōten jiten* [A reference for the larger commercial enterprises in Korean society] (Keijō: Seikaisha, 1928), p. 151.

112

9. Pusan Chikhalsisa P'yŏnch'an Wiwŏnhoe, ed., *Pusansisa* [A history of the city of Pusan] (Pusan: Cheil Printing, 1989), p. 823.

10. *Jinsenfushi*, pp. 799-800; Inch'ŏn Sanggong Hoeŭiso, *Inch'ŏn Sanggong Hoeŭiso kusimnyŏnsa* [A ninety year history of the Inch'ŏn Chamber of Commerce and Industry] (Seoul: Samhwa, 1979), p. 122.

11. The Industrial Promotion firm at Yomokdong won approval from the Ministry of Agriculture, Commerce, and Industry in May of 1906. *Inch'ŏnsisa*, p. 370.

12. *Donga Ilbo* January 21, 1922, p. 4. The Kwŏnŏpso was a unit of the Inch'ŏn Kongmul Chunggaein Chohap (Inch'ŏn Grain Brokers League) located in the Kuriki-cho Section of Inch'ŏn.

13. Akiyama Fumiyo, *Kabushiki Kaisha Jinsen Beito Torihikijo enkaku* [A history of the Jinsen Grain Exchange Company] (Inch'ŏn: Tsukijiike Publishing, 1922), p. 35. Chŏng Ch'i-guk is listed as a director, together with major Japanese millers such as Karai Eitarō, Yoshida Hidejirō, and Arai Hatsutarō.

14. The Chosen Trust Company (Chōsen Shintaku Kabushiki Kaisha) was founded in 1921 with a paid-in capital of 500,000 yen, headquarters in Inch'ŏn, and a branch in Seoul. It registered functions of brokerage, consignment sales, and real estate. Yoshida Hidejirō, long-time president of the joint chamber and the Jinsen Grain Association served as president and chair of the board. Uzu Katsu served as managing director, and Karai Eitarō & Chang Sŏk-u appeared on the board. Out of a total of 40,000 shares, Karai Eitarō held the most with 1,400 shares. Other shareholders included Yoshida, Uzu, Asano Taisaburō, and Kosugi Kinhachi. CGKKY '22: 39-40. Brief biographies of both Chŏng Ch'i-guk and Chang Sŏk-u can be found in Jinsen Shōkō Kaigisho, *Jinsen Shōkō Kaigisho gojūnenshi* [A fifty year history of the Jinsen Chamber of Commerce and Industry] (Keijō: Sawada Saichi, 1934), p. 122-123.

15. CGKKY 1922, p. 51.

16. Imai was an officer in the Jinto Brokers Association [Jinsen Torihikijo Nakagai Kumiai]. See *Donga Ilbo* October 29, 1922, p. 4 (116). Other officers included Kobayashi Tōemon, Uzu Katsu, and Nitta Yoshimin. Imai later rose from brokering to the status of a major shareholder in the Chosen Exchange. CGKKY '35: 388-389.

17. *Donga Ilbo* May 11, 1921; June 22, 1922; August 12, 1923; May 8, 1924.

18. *Donga Ilbo* May 17, 1923, August 13, 1926, and July 31, 1937.

19. Nagai Shōhin Shimbunsha, *Chōsen shōgyō sōran* [A comprehensive review of Korean commerce] (Keijo: Masafumisha,1915), p. 58; Sin T'ae-bŏm, *Inch'ŏn hansegi* [One generation in Inch'ŏn] (Inch'ŏn: Hunmi Ch'ulp'ansa, 1983), p. 196; *Jinsen Shōkō Kaigisho gojūnenshi* [A fifty year history of the Jinsen Chamber of Commerce and Industry] (Keijō: Sawada Saichi, 1934), pp. 32-38, and p. 123.

20. Jinsen Shōgyō Kaigisho, *Jinsen shōkō annai* [A guide to commerce and industry in Inch'ŏn] (Jinsen: Jinsen Shōgyō Kaigisho, 1921), pp. 173, 176; Jinsen Shōgyō Kaigisho, *Jinsen Shōgyō Kaigisho tōkei nempyō, 1926-1927* [Statistical annual of the Jinsen Chamber of Commerce, 1926-1927] (Keijo: Chikazawa Shōten, 1928), p. 234; Keijō Shōkō Kaigisho, *Chōsen kaishahyō 1935* [A list of companies in Korea, 1935] (Keijō: Keijō Shōkō Kaigisho, 1935), p. 138.

21. A record of his two stores in Inch'ŏn complete with tax accounts can be found in Jinsen Shōgyō Kaigisho *Jinsen shōkō annai* [A guide to commerce and industry in Inch'ŏn] (Jinsen: Jinsen Shōgyō Kaigisho, 1921), pp. 167, 194. Reports of the Inch'ŏn Commerce Company can be found in *Donga Ilbo* July 28, 1922, March 1, 1923, and March 6, 1923. Chang Sŏk-u served as executive director, and Chu Myŏng-gi on the board of directors.

22. A description of Sim Ŭi-sŏk's enterprise can be found in Chang Che-hŭp, *Chōsenjin shakai daishōten jiten* [A reference for the larger commercial enterprises in Korean society] (Keijō: Seikaisha, 1928), p. 150. See also *Jinsen Shōkō Kaigisho tōkei nempo 1937*, Table 105. For descriptions of the finance venture, see the following: Jinsen Shōkō Kaigisho, *Jinsenkō* [The port of Inch'ŏn] (Jinsen: Jinsen Shōkō Kaigisho, 1931), p. 208; Ko Il, *Inch'ŏn kŭmsŏk* [Inch'ŏn, then and now] (Inch'ŏn: Sŏnmin Ch'ulp'ansa, 1955), pp. 137-138.

23. *Chosŏnin sahoe*, p. 148; Jinsen Shōgyō Kaigisho, *Jinsen Shōgyō Kaigisho tōkei nempyō, 1926-1927* [Statistical annual of the Jinsen Chamber of Commerce, 1926-1927] (Keijo: Chikazawa Shōten, 1928), p. 234; *Jinsenkō*, p. 75. He received a license for brokerage on the Chosen Exchange in November of 1932 as reported in the *Donga Ilbo* November 8, 1932. He also won the sales award for the Inch'ŏn Brokers Association five years later as reported in the same newspaper of July 31, 1937. For records of his grains sales at the Exchange, see Chōsen Torihikijo, *Chōsen Torihikijo nempō* [Annual of the Chosen Exchange] (Keijo: Chōsen Insatsujo, annual) for 1936 and 1937.

24. *Chosŏnin sahoe*, p. 152; *Jinsenkō*, p. 230; Inch'ŏn Sanggong Hoeŭiso, *Inch'ŏn Sanggong Hoeŭiso kusimnyŏnsa* [A ninety year history of the Inch'ŏn Chamber of Commerce and Industry] (Seoul: Samhwa, 1979), p. 233. Yanagi-chō included 2,235 residents in 1937, of whom only twenty-one were not Korean. Jinsen Shōkō Kaigisho, *Jinsen Shōkō Kaigisho tōkei nempyō, 1937* [Statistical annual of the Jinsen Chamber of Commerce and Industry, 1937] (Jinsen: Tsukiji Publishing, 1938), table 81.

25. His election to the board of councilors at the Inch'ŏn Brokers Association was reported in the following issues of the *Donga Ilbo*: May 11, 1921; June 22, 1922; May 17, 1923; May 2, 1924, and September 9, 1926. Kim served as vice-president of the association on June 24, 1925. He also garnered an award for sales as reported on August 13, 1926.

26. CGKKY 1935, p. 328.

27. Brief biographies of Chu Myŏng-gi, Yi Hŭng-sŏn, and Yu Kun-sŏng can be found in Inch'ŏn Sanggong Hoeŭiso, *Inch'ŏn Sanggong Hoeŭiso kusimnyŏnsa* [A ninety year history of the Inch'ŏn Chamber of Commerce and Industry] (Seoul: Samhwa, 1979), pp. 233-235.

28. Jinsen Shōgyō Kaigisho, *Jinsen shōkō annai* [A guide to commerce and industry] (Jinsen: Jinsen Shōgyō Kaigisho, 1921), pp. 167, 173. The records also indicate Chu had procured a telephone for his store, quite common among Japanese enterprises but still rare at Korean operations.

29. Sin, T'ae-bŏm, *Inch'ŏn hansegi* [One generation in Inch'ŏn], (Inch'ŏn: Hunmi Ch'ulp'ansa, 1983), p. 196.

30. Jinsen Shōgyō Kaigisho, *Jinsen ni okeru seisan kōgyō* [Manufacturing industry in Inch'ŏn] (Jinsen: Jinsen Shōgyō Kaigisho, 1928), p. 651.

31. The title of the enterprise was the Chu Myŏng-gi Rice Mill [Gōmei Kaisha Chu Myŏng-gi Seimeisho]. See Keijō Shōkō Kaigisho [Keijō Chamber of Commerce and Industry, or Keishō], *Chōsen kaishahyō 1935* [A list of companies in Korea, 1935] (Keijō: Keijō Shōkō Kaigisho, 1935), p. 138.

32. *Chōsen kaishahyō 1939*, p. 190.

33. *Jinsen ni okeru seisan kōgyō*, p. 651.

34. Jinsen Shōgyō Kaigisho [Jinsen Chamber of Commerce], *Jinsen Shōgyō Kaigisho tōkei nempyō, 1926-1927* [Statistical annual of the Jinsen Chamber of Commerce, 1926-1927] (Keijo: Chikazawa Shōten, 1928), pp. 234-235; *Jinsenfushi*, p. 1098. The data for "unpolished" or "brown" rice [genmai; hyŏnmi]" and "polished" or "white" rice [seimai; chŏngmi]" are listed in koku. One koku is equivalent to 5.12 bushels. V. D. Wickizier and M. K. Bennett, *The Rice Economy of Monsoon Asia* (Stanford: Food Research Institute, Stanford University, 1941), p. 341.

35. Chang, *Chōsenjin shakai daishōten jiten*, p. 148.

36. *Jinsenfushi*, p. 1098; *Jinsen Shōkō Kaigisho tōkei nempyō, 1937*, Table 104.

37. *Chōsenjin shakai daishōten jiten*, p. 148.

38. The Korean millers in Pusan invested in larger mechanized rice milling operations later than their counterparts in Inch'ŏn, although Kim Pyŏng-jo had registered his Such'ang Rice Mill already in 1925. *Pusan sangŭisa*, p. 214.

39. *Jinsen Shōkō Kaigisho tōkei nempyō, 1937*, Tables 72 and 108.

40. Naigai Shōhin Shimbunsha, *Chōsen shōgyō sōran* [A comprehensive review of Korean commerce] (Keijō: Masafumisha, 1915). Despite the Japanese title, the text was printed with *han'gŭl* particles joining Chinese characters. Since the Chinese characters were common to both Japan and Korea, the text was accessible to both Koreans and Japanese, but the use of *han'gŭl* clearly distinguished a Korean audience for this handbook. See also Chang Che-hŭp, *Chōsenjin shakai daishōten jiten* [A reference for the larger commercial enterprises in Korean society] (Keijō: Seikaisha, 1928). Again we find a text with *han'gŭl* particles joining Chinese characters, indicating a Korean

audience.

41. *Chōsen shōgyō sōran*, p. 58.

42. *Chōsen shōgyō sōran*, p. 69.

43. *Chōsen shōgyō sōran*, p. 153.

44. "Entrepreneur" is a translation of the term *silŏpga* [in Japanese, *jitsugyōka*]. The ad for Yu Kun-sŏng's rice mill can be found in *Chōsen shōgyō sōran*, p. 148.

45. Yu remained active in education, heading a committee for a building project at the Inch'ŏn Business Institute [Inch'ŏn Sangŏp Chŏnsu Haggwŏn] as late as 1939. *Maeil Shinpo* March 3, 1939, p. 4.

46. *Chōsen shōgyō sōran*, p. 152.

47. *Pusan sangŭisa* (1982), pp. 109, 13.

48. *Paegnyŏnsa*, pp. 63-66; Jinsen Shōkō Kaigisho, *Jinsen shōkō gojunenshi* [A fifty year history of the Jinsen Chamber of Commerce] (Jinsen: Jinsen Shōkō Kaigisho, 1934), p. 11. See also Ichinosuke Tanaka, *Zen Chōsen shōkō kaigisho hattatsushi* [A history of the growth of chambers of commerce and industry in Korea] (Fuzan: Kawai Ryūkichi, 1935), p. 14.

49. Advertisement of the Inch'ŏn Korean Chamber of Commerce [Inch'ŏn Chosŏnin Sangŏp Hoeŭiso], printed in *Naigai Shōhin Shimbunsha, Chōsen shōgyō sōran* [A comprehensive review of Korean commerce] (Keijō: Masafumisha, 1915), p. 57.

50. *Chōsen shōgyō sōran*, p. 158; *Jinsenfushi*, p. 1169.

51. The early Korean port chambers lacked prominent leadership and resources, even in comparison to their colleagues in the capital of Seoul. The Seoul Korean Chamber enjoyed leadership of aristocrats in finance such as Cho Sŭng-t'aek of the Hanil Bank and Cho Chin-t'ae of the Chŏnil Bank. A roster of leadership in 1911 at the Seoul chamber can be found in Makiyama Kōzō, *Chōsen shinshi meiran* (A register of Korean gentlemen) (Keijō: Nihon Dempo Tsūshinsha Keijō Jikyoku, 1911), pp. 311-312. Cho Chin-t'ae served in high government office prior to annexation, and then moved quickly into a variety of financial and trade investments. The massive Oriental Development Company [Tōyō Takushoku Kabushiki Kaisha] of Japan recognized his status with appointment to the board as auditor [*kansa*]. *Chōsen shinshi meiran*, p. 102. Meanwhile, commoners with a commercial background took the helm at the Inch'ŏn and Pusan chambers.

52. *Chōsen shōgyō sōran*, p. 57. The handbook was printed in Chinese characters connected by *han'gŭl* particles. However, the authors did use Japanese for the title of the book.

53. The Government-General published the Chosen Chamber of Commerce Decree [Chōsen Shōgyō Kaigishorei] on July 15, 1915. The text of the decree can be found in Government General of Chosen, *Annual Report on Reforms and Progress in Chosen (Korea), 1915-1916* (Keijo: Government General of Chosen, 1917), p. 83; *Paegnyŏnsa*, pp. 81-83.

54. *Jinsenfushi*, pp. 158-159; *Jinsenkō*, 1931, pp. 64-65. The Corporation Decree [*kaisharei*] of the Government-General in 1910 banned "firms" without certain capital requirements, prompting reorganization of the Merchants Firm as a "cooperative [*tanhap*]." *Jinsenfushi*, p. 1176. Note the following translations: Inch'ŏn Merchants Association [Inch'ŏnhang Sinsang Hyŏphoe], Merchants Firm [Sinsang Hoesa], Inch'ŏn Brokers' Union [Inch'ŏn Kaekchu Tanhap], and Inch'ŏn Brokers' Association [Inch'ŏn Mulsan Kaekchu Chohap].

55. *Donga Ilbo* November 3, 1937, p. 6.

56. *Jinsen Shōkō Kaigisho tōkei nempyō, 1937*, Table 69.

57. See for instance the *Donga Ilbo* of May 11, 1921, p. 4, and July 31, 1937, p. 8.

58. As president of the Merchants Firm [Sinsang Hoesa], Chŏng Yŏng-hwa won approval of the organization from the Korean Ministry of Agriculture, Commerce and Industry in 1908. He later served as president of the Inch'ŏn Brokers Cooperative [Inch'ŏn Kaekchu Tanhapsa] in 1916. *Jinsenfushi*, p. 1182; *Inch'ŏnsisa*, p. 370.

59. *Inch'ŏnsisa*, p. 370. The Industrial Promotion Firm was an early Inch'ŏn grain brokerage of brokers from Kyŏngsang Province, experienced in trading with the Japanese. *Kusimnyŏnsa*, pp. 101-102.

60. "By these regulations, those engaged in the manufacture and trade of products deemed akin by the Governor-General were required to form a trade association. Those engaged in the manufacture or sale of kindred products of important nature in any one particular district were also required to organize an association [*dōgyō kumiai*] embracing those products in order to promote their mutual interests, and its legal being receiving recognition, it can bring an action to enforce the payment of its fee. Such association is also authorized to engage in cooperative purchase of raw material and consignment sale of their products. For the formation or alteration of an

61. *Jinsenfushi*, pp. 1177-1187.

62. *Jinsenfushi*, pp. 1182-1183.

63. Korean brokers gained limited incorporation at the Jinsen Grain Exchange, where Yun Pyŏng-jun and six other Koreans won seats among the twenty-eight brokers. Jinsen Beitō Torihikijo, *Jinsen Beitō Torihikijo enkaku* [A history of the Jinsen Grain Exchange] (Jinsen: Tsukiji Printing, 1922), p. 36.

64. *Donga Ilbo*, December 1, 1923. The Jinsen Grain Association [Jinsen Kokubutsu Kyōkai] was mainly a Japanese organization of traders and brokers at the port.

65. A description of the Inch'ŏn Brokers Association [Inch'ŏn Mulsan Kaekchu Chohap] can be found in *Jinsenfushi*, pp. 1176-1177, and also in the *Donga Ilbo*, December 1, 1923. The latter newspaper also regularly published news of their annual plenary conventions, elections of officers, and special awards. See for instance, *Donga Ilbo* August 9, 1923; December 6, 1923; May 2, 1924; June 24, 1925; August 13, 1926; and September 9, 1926.

66. The Rice Sales Association [Misang Chohap] under president Chu Myŏng-gi, and the Grain Association [Kongmul Hyŏphoe] under president Yi Chŏng-hwa were listed among trade associations in Inch'ŏn as early as 1907. *Jinsenfushi*, pp. 1080-1081.

67. Karl Moskowitz has documented immigration plans and results in his "The Creation of the Oriental Development Company: Japanese Illusion Meets Korean Reality," pp. 73-109 in James B. Palais, ed., *Occasional Papers on Korea*, no. 1, (Seattle: Joint Committee on Korean Studies of the American Council of Learned Societies and the Social Science Research Council, 1974).

6

Zaikai

The Japanese business community or *zaikai* at Inch'ŏn stood in opposition, at other times in competition, and sometimes in company with the chaegye. Unlike the colonized Korean community, the zaikai offers a more conventional model of a private sector within the prewar political economy of Japan, and a clearer foil of contract to covenant, of officials and citizen or *kwanmin* to *kunsin,* and of engagement rather than isolation from regional markets. Japanese pioneers pressing colonial incorporation included not only soldiers and diplomats, but also traders, brokers, and millers. More significant than their ships, capital or merchandise, these colonists in concert with the state brought new patterns of authority to the market, evident in legislation and procedure, and new patterns of business-state relations, evident in the chartered banks, exchanges, and business associations. Early institutions such as the Daiichi Bank and later the Oriental Development Company, together with the departments of the Residency and Government-Generals mandated the patterns with powers of coercion and attraction, the former through law and the latter through capital and markets. An unfair competition with the zaikai made the patterns feasible and far more palatable to Korean brokers than political coercion. Simply mandating a joint chamber of commerce was one thing. Legislating Korean participation in chamber leadership, access to government planning, dispute resolution in the business community, and consultation opportunities was another.

A crisis confronting both chaegye and zaikai at Inch'ŏn in the 1920s introduces contention among mercantile interests in an emerging civil society. A government proposal to move the Jinsen Grain Exchange to the capitol in a merger with the Seoul Stock Exchange caused a furor. Colonial administrators pressed a policy from the home islands of consolidating futures trading in grains and stock certificates within one inclusive exchange to strengthen oversight of brokers' commissions, tax collection, fulfillment of contracts, and controls on speculation. The government argued for the common good but few in Inch'ŏn agreed. What lay behind the debate over the commonweal was the fact that a merger could benefit major shareholders of the Exchanges, which were privately held, joint-stock firms. A coalition of Korean and Japanese grain millers and merchants quickly mobilized to protest the move and save the centerpiece of their market. A profile of zaikai enterprise and association at the port helps explain both opposition and advocacy for the proposal, while a subsequent chapter on the Exchange introduces the controversy and its significance for the role of the business community in the emerging civil society of the colony.

Just as the Korean brokers in the colony continued precedents from the late Kingdom, so also the Japanese traders and brokers at Inch'ŏn worked within patterns of Japanese business-state ties abroad in place on the peninsula well before 1910. For instance, Japanese traders immigrating to Inch'ŏn through the turn of the century enjoyed extensive support. Transport firms such as the Japan Steamship Mail Company and the Osaka Commercial Steamship Company and banks such as the Daiichi assured safe passage for trader and family, his goods, and his capital.[1] The Daiichi Bank opened its first Korean branch in Pusan in July of 1878. Three decades later, the Bank of Chosen took over the Daiichi's extensive network of branches across the peninsula to serve as the central bank on the peninsula.[2] A pattern of public support for private firms coincided with the norm of close cooperation between state and private capital distinguishing the political economy of Meiji Japan, particularly in efforts abroad.[3] Umbrella associations such as chambers of commerce brought together businessmen across trades to provide a second level of support for the trader coming to Inch'ŏn. Finance and commerce leaders such as Shibusawa Eiichi of the Daiichi in Japan, and Ōkura Kihachirō in Pusan lent their prestige to the prominent Japan-Korea Trade Association in the 1890s.[4] Association chapters in the major commercial cities in Japan and the treaty ports of Korea promoted trade on all levels with Korea. State support of shipping, railroads, banks, and business associations fostered the consolidation of Japanese business circles in the treaty ports and capital.[5]

If firms, associations, and chartered exchanges and banks comprised a critical circle of enterprise for the port chaegye, a far more complex circle embedded Japanese enterprise. Indeed, it was this circle that was superimposed on Korean precedents of guild organization, political controls in the market, and ethnic identity. Lacking comparable state support, a Korean business community was exposed to the structure and ideas of Japanese capitalism initially as middlemen fighting to retain a monopoly in the grain trade, then briefly as competitors with a small Japanese community, and finally as unequal partners within a single chamber at Inch'ŏn, Pusan, and elsewhere. Institutional development at Japanese mills and trade associations stabilized and extended the power of the Japanese traders at the ports. The formation and functions of the institutions, and their ties with colonial state and local brokers help explain the pattern of distinction, subordination, and limited cooperation distinguishing the port chaegye.

Mills and Merchants

The proposed transfer of the Jinsen Grain Exchange to Seoul divided the Inch'ŏn zaikai into contesting factions of leading Japanese mercantile interests listed in Table 6.1. Among pioneers in the grain trade, the founder of the Exchange, Karai Eitarō, and Yoshida Hidejirō, longtime leader in associations and milling proved formidable foes to the aggressive merger effort of Jinsen Exchange president Arai Hatsutarō. With the oldest among the huge milling and brokerage operations in Inch'ŏn, Rikimu Kurosamorimon appeared among the most vocal and adamant opponents to the transfer. Katō Heitarō, dubbed the "King of Polished Rice" with the largest mill in the port and similar operations at Chinnamp'o and Pusan, played a more subdued role of opposition despite his formidable presence, and later emerged among the leading stockholders in the combined Exchange. Meanwhile Grain Exchange brokers such as Nitta Yoshimin, Asano Taisaburō, and Uzu Katsu kept at their trade throughout the controversy, and then prospered with the combined exchange. If firms and association largely defined the chaegye circle of enterprise, the zaikai appear prominent in the direction and even ownership at a further level of chartered government firms as well. As founder and long-tenured president of the Jinsen Grain Exchange, Karai Eitarō had raised the necessary capital and saw the enterprise through its difficult early years.[6] Karai rose to the presidency of the Japanese Chamber of Commerce at Inch'ŏn in 1909, and remained prominent in the chamber thereafter. Born in Fukuoka in 1858, he studied foreign trade at Meiji Gakuin before coming to Inch'ŏn in 1904 to work with

TABLE 6.1 Japanese Enterprise in Inch'ŏn

Name	Enterprise	Association
Yoshida Hidejirō	Yoshida Rice Mill, Chosen Central Rice Oil	Jinsen Chamber Pres.
Arai Hatsutarō	Araigumi	Jinto Pres., Chosen Engineering & Construction, Chosen Mining
Kosugi Kinhachi	Chosen Printing Chosen Stock & Finance	Seoul Exchange Pres.
Katō Heitarō	Katō Rice Mill Chosen Polished Rice	Jinsen Chamber, Jinsen Grain Association
Rikimu Kajirō & son	Rikimu Bussan	Jinsen Chamber
Nitta Yoshimin	Chosen Agency Nitta Commerce Keijo Industrial	Jinto Brokers
Asano Taisaburō	Asano Partnership	Jinto Brokers
Uzu Katsu	Chosen Finance, Chosen Enterprise & Finance	Jinto Brokers

Okuda Teijirō, a prominent early miller at the port.[7] Karai organized, mostly owned, and served as president of Jinsen Mutual Finance Company with a paid-in capital of 35,000 yen,[8] and appeared as the leading shareholder in Chōsen Trust led by Yoshida Hidejirō with a paid-in capital of 500,000 yen already in 1922.[9] Karai was president of the Inch'ŏn Marine Products Company with a capital of 500,000 yen, and of Chōsen Match Company with a paid-in capital of 200,000 yen in 1921.[10] Active also in business interest associations, Karai was a leader in the early years of the Jinsen Polished Rice Association, and the Jinsen Grain Association. Together with these related activities, the Exchange remained a central interest and investment for Karai throughout his business career in the port city.

A native of Kyushu, Yoshida Hidejirō came to Inch'ŏn in 1897 with a trade firm and soon joined the enterprising Okuda Teijirō, as well as establishing his own enterprises in Wŏnsan and Inch'ŏn.[11] He appeared on the board and as a major shareholder in the Chosen Mail Steamship Company in 1922, one of the largest enterprises on the peninsula with a paid-in capital of three million yen,[12] and as Inch'ŏn representative of the Osaka Fire and Marine Insurance Company.[13] He later owned and operated the Yoshida Rice Mill with a capital of 50,000 yen, and the Yoshida Warehouse Company with a capital of 125,000 yen.[14] He was also president, chair of the board, and largest shareholder in what had been Okuda Teijirō's early investment, the Okuda Rice Mill.[15] He was also the chairman of the Asahi Brewery in Inch'ŏn, established in October of 1919, and listing a paid-in capital of 450,000 yen by 1937.[16] Among his later ventures, Yoshida established the Chosen Central Rice Oil Company at Inch'ŏn in 1936 with a paid-in capital of 400,000 yen.[17] Beyond this formidable base of enterprise, what distinguished the opposition of Yoshida was his prominence in associations at Inch'ŏn. He led the joint chamber of commerce as president from 1921 to 1934, and again from 1937 to 1939,[18] and the Jinsen Grain Association as president from July 1921 to January 1928.[19]

Two other leaders in the trade at Inch'ŏn differed in both the scale of their enterprise and their roles in the transfer controversy. Spearheading a more radical opposition to the transfer, Rikimu was prominent in the "Coalition to Halt the Transfer," while Katō Heitarō was content to be listed only on the Action Committee of the more moderate "Federation of Public Officials" in Inch'ŏn opposing the changes. The young Rikimu Kurosamorimon, born in 1901, owned and operated his father's Rikimu Rice Mill in Inch'ŏn. Nearly twenty years his senior, Katō Heitarō owned the Katō Rice Mill Company. The two largest mills in the port city, both operated a daily capacity of 1,600 koku of polished rice per day, with Katō's mill listing a further capacity for 1,600 koku of hulled rice compared to only 500 koku at Rikimu's mill. Both mills boasted of the latest Engle milling machines, with Katō listing 16 machines, and Rikimu 21 machines.[20] Rikimu's father, Rikimu Kajirō had opened a mill in Inch'ŏn already in 1903, and with the help of his son just back with a degree from Keio University, incorporated the milling operation into a general trade company in 1927 titled "Rikimu Bussan." Beyond milling, the operation included real estate brokerage from its turn of the century days, and financing from the 1920s. By 1935, the firm was listed as both an industrial and financial operation with a paid-up capital of 700,000 yen at its headquarters in the Hana-chō section of Inch'ŏn. Operations included hulling and polishing of rice, consignment and general sales of grains, dealership for other trades, consignment and sales of coal, real estate, and financing.[21] Among the largest private warehouse companies at the port, Rikimu Bussan owned a facility with 500 square meters in Hana-chō, a second facility with 653 square meters in Hana-chō, a third in Hon-chō, and a fourth in Kaigan-chō near the Jinsen Grain Exchange.[22]

Born in Yamaguchi-ken in 1882, Katō Heitarō came to Korea already in 1896 following the Sino-Japanese War. He had established rice mills in Chinnamp'o to the north already in 1918, and in Inch'ŏn and Pusan the next year.[23] He operated the Inch'ŏn mill as a branch of the Katō Rice Mill limited partnership based in Chinnamp'o, with a capital of 300,000 yen already in 1922.[24] Katō took over and refounded the joint-stock Chosen Polished Rice Company in December of 1935 with headquarters in Seoul, and branches in Chinnamp'o, Inch'ŏn, Pusan, Kunsan, and Haeju.[25] Operations included rice consignment and sales, milling, transport and warehousing, and finance. The firm registered a paid-in capital of 4.25 million yen in 1939, the largest of the milling companies, with the Katō Rice Mill Partnership and Katō himself holding 60% of the shares. The same principals were also major shareholders in two government-affiliated firms, the combined exchange titled the Chosen Exchange, and the Chosen Rice Storage Company.[26] Apart from his wide range of investments, Katō remained the rice king in Inch'ŏn to the end. The government's Chosen Grain Storage Company operated warehouses across the port in 1937, but Kato's Inch'ŏn Branch of the Chosen Polished Rice Company was far and away the largest private operator.[27]

Aligned against the elder statesmen of the Inch'ŏn zaikai, Arai Hatsutarō assumed the presidency of the Jinsen Grain Exchange in 1927 in the wake of demonstrations and growing civic anger against the proposed transfer. He renewed the effort, successfully concluded the merger, and then headed the combined exchange until its dissolution during the Pacific War.[28] Born in Toyama Prefecture central Japan in 1868, Arai arrived in Korean in 1904 for construction of the Seoul-Pusan Railroad.[29] After further work on a railroad bridge on the Yalu River and projects in Manchuria, he turned his efforts to the grain trade and joined Yoshida Hidejirō, Karai, and Chŏng Ch'i-guk on the board of the Jinsen Grain Exchange in the years following annexation.[30] Arai held 50% of the shares in Araigumi, a joint-stock engineering and construction firm with a paid-in capital of 250,000 yen.[31] He served as an auditor on the board of the Chosen Rice Storage Company, and a director and major shareholder in the huge Chosen Polished Rice Company of Katō Heitarō.[32] Arai also appeared on the boards of two other firms with strong government connections in the grain trade, the Keijo Storage and Finance Company, and the Keijo Exchange Market Company.[33] Active in construction, mining, and grains, Arai was president of the Chosen Engineering and Construction Association, and on the boards of the Chosen Construction Association, and the Chosen Mining Association. There were leisure activities for the colonists of his stature, and Arai served as president of the Chosen Horse Racing Club as well.[34] If Katō Heitarō was the rice king, and Yoshida the leader of the Inch'ŏn zaikai, Arai was the standard bearer at the Exchange generating credibility among investors and government officials.

It was not only the leading millers who found a place in the heady circle of firm, association, and government-affiliated companies, but also a few of the Japanese brokers themselves. Nitta Yoshimin began as a broker at the Jinsen Grain Exchange [Jinto] and an officer in the Jinto Brokers Association, and moved from leadership in Inch'ŏn to head of the brokers of the combined Chosen Exchange from 1932, representing the Brokers Association before officials of the Government-General and owners of the Exchange.[35] With the closing of the Inch'ŏn grain branch of the Chosen Exchange in 1939, he was left to explain the role of brokers in the newly established Chosen Grain Company.[36] Nitta parlayed his brokerage and association contacts into multiple investments with firms surrounding the Chosen Exchange in the Kogane-chō section of Seoul. He chaired the Chosen Exchange Agency Firm from its inception in May of 1937 with a paid-in capital of 500,000 yen and specializing in exchange and representation for short-term negotiable stocks. The Brokers Association of the Exchange appeared as its largest stockholder with 1,500 of the 20,000 shares.[37] Nitta founded his own Kogane-chō firm as well in October of 1936 with a paid-in capital of 250,000 yen, the Nitta Commerce Company which operated a branch office in Inch'ŏn.[38] He was chair of the board and president of the Keijo Industrial Company, a brokerage, real estate, and finance firm established in November of 1938 and a paid-in capital of 90,000 yen. Directors of the company included two Korean brokers from the Chosen Exchange, Cho Chun-ho and Kang Ik-ha.[39] Nitta also appeared as a major investor in two other firms associated with the trade in grains and stocks, the Chosen Stock and Finance Company with a paid-in capital of one million yen, and the Keijo Storage and Finance Company.[40] At the latter firm Nitta joined Arai Hatsutarō, President of the Chosen Exchange, as a member of the board.

Asano Taisaburō likewise blended brokerage with association, and also began at the Jinsen Grain Exchange [Jinto]. A native of Yamaguchi-ken prospering in finance and brokerage at Inch'ŏn for many years, he rose to the presidency of the Jinto Brokers Association in 1922, and later was prominent in early discussions about the transfer of the exchange to Seoul.[41] Asano was able to diversify with the Asano Partnership from April of 1934 as a Seoul real estate operation, but also a holding company for other investments in the grains and stocks.[42] With only five shareholders and a capital of 700,000 yen, this closely held firm in turn invested in three major Kogane-chō brokerage operations. Asano gained a seat on the board of directors at the Chosen Exchange already in 1932, and by 1935, both Asano himself and his Asano Partnership were listed among the major shareholders with a total of some 3,000 shares, the third largest block of shares in the firm.[43] Together with Nitta Yoshimin, the Asano Partnership was also a major stockholder in the Chosen Stock and Finance Company, and the Keijo Storage and Finance Company.[44]

Another broker from the Jinsen Grain Exchange and officer in its Broker Association also gravitated towards finance.[45] Maintaining his brokerage at the Exchange, Uzu Katsu was active in major financial ventures such as the early Chosen Trust, and later Chosen Finance and the Chosen Enterprise and Finance Company. Uzu had served under president Yoshida Hidejirō as managing director of the Chosen Trust Company in 1922. Major shareholders at the time included Karai and Yoshida, but also Uzu, Asano Taisaburō, and a leading broker and future president at the Seoul Exchange, Kosugi Kinhachi.[46] The Chosen Finance Company was founded in the same year in Inch'ŏn, and twenty years later had prospered with a paid-in capital of 500,000 yen. Uzu appears as both president and largest shareholder with 25% of the total shares.[47] By 1942, the Chosen Finance Company was listed among the major shareholders in the Chosen Exchange.[48] A second enterprise, the Chosen Enterprise and Finance Company was also founded in November of 1921, and by 1942 registered a paid-in capital of 500,000 yen. Uzu appears similarly as president and the major shareholder with 25% of the total shares.[49] Despite his investment in Inch'ŏn-based financial circles, Uzu did not appear prominently in the controversy over the transfer of the Jinsen Grain Exchange, and like Katō, appears later among the major owners of the combined Chosen Exchange. Despite his growing wealth, Uzu Katsu retained a grain broker's seat on the Chosen Exchange until its closure in 1939.[50]

Japanese Chamber

Enterprise offers a profile of capital and assets, but association tells us more of ideas among the business community. An infrastructure of peak and trade specific interest associations permitted rapid mobilization of the colonial zaikai at Inch'ŏn where a chamber of commerce was in place almost two decades prior to annexation. A prosperous trade, coupled with the formation of chambers in the home islands contributed to the founding of Japanese chambers of commerce in Inch'on, Pusan, and Seoul by 1893.[51] The Inch'on chamber opened membership to nearly all Japanese apart from factory and restaurant workers, implemented a stringent program of dues to insure adequate revenues, and promoted links with the Japanese Residents Association, the Consulate, and Japanese chambers in other cities.[52] The membership and ideas of the new Inch'on chamber proved effective in promoting Japanese commercial interests at the port, and professed goals of maintaining profits and facilitating commerce for its members left no doubt about its interests.

The chamber for Japanese nationals at Inch'on coalesced around well-defined interests of profit and expanded trade, and carefully cultivated the support of the local residents association and the Consulate. The high priority given the grain trade at the Inch'ŏn chamber was evident in their leadership of a joint campaign with the Wŏnsan and

Pusan chambers against grain embargoes in 1893. A resolution presented to the Korean government through the Japanese Consul enumerated violations of the treaty agreement on commercial relations, complaining that the embargo illegally prohibited the Japanese from purchase of rice, from sales of rice in warehouses, and from export of rice already purchased. They also protested punishment meted out to local barge personnel assisting the Japanese in purchases, and concluded with a demand for indemnities.[53] In the decade between the Sino-Japanese and Russo-Japanese Wars, the chamber campaigned for Japanese commercial rights against the perceived advantages of Chinese and Western traders. A list of formal chamber recommendations to the government from 1905 reflects strenuous efforts to expand state support for transport and financing of grain exports, and for elimination of tariffs.[54] The chambers grew bolder with the arrival of Japanese authority on the peninsula from 1905, quickly launching almost a decade of lobbying efforts to eliminate all tariffs on grain exports. Annual recommendations and persistent lobbying efforts contributed to the removal of duties by 1913.[55]

Japanese chambers on the peninsula showed little resemblance to their short-lived Korean counterparts. Differences began with the membership. Brokers dominated the Korean chambers outside of Seoul, but membership at the Japanese chambers was far more diverse. Japanese chambers assembled a variety of mercantile interests, including people in shipping, warehousing, finance, and trade. Differences continued in chamber efforts to coordinate a national business lobby across the peninsula. The Korean chambers found little success in coordinating nation-wide efforts, but among the Japanese, a Joint Chamber Assembly of 1911 in the Namdaemun area of Seoul brought together Japanese chambers from across the peninsula to demand elimination of duties on rice exports.[56] One finds further differences in the international network of the two ethnic chambers. The Korean chambers could not look to support beyond the peninsula, but Japanese chambers fostered ties with major firms and business leaders in the colony and home islands through chamber to chamber contacts, as well as through the Japan-Korea Trade Association. The variety of expertise and experience, as well as ties to more established chambers in the home islands, enabled the chamber to foster a more professional circle of mercantile interests in Inch'ŏn.

The chamber linked metropole and colony in the interstate market system as a front-line support group for the advance of larger and mid-sized investors. Combined chambers from 1916 would serve as a forum for class alliances between zaikai and chaegye, between alien and local mercantile interests in the port city. One significant pattern at the Japanese Chamber at Inch'ŏn was the emphasis on law and contract whether in formal recommendations to the government, or in lobbying their interests within treaty limits to insure an advantage in interpretation and implementation of the agreements.[57] Nor can we ignore their circumscribed but nonetheless significant political role. The growing leverage of the Japanese chambers in economic policy on the peninsula regarding tariffs, railroads, and harbor improvement, and expanding commercial interests of the chamber members reflected changes in authority and exchange on the peninsula prior to annexation. Chambers served a semi-official role of supervision and organization of the private sector, insuring close supervision of the expatriate business community by the Consulates in the last years of the kingdom, and by the colonial bureaucracy in the colony. Chambers also afforded multiple opportunities for coordinating investment strategies between home islands and peninsula prior to annexation.

Legislation decreeing a joint chamber of Korean and Japanese business circles closed the chapter on the Korean chamber, and opened a chapter of distinction and cooperation. The decree of 1915 stipulated Japanese appointments to the presidency, vice-presidency, and most of the positions on the governing councils of the combined chambers at the ports. The new joint chamber, or Jinsen Chamber of Commerce or "Jinshō [Jinsen Shōgyō Kaigisho]" prospered under colonial rule, as apparent in annual budgets growing from 9,000 yen in 1919 to 22,700 yen by 1933.[58] Koreans were permitted one vice-presidency, one seat on the five member executive council, and six seats on the 24 member Chamber Council by 1934.[59] Former Pusan broker and Korean Chamber president Chŏng Ch'i-guk served as the first Korean vice-president of the combined chamber from 1916 to 1921. Grain broker Sim Nŭng-dok served as the vice-president from 1923 until his death in 1927,[60] followed by Chu Myŏng-gi until 1932, and then by yet another broker, Kim Yong-gyu.[61] Membership in the mandatory chamber was based on amount of taxes and by 1935, 332 Koreans and 361 Japanese were counted among voting members.[62] But the Japanese reserved the presidency of the chamber for themselves with grain trade magnates such as Okuda Teijiro (1916-1919) and Yoshida Hidejirō (1921-1931) at the helm of the chamber.

The joint chamber professed a familiar mix of private and public goals. Grain interests certainly found a place at the Chamber as evident in their recommendations to various ministries of the Government General through 1930.[63] Complaints about grain inspection procedures were directed to the Ministry of Agriculture, Commerce, and Industry in 1917, and to the local province administration in 1925. The Chamber petitioned for removal of duties on imports of foreign rice in 1927, and protested inequities at the Jinsen Rice Exchange or "Jinto" in a letter to the Government-General in 1930. As we shall see below, a furious effort by the Chamber to stop the proposed move of the Jinto to Seoul ultimately saved the exchange for Inch'ŏn. There is also support for extension of the new interstate market system evident in recommendations [kengi] for transportation and links with markets in the empire as the Chamber frequently pressed for improved harbor facilities, reduced freight charges on the railroad, and extension of railroad facilities.[64]

Cooperation between Japanese and Korean mercantile interests at the combined chamber highlights the fact that even medium-scale and small-scale enterprise among Koreans in the grain trade entailed close interaction with Japanese traders and colonial finance and transport networks. The organization of the chamber also provides evidence of growing professionalism among Korean business circles at the port. The combined chamber permitted a contractual, legally defined relationship between business community and the state, sufficient funding for effective lobbying, and a common commitment to competitive practices within organized grain markets monitored by Chamber and other trade associations. Chamber recommendations gave clear evidence of a distinctive business interest and expertise, apart from the colonial state, and well-positioned within the new interstate system of the Empire.

Grain Association

Japanese grain traders and brokers worked to gain direction of the grain trade through both enterprise and association. State recognition of their associations gave credibility and assured access to both the embassy and later the Government-General. Dominant in enterprise and association, they could then accommodate Korean brokers in the trade to gain their cooperation in expanding the market. A party at Karai Eitarō's villa sponsored by the Brokers Association of the Jinsen Grain Exchange in the spring of 1921 included the major Japanese grain merchant associations, and a contingent from the Inch'ŏn Brokers

Association.[65] The latter association met in plenary session the next year at their new headquarters in Minato-chō, shared with the Jinsen Grain Association, and also Chu Myŏng-gi's Rice Sales Association.[66] In a newspaper interview of 1923 at the new building, President Katō Heitarō explained the purpose of his Jinsen Grain Association: eliminate destructive competition and dishonest practices, and expand the volume of exports. But he added further plans such as promoting ties with the market in Osaka and "appropriate competition" with Korean grain dealers.[67]

Ties with Korean brokers had not always been so cordial. Historians of the Grain Association traced its founding to competition with the Inch'ŏn brokers who had already organized at the turn of the century to retain authority over inspections and measurement of grains for export. Seeing Hong Chae-bŏm's Merchant's Firm as a Korean initiative to monopolize tasks of standardization and measurement, Japanese traders responded with their own organization.[68] Okuda Teijirō, Karai Eitarō and thirty-eight other traders petitioned the Japanese Consul at Inch'on for recognition of the Jinsen Grain Association in August of 1903, citing goals of profits and market expansion which left no doubt about a business "interest."[69] Duties would include efforts to standardize trade practices, correct the destructive effects of market competition within the trade, increase the volume of exports, advertise the profitability of the trade, mediate disputes, and inspection, warehousing, and market development tasks at Inch'ŏn. It was an effort to establish an institution with a clearly defined mandate and regularize market practices. Okuda signed the petition as representative of the Grain Association. The president of the Japanese Residents Association of Inch'ŏn added his signature as a sign of support and solidarity, before submission to the Japanese Consulate in Inch'ŏn. Consul Katō approved each of the functions in turn, and added that standardization of measures would be based on the Fukuyama grain market in Tokyo. He welcomed their commitment to correct the excesses of free competition, since it coincided with Diet legislation of 1900 regarding trade associations.[70] Together with establishment of the Jinsen Grain Exchange earlier in 1899, the Grain Association assured leadership of the central institutions of the grain trade in state authorized organizations.

Association tasks included inventories of grain stocks and warehouse usage, but occasionally the group served as a sounding board for the interests of brokers.[71] Inch'ŏn brokers feared the attraction of the Seoul market and possible shift of the Inch'ŏn exchange to the capitol. The

Association published a unanimous resolution against the proposal before the Government-General to permit Inch'ŏn brokerage houses to establish branch offices in Seoul.[72] But the Grain Association remained a semi-official organization, busy with inventories and reports, rather than a more focused interest association of specific brokers. Annual budgets at the Jinsen Grain Association doubled in the three decades between 1903 and 1932, growing from 66,000 yen in 1903 to 128,000 yen in 1932. Members processed about 25% of the total rice exports through Inch'on in 1928, 13% in 1930, and 20% in 1932.[73] The Grain Association also operated one of the largest warehouses at the port with one thousand square meters of space, in Kaigan-chō near the Grain Exchange.[74] A developing relationship between state and trade association, initially between Consul and the early Grain Association, later between Government-General and a mature Grain Association, provides further evidence of a new type of business/state relation, distinguished by semi-official tasks now formalized in well-defined legislation, and undertaken within institutions under close public scrutiny.

Like the chambers, the trade association exemplified the bridging of public and private interests, and again, professionalism contributed to recognition of the private sector, and to the credibility necessary for state recognition. The associations also pioneered strategies of accommodation between zaikai and chaegye. Larger Korean rice millers such as Chu Myŏng-gi or Yi Hŭng-son later won membership in the Grain Association itself.[75] Koreans maintained their own Inch'ŏn Brokers Association, and found a place as well in the Japanese Jinsen Grain Association. Distinction did not lead to isolation. Resumes of enterprise, prominence in local civic organizations, and citizenship in the joint Chamber gained recognition.

Conclusion

Japanese business and state on the peninsula allowed a limited role for the local brokers for at least two reasons: the need for local expertise, and the lack of sufficient numbers of Japanese brokers to replace them. Alliances between capital of core and periphery give continuity to the process of incorporation. An emerging class of mercantile interests among the Inch'ŏn brokers came to depend on Japanese traders and trade networks, and the reliance extended beyond market transactions. Professional organization of the Japanese in chambers and trade associations forced similar reorganization among the Korean brokers, but the history of Korea's incorporation offers some anomalies. We do not find the pattern of core state penetration and then assimilation familiar in French Indochina, nor the model of accommodation and limited local autonomy prominent in British colonies such as India or dependencies on the Malay peninsula.[76] One might also suggest a third model of exclusion by a neighboring power in which a colonizing immigrant group simply assumes all direction in the economy and polity, but even the alliance of Meiji and colonial states with the associations and enterprise of Japanese mercantile interests did not drive local brokers out of the grain trade in Korea.

Our review suggests rather separate, ethnically distinct Korean business associations in kingdom and colony, that is, subordination without absorption. A long Korean experience of commerce prior to the Kanghwa Treaty, and of ethnically separate trade associations in the decades prior to annexation, together with Japanese accommodation encouraged by the pace and scale of penetration helps account for the pattern of ethnic distinction in milling without isolation. Japanese transport and finance networks, and the Chamber itself all played a role in the subordination and integration of the brokers with Okuda's grain association. The multi-leveled network of support for the grain trader made possible the professional organization of a Japanese business community in the port. Banks, an exchange, shipping and railroads align with a familiar pattern of colonial expansion found in dependencies of Western powers. A further network of business interest associations, in tandem with the larger firms of the private sector can also be found in other cases of core expansion to peripheral areas, although seldom with the same degree of cohesion and coordination between state and enterprise.

How did coordination among combined chamber and Jinsen Grain Association affect the local brokers and their own Inch'ŏn Brokers Association? Korean brokers at the end of the nineteenth century did not enjoy the advantage of projecting their commerce abroad. Working rather within Korea's borders, they came to know the interstate system through contact with foreign traders. The Japanese and combined chambers, together with the Jinto and Grain Association quickly cast, and then tightened a net linking Inch'ŏn's grain market with Tokyo, Osaka, and Nagasaki. Soon after Japanese businessmen at Inch'ŏn had penetrated the local markets under the banner of free trade, the Japanese began to speak less of "open markets" and more of "organized markets."

Founders of grain trade associations openly professed the new ideal of avoiding destructive competition among merchants within similar trades. A market ideology of controlled competition within the guidelines of business associations and government ministries left a place for the Korean brokers in the grain trade. Brokers confronted not the open competition of international commerce, but rather competitive but structured markets with close linkages to grain markets in Tokyo and Osaka evident in the grading of rice, quality controls, and transportation routes. Such was the character of the interstate system in the grain markets at Inch'ŏn.

Ishida Takeshi[77] wrote of a "governmentalization" of interest groups in prewar Japan where "the specific purposes of interest groups become fused with government purposes." Although the author highlighted cooperation of the business sector in the years leading up to World War II, his work documents the broader issue of porous borders between state and society in Japan cited at the beginning of this study. Contract was embedded in social and cultural covenants, although far different than the Confucian covenants of trade critics in Korea, and distinction between officials and citizens often gave way to interpenetration and collaboration, but certainly not to precedents of monarch and minister familiar in the Chosŏn Dynasty. This is the irony of Korean incorporation into a Japanese intermarket and interstate regional order of international trade, where markets gained only a limited autonomy in the reembedding within a Japanese system oriented to the state. Patterns of distinction for the chaegye, and then reintegration under a new set of market controls were shaped not only by Korean precedent and capitalist premises of private property and profit, but also by the terms of the alliance of colonial state and zaikai promoting the grain trade, evident in the coincidence of Chamber and Grain Association priorities with state goals.

Notes

1. The Japan Mail Steamship Company [Nippon Yūsen Kabushiki Kaisha] inaugurated regular service to Inch'ŏn in 1891, followed by the Osaka Commercial Steamship Company [Osaka Shōsen Kabushiki Kaisha] in 1895. Jinsen Nijūgonen Kinenkai, ed., *Jinsen kaikō nijūgo nenshi* [A twenty-five year history since the opening of the port of Inch'ŏn] (Osaka: Shiobarakin, 1922), p. 32. This volume will be cited as *Jinsen kaikō*.

2. The Daiichi performed a wide variety of functions for the Japanese and Korean governments between 1878 and 1910: (1) collection of Japanese import duties; (2) purchase of gold and silver in Korea for the Japanese government; (3) bank drafts on the peninsula; (4) management of Japanese government loans to the Korean government. But three further tasks bridged the roles of central bank for this Japanese institution on the peninsula: (5) currency management; (6) a treasury for the Korean government funds; (7) and finally, functions of a central bank on the peninsula during the Protectorate. See Daiichi Ginkō, *Daiichi Ginkō gojūnen shōshi* [A brief history of fifty years of the Daiichi Bank] (Tokyo: Tokyo Insatsu, 1926), p. 73; So Kwang-un, *Han'guk kŭmyung paegnyŏn* [A century of finance in Korea] (Seoul: Ch'angyosa, 1972), pp. 61-69. One task of the Daiichi suggests the extent of Japanese economic strength at the treaty ports: depository for receipts of the Korean Customs office. Martina Deuchler, "The Opening of Korean Ports," *Korea Journal* vol. 9, no. 1 (January 1969): 11-20.

3. William W. Lockwood, "The State and Economic Enterprise in Modern Japan, 1868-1939," in Simon Kuznets, Wilbert E. Moore, and Joseph J. Spengler, eds., *Economic Growth: Brazil, India, Japan* (Durham: Duke University Press, 1955), pp. 537-602; Arthur E. Tiedemann, "Big Business and Politics in Prewar Japan," in James William Morley, ed., *Dilemmas of Growth in Prewar Japan* (Princeton: Princeton University Press, 1971), pp. 267 - 316; William Fletcher, *The Japanese Business Community and National Trade Policy, 1920-1942* (Chapel Hill: The University of North Carolina Press, 1989).

4. Johannes Hirschmeier, "Shibusawa Eiichi: Industrial Pioneer," in William W. Lockwood, ed., *The State and Economic Enterprise in Japan* (Princeton: Princeton University Press, 1965), pp. 209-247.

5. Japanese investors purchased the rights to build the Seoul-Inch'on Railway from the original American investors, and completed the line by July of 1900. Japanese investors with government help soon undertook the more ambitious task of constructing a Seoul-Pusan railway, completed by November of 1904. Chōsen Sōtokufu Tetsudō Kyoku, *Chōsen tetsudōshi* (A history of railroads in Korea) (Keijō: Chōsen Sōtokufu, 1923), pp.49-58; Janet Hunter, "Japanese Government Policy, Business Opinion, and the Seoul-Pusan Railway, 1894-1906," *Modern Asian Studies* 11 (1977): 573-579.

6. The Jinsen Rice and Soybean Exchange [Kabushiki Kaisha Jinsen Beitō Torihikijo] was established on March 10, 1896. *Inch'ŏnsisa*, pp. 457-462; Jinsen Beitō Torihikijo, *Jinsen beitō*

7. Biographies of Karai can be found in two publications of the Jinsen Shōkō Kaigisho: *Jinsenkō*, pp. 50-51, and in *gojunenshi*, p.120; see also Tanaka Ichinosuke, ed., *Zen Chōsen shōkō kaigisho hattatsushi* [A history of the growth of chambers of commerce and industry in Korea] (Fuzan: Kawai Ryūkichi, 1935), pp. 35-36.

8. CGKKY 1922: 51.

136

9. CGKKY 1922: 39-40.

10. TGKY 1921: 20.

11. See the following biographies: Tanaka Ichinosuke, *Zen Chōsen shōkō kaigisho hattatsushi* [A history of the growth of chambers of commerce and industry in Korea] (Fuzan: Kawai Ryūkichi, 1935), p. 36; Kamesaka Tsunesaburo, ed., *Who's Who in Japan 1939-40* (Tokyo: The Who's Who in Japan Publishing Office, 1939), p. 1101; and Abe Kaoru, *Chōsen kōrōsha meikan* [A register of eminent people in Korea] (Keijō: Minshū Jironsha, 1935), p. 477.

12. CGKKY 1922: 91-92.

13. His role with the Osaka Fire and Marine Insurance Company [Osaka Fasai Kaijō Kabushiki Kaisha] is noted in Jinsen Shōgyō Kaigisho, *Jinsen shōkō annai* [A guide to commerce and industry in Inch'ŏn] (Jinsen: Jinsen Shōgyō Kaigisho, 1921), p. 175.

14. The Yoshida Rice Mill [Yoshida Seimeisho] in Inch'ŏn was registered in TGKY 1921: 31. The Yoshida Warehouse Company [Yoshida Sōkō Kabushiki Kaisha] with headquarters in Wŏnsan was listed in CGKKY 1922, p. 100.

15. The Okuda Rice Mill [Okuda Seimaisho] in Inch'ŏn registered a paid-in capital of 75,000 yen in 1922, and included Okuda among the major shareholders. CGKKY 1922: 193

16. *Jinsen Shōkō Kaigisho tōkei nempyō, 1937*, Tables 98, 106.

17. *Jinsen Shōkō Kaigisho tōkei nempyō, 1937*, Table 97; Keijō Shōkō Kaigijo, *Chōsen kaishahyō 1939* [A list of firms in Korea, 1939] (Keijō: Keijō Shōkō Kaigijo, 1939), p. 258; DKB 1942, p. 58. The Chosen Central Rice Oil Company [Chōsen Chūyū Beiyū Kabushiki Kaisha] in 1942 was listed Yoshida with among the large shareholders but no longer as president.

18. In a remarkable tribute to his leadership in the Inch'ŏn zaikai, the chamber unanimously returned the now senior Yoshida to the presidency of the chamber in 1936. *Donga Ilbo*, June 10, 1936. p. 8.

19. Jinsenfu, *Jinsenfushi* [A history of the city of Inch'ŏn] (Keijō: Chikazawa Shōten, 1933), p. 1184.

20. Inch'ŏn Sanggong Hoeŭiso, *Inch'ŏn Sanggong Hoeŭiso kusimnyŏnsa* [A ninety year history of the Inch'ŏn Chamber of Commerce and Industry] (Seoul: Samhwa, 1979), p. 233.

21. TGKKY 1935, p. 187; Keijō Shōkō Kaigijo, *Chōsen kaishahyō 1939* [List of firms in Korea, 1939] (Keijo: Gyōsei Gakkai Insatsujo, 1939), p. 181; DKB 1942, p. 70. A note on his finance operation in Inch'ŏn can be found in *Kusimnyŏnsa*, p. 263. Rikimu Bussan is listed among the eight leading financial institutions in Inch'ŏn in 1937. *Jinsen Shōkō Kaigisho tōkei nempyō, 1937*, Table 95.

22. *Jinsen Shōkō Kaigisho tōkei nempyō, 1937*, Table 72.

23. A biography can be found in *Chōsen kōrōsha meikan*, p. 645.

24. The title of the firm was Katō Rice Mill Limited Partnership [Gōmei Kaisha Katō Seimei] in CGKKY 1922, p. 193; CGKKY 1932, p. 184.

25. The firm had earlier been listed under the management of Tennichi Tōjirō, who at the time was president of the Keijo Stock and Produce Market Company [Kabushiki Kaisha Keijō Kabushiki Genbutsu Torihiki Sijō], i.e., the Stock Exchange in Seoul. The Chosen Polished Rice Company had been originally established in 1918 with a capital of 300,000 yen and based in Seoul with branches in Kunsan and Inch'ŏn. Operations included mining and sales of coal, as well as milling, consignment, and sales of rice. Tennichi owned 3,580 of a total of 10,000 shares. CGKKY 1922, pp. 192-193; CGKKY 1928, p. 176.

26. DKB 1942, p. 5. The Chosen Rice Storage Company [Chōsen Beikoku Sōko Kabushiki Kaisha] was listed in 1942 with a paid-in capital of 3 million yen. DKB 1942:, p. 18.

27. *Jinsen Shōkō Kaigisho tōkei nempyō, 1937*, Table 72.

28. TGKY 1942, p. 47.

29. Biographies can be found in Kamesaka, *Who's Who in Japan*, p. 40, and in Abe, *Chōsen Kōrōsha meikan*, p. 73.

30. *Enkaku*, p. 35.

31. Araigumi [Araigumi Kabushiki Kaisha] was established in November of 1931 with an authorized capital of one million yen, and headquarters in Seoul. CGKKY 1935, p. 387. The president of the firm, Arai Kengo, held a further 40% of the shares.

32. A list of directors of the Chosen Rice Storage Company can be found in TGKY 1942, pp. 48-49. Data on the Chosen Polished Rice Company is available in the same volume, p. 42.

33. Data on the Keijo Storage and Finance Company [Keijō Sōko Kinyū Kabushiki Kaisha] led by Ogasa H. can be found in TGKY 1942, p. 13, and DKB 1942, p. 18, and DKB 1943, p. 20. The Keijo Exchange Market Company [Keijō Torihiku Shijō Kabushiki Kaisha] is listed in CGKKY 1928, p. 262.

34. Arai's positions in the Chosen Engineering and Construction Association [Chōsen Dobuku Kenchiku Kyōkai], the Chosen Construction Association [Chōsen Kenchikukai], and the Chosen Mining Association [Chōsen kōgyōkai] are listed in *Who's Who in Japan*, p. 40, and the *Chōsen kōrōsha meikan*, p. 73. See also his role in the Chosen Animal Husbandry Association [Chōsen Chikusankai] and the Chosen Horse Racing Club [Chōsen Keiba Kurabu].

35. *Donga Ilbo* October 29, 1922, p. 4; May 31, 1934, p. 4.

36. *Donga Ilbo* March 12, 1939, p. 6.

37. TGKY 1942, p. 51; DKB 1943, p. 12.

38. Data on the Nitta Commerce Company [Nitta Shōji Kabushiki Kaisha] can be found in TGKY 1942, p. 58.

39. An entry for the Keijo Industrial Company [Keijō Sangyō Kabushiki Kaisha] can be bound in TGKY 1942, p. 13. Cho Chun-ho and Kang Ik-ha were listed among the grain brokers at the Chosen Exchange from 1936 to 1939. Chōsen Torihikijo, *Chōsen Torihikijo nempō* [Annual of the Chosen Exchange] (Keijo: Chōsen Insatsujo, pertinent years).   Nitta Yoshimin distinguished himself in those same years with a leading share of sales in both stocks and grains at the Exchange.

40.   The Chosen Stock and Finance Company [Chōsen Shoken Kinyū Kabushiki Kaisha] was chaired by Kosugi Kinhachi. TGKY 1942, p. 41. The Chosen Exchange held 13,690 shares out of a total of 20,000, and the Chosen Exchange Agency Firm held 1,150.   Executive Director Ogasa H. headed the venerable Keijo Storage and Finance Company [Keijō Sōko Kinyū Kabushiki Kaisha], originally founded in 1921.   DKB 1942, p. 18; 1943, p. 20.

41. *Donga Ilbo* April 21, 1925, p. 4, and October 19, 1926, p. 6. Reports of his election can be found in the *Donga Ilbo* of February 17, p. 4, and February 24, 1922, p. 4.   His biography is printed in *Chōsen kōrōsha meikan*, p. 143.

42.   The Asano Partnership [Asano Gōmei Kaisha] was listed as an unlimited partnership, led in 1942 by Asano Tarō. TGKY 1942, p. 3.

43.   CGKKY 1932, pp. 363-364; CGKKY 1935, pp. 388-389.

44.   TGKY 1942, p. 41; DKB 1942, p. 18.

45.   His election as officer of the Jinto Brokers Association is reported in *Donga Ilbo*, October 29, 1922, p. 4.

46.   Data on the Chosen Trust Company [Chōsen Shintaku Kabushiki Kaisha] can be found in CGKKY 1922, pp. 39-40.

47.   The Chosen Finance Company [Chōsen Kinyū Kabushiki Kaisha] functioned as a real estate and holding firm.   TGKY 1942, p. 37.

48. TGKY 1942, p. 47.

49.   The Chosen Enterprise and Finance Company [Chōsen Kigyō Kinyū Kabushiki Kaisha] is listed in DKB 1942, p. 86.

50. *Chōsen Torihikijo nempō*, 1936-1940.

51.   Details on the founding of the Jinsen Japanese Chamber of Commerce [Jinsen Nihonjin Shōgyō Kaigisho] can be found in *Gojūnenshi*, p. 7-11; *Jinsenfushi*, pp. 1168-1172; and in *Hattatsushi*, pp. 15-17.   Despite a larger membership, the Japanese chamber at Inch'on reported a budget of only 6,500 yen in 1915, while the chamber at Pusan reported a budget of 7,800 yen. *Pusan sangŭisa*, p. 112.

52.   They also changed the title from the "Japanese Chamber of Commerce at Jinsen," to the "Jinsen Chamber of Commerce" in October of 1911.

53. *Gojūnenshi*, p. 9.

54.   A list of recommendations [*kengi*] can be found in *Gojūnenshi*, pp. 47-50, and in *Jinsen kaikō*, pp. 8-12.

55. The government levied a five percent ad valorem duty on the import of grains and corn in 1912. There was no duty on exports of rice from 1913, but a 5% ad valorem duty levied on exports of soybeans and wheat. Government-General of Chosen, *Laws and Regulations relating to the Customs of Chosen and Japan Proper* (Tokyo: Tōa Insatsu, 1912), p. 50.

56. Keijō Nihonjin Shōgyō Kaigisho, *Shōgyō Kaigisho nempō 1911* [Annual of the Chamber of Commerce, 1911] (Keijō: Keijō Nihonjin Shōgyō Kaigisho), pp. 108-121.

57. Edward Chen offers a wider perspective on law and empire in his article, "The Attempt to Integrate the Empire: Legal Perspectives," in Ramon H. Myers and Mark R. Peattie, eds., *The Japanese Colonial Empire, 1895-1945* (Princeton: Princeton University Press, 1984).

58. *Jinsen shōkō annai*, p. 149; *Jinsen shōkō gojūnenshi*, p. 21.

59. *Jinsen Shōkō Kaigisho gojūnenshi*, p. 16. I translate *jōgiin* as "executive council," and *giin* as Chamber Council.

60. Chang Che-hŭp, *Chōsenjin shakai daishōten jiten* [A reference for the larger commercial enterprises in Korean society] (Keijō: Seikaisha, 1928), p. 150. Sim was active earlier in the Merchants' Firm at Inch'on. See Yi Pyŏng-ch'ŏn, "Kaehanggi woeguk sang'in ŭi naeji sanggwŏn ch'imip [Penetration of interior commercial rights by foreign merchants in the treaty port era]," *Kyŏngje Sahak* no. 9 (December 1985). A brief biography of Sim and his descendants can be found in Il Ko, *Inch'ŏn kŭmsok* [Inch'on, then and now] (Inch'ŏn: Sŏnmin Ch'ulp'ansa, 1955), pp. 137-138.

61. A brief biography of Kim Yong-gyu can be found in *Jinsen Shōkō Kaigishō gojūnenshi*, p. 22.

62. *Donga Ilbo* August 9, 1935, p. 5.

63. Recommendations [*kengi*; *konŭi*] are summarized in Tanaka, *Zen Chōsen shōkō kaigisho hattatsushi*, pp. 24-27.

64. A review of recommendations at the Fushō [Fuzan Shōgyō Kaigisho] or combined chamber in Pusan indicates a greater variety of interests beyond grains.

65. *Donga Ilbo* May 26, 1921, p. 4. Sponsored by the Jinto Brokers Association [Jinto Torikhikijo Nakagainin Kumiai], the party included the Inch'ŏn Brokers Association [Inch'ŏn Mulsan Kaekchu Chohap], the Jinsen Rice Merchants Association [Jinsen Beishō Kumiai], and the Jinsen Grain Merchants Association [Jinsen Kokumotsu Shōbai Kumai].

66. *Donga Ilbo*, June 22, 1922, p. 4.

67. *Donga Ilbo*, December 1, 1923, p. 3.

68. *Inch'ŏnsisa*, p. 463. We cited above the following succession of brokers' organizations at Inch'ŏn: Inch'ŏn Merchants Association [Inch'ŏnhang Sinsang Hyŏphoe], Merchants Firm [Sinsang Hoesa], Inch'ŏn Brokers Union [Inch'ŏn Kaekchu Tanhap], and Inch'ŏn Brokers Association [Inch'ŏn Mulsan Kaekchu Chohap].

140

69. A history of the Jinsen Grain Association [Jinsen Kokubutsu Kyōkai] can be found in *Jinsenfushi*, p. 1178.

70. I translate *dōgyō kumiai* as "trade associations."

71. Examples of Association surveys of inventories can be found in *Donga Ilbo*, May 17, 1923, August 9, 1923, and August 30, 1923.

72. *Donga Ilbo* November 22, 1922, p. 4. Kawai Tada of the combined Chamber [Jinto Shōgyō Kaigisho] and Tsujikawa Tōmicho of the Jinto Brokers Association [Jinsen Torihikijo Nakagainin Kumiai] presented speeches against the proposal for branches.

73. *Jinsenfushi*, p. 1187. The ratios are based on total exports of 1.484 million koku in 1928, 1.224 million koku in 1930, and 1.527 million koku in 1932. *Kusimnyŏnsa*, p. 232.

74. *Jinsen Shōkō Kaigisho tōkei nempyō, 1937*, Table 72.

75. *Jinsenkō*, advertisement for the Jinsen Grain Association.

76. Stephen A. Roberts, *The History of French Colonial Policy, 1870-1925* (London: Frank Cass and Co., 1929), pp. 634-679; D. K. Fieldhouse, *Colonialism, 1870-1945: An Introduction* (New York: St. Martin's Press, 1981), pp. 29-39.

77. "The Development of Interest Groups and the Pattern of Political Modernization in Japan," in Robert E. Ward, ed., *Political Development in Modern Japan* (Princeton: Princeton University Press, 1968), p. 297.

7

Exchange

The Kanghwa Treaty opened a new era of managed markets on the peninsula. A shift in exchange towards banking and finance, contract and procedure, and regional markets with grain exchanges spurred the transformation from constrained to more autonomous markets. Apart from market functions deeply affecting the price and supply of grains, the Grain Exchange at Inch'ŏn served as a nexus of business-state relations critical for both state agrarian policy and successful private enterprise at the port. In addition to regularizing and expanding trade volummes, the Jinsen Grain Exchange or "Jinto" specialized in futures trading of one to three months, as opposed to "spot" or over the counter trade at other regional exchanges. Although Korean brokers had long been accustomed to consignment sales, the advent of contracting in large lots of grains for specific dates of delivery demanded new procedures and new sources of capital. Changing ideas paralleled changing structures in the shift from subsistence to profit, barter to currency, or spot to futures.

The pinnacle of circles of enterprise at Inch'ŏn, the Jinto was the arena for competition and cooperation within both zaikai and chaegye, and between them. Prosperity and growth for both association and enterprise depended on efficiency and continuity at the Exchange based on reliable contracting and delivery. It functioned as the central forum for a colonial administration committed to expanding the trade, and for mercantile interests of zaikai and chaegye looking for profit. Designed to bridge official and private sectors of the colonial grain trade through a managed and closely monitored semi-official but privately owned and managed firm, the Exchange was responsible to the state, to its owners, and to the public. The specter of losing the Exchange to Seoul mobilized not only the business community, but also the citizens [*simin*] of Inch'ŏn, adding a "public" counterpoint to the priorities of official and private sectors in the transfer. Semi-official, privately owned and managed, yet critical for the common good, the Exchange offers an institutional focus for the colonial resolution of the tension between public good and private profit.

Mediation of official and private interests distinguished other colonial institutions as well in the agrarian economy, for the rice policy [Senbei taisaku] of the Government-General had to serve both public and private interests. Announcing the appointment of Ariga Mitsutoyo of the Chosen Industrial Bank to chair a committee on rice policy in 1929, a Minister of the Political Affairs Bureau explained, "Ariga is a good choice because his work at the Bank is both semi-official and semi-private [*hankan-hanmin*]."[1] The semi-official status of institutions such as the Jinto critical for implementation of a rice policy reduced the financial and bureaucratic investment of the Government-General and enhanced their linkages with Japanese and Korean capital in the grain trade, but also made direction far more complex. From the business side, the civilian presidents of the Jinto and the Stock Exchange at Seoul acknowledged the government's stake in their enterprise: "We realize there are special political measures necessary, since the Exchanges in Korea have always had a special relationship with the polity, as well as with the business community."[2] The ambitious task of designing a merger to meet the demands of stockholders, foster the credibility of the local market, and achieve uniformity with markets in the home islands frustrated the colonial administration through 1928.[3]

Established in 1899, the Jinsen Grain Exchange quickly came to dominate the trade at Inch'ŏn and remained prominent through the 1920s despite increasing competition from Exchanges at other grain gateways such as Pusan and Kunsan. The first twenty years of the Jinto under Karai Eitarō spanned both the last years of the Kingdom and the first decade of the colony. Integration of grain and stock exchanges in Japan, the demand for a more centralized forum for grain futures in a growing trade, and owners' hopes for profit prompted calls in its last decade (1922-1931) for transferring the Jinto to Seoul. A compromise solution authorized a corporate consolidation of the Jinto and the Stock Exchange in Seoul [Kabushiki Kaisha Keijō Kabushiki Genbutsu Torihiki Sijō] in the new "Chosen Exchange," with the grain exchange at Inch'ŏn reduced to a branch of the Seoul firm. Merger opponents kept the exchange in Inch'ŏn but they lost the company to Seoul. The Chosen Exchange operated both a stock exchange in Seoul and a grain exchange in Inch'ŏn until wartime controls closed the grain branch in 1939, and finally the stock exchange in Seoul in 1943.

The early years (1899-1921), transfer controversy (1922-1931), and branch years (1932-1939) at the Exchange parallel the growth and then relative decline of the grain trade during the industrialization of the 1930s. Beyond grains, the decade of the "Jinto Problem" in the 1920s links the growing market dynamic to the beginnings of civil society as contention, conflict, and compromise across a decade of proposals and protests introduce a new world of enterprise, association, and colonial state now divided by issues of public versus the private good. A decline in grain prices at Inch'ŏn, a surplus of domestic grains in the home islands, and a shift towards industrial priorities on the peninsula forced a restructuring of the Jinto. A total of 340,000 koku of rice exported from the port in 1920 fetched some 12.5 million yen, and one million koku exported five years later earned 47 million yen. But prices declined quickly later in the decade with 1.2 million koku of rice exports earning only 27 million yen in 1930.[4] Having survived earlier recessions, port brokers with life savings invested in mills and small warehouses could endure shifting demand but not a Government-General effort to demote the port.

Apart from divisions caused by priorities on industry over agriculture, and controls versus expansion of rice exports, the Jinto Problem brought attention to two very emotional issues at the port: the "unequal treatment [fubyōdai daigū]" of brokers at the Jinto in contrast to brokers at other produce exchanges, and the "rikken [interests and rights]" of the Jinto and citizens of Inch'ŏn. Eldest son of the pioneer broker Sim Nŭng-dŏk, Sim Ŭi-suk denounced the Jinto transfer and proposed new requirements on brokerage: "I grieve for the Jinto, and I grieve for Korea." Rice he argued, "is the foundation of Korean industry, and agriculture for industrial growth." Exasperated with the administration's shift from rice promotion to rice and Jinto demotion, he acknowledged the need for rationalization, but only for the benefit of the "Korean populace [Chōsen minshū]."[5] Rice king Katō Heitarō contrasted the constrained Jinto with "competitive produce markets" at Pusan, Kunsan, and Taegu which produce a baseline for sales.[6] More concerned with market management and more blunt than Sim, Katō berated the administration plan for taxes at the Jinto and new demands on collateral for the brokers as constraints with neither a government policy nor a principal.

The lively debate in the liberal decade of "Cultural Rule" reveals more than deep dissent among the business elite of the port. It also highlights links between market priorities of the official and private sectors with the commonweal of smaller merchants, and indeed of the "citizenry" in the port city of Inch'ŏn. Dissent is no longer confined to literati of an earlier era, but now flourishes among a well-established and respected business elite who gain a hearing at both government and private associations of Inch'ŏn citizens. Protesters got more than a hearing. They forced a compromise of the government's original plan securing the grain exchange for Inch'ŏn despite the corporate merger of the Jinto with the exchange at Seoul. To the advocates' promise of a consolidation of two major markets, opponents countered it was a merger solely of companies and the demise of the Inch'ŏn market. Priorities of both market and society governed the debate, whether among advocates promising growth and greater efficiency, or opponents fearing the loss of capital, consumers, and jobs.

Grain Exchange

Rice paddy and Grain Exchange stood at opposite ends of a long chain of production and marketing for export. Incorporation begins with adventurers, entrepreneurs, and diplomats, but soon demands more complex networks of banks and exchanges to secure markets and supply sources across core and periphery. Such networks remain the key to effective incorporation, and among them the Jinto played its role of stabilizing the trade in grains with more secure contracting and more reliable brokerage. A commerce in grains would no longer depend solely on trust buttressed by personal relationships, but rather on contracts protected by law and organization. Institutions provide stability and continuity in a trade beyond individuals and their enterprise. Continuing the work of the Jinto and the Seoul Exchange, the Chosen Exchange was organized in 1932 within a web of ten government-chartered firms [tokushu kaisha] comprising the central institutions of market and exchange on the peninsula, listed in Table 7.1. Chartered by government decree with officers either directly appointed or approved by the government, and with investment from government supported banks or other chartered firms, the ten institutions represented the core instruments of government policy in the colonial economy of Korea. Yet each of the firms stood independently in the market as a joint-stock firm

TABLE 7.1 Government-Chartered Firms [*tokushu kaisha*], 1941

Firm	*Est.*	*Capital**
Oriental Development	1908	42.5
Bank of Chosen	1909	35.0
Chosen Industrial Bank	1918	52.5
Chosen Savings Bank	1929	3.75
Chosen Exchange	1932**	1.5
Chosen Trust Bank	1932	2.5
Chosen Forestry Development Co.	1937	4.0
Chosen Magnesite Development Co.	1939	15.0
Chosen Grain Market Company	1939	0.9
Chosen Mining Promotion Co.	1940	2.5

* Paid-in capital cited in millions of yen.
** Predecessor Jinsen Grain Exchange founded in 1899.
Source: Tōyō Keizai Shinpōsha. *Dairiku kaisha benran, 1942* [Handbook of companies on the continent, 1942] (Tokyo: Tōyō Keizai Shinpōsha, 1942), p. 253.

with a diversity of government and private investors, with the two major banks regulating the availability and flow of capital.

The Bank of Chosen functioned as a central bank. Rural agricultural banks of the 1910s were reorganized into a second major colonial institution, the Chosen Industrial Bank in 1918, which served as the central creditor for the Finance Associations [Kinyū Kumiai] and the Irrigation Associations critical for agrarian development. A third chartered firm, the Oriental Development Company developed and operated agricultural estates across the country with its own warehouses and credit system for producing and marketing rice. As evident in Table 7.1, the Bank of Chosen, Industrial Bank, and Oriental Development Company were organized either before or at the beginning of the colonial period. Although the Jinto was reorganized as the Chosen Exchange in 1932, its founding in 1899 predated all of the chartered firms. Finally, a set of firms for extraction of natural resources was established just prior to the Pacific War, including the Grain Market Company. The latter wartime organization took control of the purchase and sales of now rationed grains, closing the grain market and ending the functions of the Inch'ŏn grain office of the Chosen Exchange.

Nishiwaki Chōtarō, president of the precolonial Japanese Chamber of Commerce at Inch'ŏn strongly endorsed the establishment of the Jinsen Grain Exchange in 1896.[7] But it was the founder, president and longtime director of the Jinto, Karai Eitarō who raised the necessary capital and saw the enterprise through its difficult early years. Karai and partners began with an idea, 30,000 yen, a broad mandate for the exchange of multiple products, and the permission of the Japanese Consul to open in March of 1896. Problems with deliveries of textiles, fish, as well as grains finally forced the Consulate to close the Exchange six months later, a victim of not only supply problems, but also volatile prices and speculation. Karai gained the Consul's support to reopen solely as a grain exchange in 1899 with more warehouse space and expanded brokerage. The Karai group raised the paid-in capital to 45,000 yen by 1904, later prospered with the elimination of duties on rice exports from 1913, and listed a paid-in capital of 1.5 million yen by 1922.[8] Their Jinto assured Japanese traders of a supply of Korean grains, and also served as a central clearinghouse affecting supply, demand, and pricing in the colony. The firm listed the following goals: (1) promote grain exports; (2) standardize quality and price of grains; (3) improve the quality of local produce for export; (4) prevent spoilage and stock losses; (5) establish a model for other ports.[9] Operating as the center of brokerage in the colonial port, it was mandated by the Government-General with collection of a ten percent commission tax on grain sales.[10]

Some two decades after its founding, the Jinto had established itself as a leading grain exchange, now under the leadership of Arai Hatsutarō and others. Processing a major share of rice and soybean exports to Japan, the Exchange registered transactions worth 15.5 million yen in

1916, 69 million yen in 1920, and 285 million yen in 1930.[11] Futures contracting had brought growth, relative distinction from other exchanges, and scandals. Parallel to the normal functions of over the counter sales, a small number of brokers were authorized to buy and sell contracts of one to three month futures on high, medium, and low quality grain lots, with a minimum purchase of one hundred koku (i.e. about five hundred bushels).[12] A group of twenty-eight authorized brokers, including seven Koreans, held official seats on the Exchange.[13] Prominent Japanese businessmen in Inch'ŏn such as Karai himself, Yoshida Hidejirō, and Korean broker Chŏng Ch'i-hak served on the board of directors in 1922.[14] Although Japanese nationals dominated ownership, Koreans such as Chang Tu-hyŏn and the aristocrat Yi Pyŏng-hak ranked among the major investors in the Exchange by 1928, and again in the reorganized Chōsen Exchange a few years later.[15] Closely linked to other chartered firms, the Jinto was a major stockholder in both the Chosen Industrial Bank and the Chosen Commercial Bank.[16]

Although private ownership continued after 1932, brokers at the Jinto and subsequent Chosen Exchange dominated day to day operations. Indeed, one major issue in the reorganization of the exchanges was ownership itself, with alternatives of state ownership as found in Japan, private ownership as was the case in Korea, or association status under a board of brokers or brokerage houses more common in Europe and the United States. A profile of operations at the Jinto can be gleaned from newspaper reports of the Jinto Brokers Association under Asano Taisaburō, Kobayashi Tōemon, and later Nitta Yoshimin.[17] As the major coalition of brokers in the port, the Association enjoyed a clearer mandate than the Jinsen Grain Association, and far more prominent members than the Inch'ŏn Brokers Association of their Korean counterparts.

Japanese nationals dominated the Jinto Brokers Association, although it also included Koreans who served as Jinto brokers.[18] Receptions and parties including the Jinto Brokers Association won press coverage, and attendance by both government officials and Jinto owners,[19] but both the press and government found interest as well in the priorities of the Association. The Association pressed for better accounting systems, for higher handling fees, and for more efficient collection of government commissions.[20] Koyabashi Toemon led a campaign for higher handling fees with petitions to the Government-General in 1926, and mobilized the protest against a reduction in handling fees on futures trading proposed by Jinto owners.[21] We also find the Jinto Brokers Association addressing larger market issues such as the merits of a fixed price system or of a merger of the Jinto with the Exchange at Seoul, and its effect on other markets on the peninsula.[22]

The larger issue of "interests and rights" in the Jinto transfer provided common ground for citizens, brokers, and indeed shareholders in the Jinto to sustain the market position of Inch'ŏn against encroachments from Seoul. But the immediate issue of discrimination captivated the attention of brokers during the decade of controversy as they raised the banner of "unequal treatment." For instance when Jinto owners had unilaterally decided to drop commissions of futures trading, the Brokers Association protested the change reduce their incomes by half. A further proposal of a personal insurance fee of 10,00 yen prior to transactions sparked further debates.[23] Reforms in the transfer package to strengthen the credibility of futures transactions by raising the collateral or personal insurance of the individual brokers, together with responsibilities for collection of government fees prompted further anger at the Jinto Brokers Association, and added to the indignation brewing among the wider population.[24] The powerful Katō Heitarō had little to fear with his multiple mills and huge role in the grain trade, but the Jinto Brokers Association itself could very well have been rendered obsolete in a transfer to Seoul.[25] A few such as Nitta Yoshimin, a Jinto brokers and officer in the Jinto Brokers Association, found themselves in the delicate position of protesting reforms yet hoping remain a part of the ultimate solution. As vice-president of the Brokers Association in 1930, Nitta Yoshimin did not dispute the need for reforms, but did protest the economic burden laid on the brokers with the higher insurance fee.[26] Sim Ŭi-suk, Nitta, and Katō all concurred on the need for rationalizing the futures operation with stronger institutional controls, but insisted on competitive brokering opportunities.

A corporate merger into the Chosen Exchange in 1932 reduced the number of authorized seats at the exchange, although up to 30 brokers were permitted to engage in futures transactions, and up to 50 brokers could work in spot transactions.[27] Yu Kun-sŏng, Kim Kwang-jun, and Yu Rae-hang ranked among the twenty-one authorized stock brokers at the Exchange from 1936 to the close of the grain operation in 1939, with Yu Kun-sŏng, Yu Rae-hang, Cho Chun-ho and Kang Ik-ha listed among the twelve grain brokers.[28] After processing between 12 and 17 million koku annually from 1932, the grain office of the Exchange prospered with annual totals of 30 million koku in 1936 and 39 million koku in 1937.[29] Local investment continued with Koreans Kim Chŏng-ik and Yu

Ki-yong listed as the leading stockholders in the Exchange in 1935, although with a combination of only 12,000 shares in a widely held Exchange listing a total of 300,000 shares.[30] In place of large individual shareholders, holding companies of brokers and former stockholders came to dominate ownership in the closing years of the Exchange. Prominent among former leaders in the Exchange and later owners and leaders in holding companies were brokers Asano Taisaburō and Nitta Yoshimin, but also an early major stockholder such as Kosugi Kinhachi. As a director and then president of the Exchange in Seoul, Kosugi played a major role in the merger, and then served as vice-president of the Chosen Exchange from 1932.[31]

In addition to the ten chartered firms including the Exchange, a further web of twenty-seven quasi-chartered [*juntokushu kaisha*] firms further extended the government's role in the economy. Tensions between private capital and public good evident at the exchanges were resolved with government acquisition in the warehousing of grains. The solution was predicted in an report of the government vernacular newspaper, the *Maeil Shinbo* which cited the problem of a privately managed firm deciding public priorities in distribution of grains during a time of scarcity.[32] To support prices and insure supplies, the Government-General in 1930 began subsidizing construction of smaller warehouses close to production sites, and reorganized port warehouse facilities into the Chosen Grain Storage Company. Rather than building a new set of facilities at the outset, the company leased storage facilities of the Chosen Development Bank and Commerce Bank, and of other port warehouse companies.[33] The purpose of the firm was stated clearly: to insure the supply of Korean grains for export. Its functions included transport, storage, consignment sales & purchases, and fire insurance with branches in Inch'ŏn, Chinnamp'o, Pusan, Kunsan, and Mokp'o.[34] The Chosen Grain Storage Company was listed as an affiliate of the Oriental Development Company, with a paid-in capital of 250,000 yen in 1932, but two million yen ten years later.[35] The Bank of Chosen held 13% of the shares, the Industrial Bank 12%, the Oriental Development Company seven percent, and the ubiquitous Katō Heitarō of the Chosen Polished Rice Company three percent of the shares. By 1937, the company operated a comprehensive set of older wood buildings at Inch'ŏn, as well newer brick warehouses in every neighborhood.[36]

The exchange and the storage company served both political and economic goals by institutionalizing the grain trade and its links to the home islands, and providing a channel for continuous and reliable investment in Korean land and production. The same organization helped shape and extend the role of the Japanese at the port, and foster the rise of Korean mercantile interests. Karai's Jinto bridged public and private interests by linking private investment to a state-support system which brought growth to the port and prosperity to the Empire, and insured Japanese dominance in the grain trade through control of management and brokerage. Certainly Karai and subsequent investors would profit, but so too would the associated brokers, Japanese traders, and merchants and consumers in Osaka. As evident in the furor over transfer of the exchange to Seoul, the Jinto also benefitted the citizens of Inch'ŏn as the center of brokerage for the major enterprise of the port. Secondly, the Exchange both employed and fostered professional expertise and resources available to the Japanese who could rely on the organizational experience of exchanges in the home islands in developing procedures, coordinating warehousing with purchases and sales, and insuring secure transport. Such professionalism contributed to the relative autonomy of the business community at the port from the state, and to the credibility necessary for continued state recognition and support. Thirdly, the Jinto advanced the process of incorporation through dominance and then integration of the Korean grain brokers. The Exchange assured a prominent Japanese role in determining issues of supply and prices at the port, and in the brokerage activities necessary to expand the trade, but also designated brokerage positions to Koreans to insure penetration of the national market.

Transfer Debate

A scandal at the Jinto in 1919 sent shock waves through the port.[37] Saddled with expensive futures contracts coming due at a time of depressed market prices, some brokers at the Exchange defaulted by paying their suppliers with worthless checks. Defaults of 1.7 million yen exceeded the 1.2 million yen of assets at the Exchange and threatened to bring down the whole enterprise. Government investigations and a recapitalization campaign closed the Exchange from March until August of 1919, and resulted in strict new government regulations on exchange transactions, a paid-in capital of 100,000 yen, and a new president, Wakamatsu Tōsanjirō, formerly of the Foreign Ministry.[38] Confusion in world markets at the end of World War I contributed to sharp price fluctuations in general, but other factors also contributed to the extreme volatility of prices on advance contracts for grains. Fluctuating demand in Japan for local and foreign rice at the Dojima Market in Osaka largely determined prices in Inch'ŏn. Local production and supply, affected in turn by climate and local demand, also played a role in determining prices.

But a third factor of speculation had plagued the exchange from the outset and spurred various government efforts at reform. Price fluctuations due to the size and quality of supply, or to variations in demand could be moderated in part by government controls on credit, tariffs on grain imports or embargoes on exports, but the activities of Korean and Japanese speculators eluded government controls.[39] The cabinet in Japan had addressed the latter problem and improved control over government commissions on transactions with consolidation of grain and stock exchanges in the home islands under government ownership and scrutiny. Speculation at the Jinto, reforms in the home islands, government hopes for greater control, and demands of exchange owners for greater profit supported an initiative to merge the Jinto with the stock exchange at Seoul. The initiative played out as the central drama dominating the press and dividing the business community in Inch'ŏn across nearly a decade from 1922, with periods of division into opposing camps, contention, and ultimately a compromise against the transfer but for the merger.

Contending forces began to emerge in 1922 when representatives of the combined Chamber of Commerce and the Jinto Brokers Association protested a proposal before the government to permit Inch'ŏn brokerage houses to open branches in Seoul.[40] Then in November of 1923, Hirai Nosaburō led 31 Jinto stockholders in a proposal to the Jinto board of directors for the transfer of the Jinto to Seoul in a merger with the Seoul Exchange.[41] As they drew up forces against the transfer proposal, the Jinsen Chamber and the brokers claimed the high ground of the public good, identified themselves with the "wider business community [*ilban chaegye*]," and gained the support of the "citizens of Inch'ŏn [*Inch'ŏn simin*]." Facing a divided zaikai and an angry populace, the Government-General tolerated the debate, reaffirmed its authority over any change in the status of the Exchange, and appeared reluctant to press a solution.[42] Juggling roles of referee, reformer, and ultimate authority, the government remained the center of the controversy and target of petitions. Opposing camps consolidated in the winter of 1923 as the president of the Stock Exchange at Seoul supported the transfer, the Jinsen Chamber met in emergency session, reports surfaced of a citizen protest at the port, and the "Coalition to Halt the Transfer" led by the volatile twenty-one year old Rikimu Kurosamorimon submitted the first of many petitions to the Colonial Office of Development.[43] Two years later the Jinto Brokers Association under Kobayashi mobilized further support against the merger, while the eminent Karai Eitarō and chair of the Council at the Inch'ŏn Brokers Association, Chang Sŏk-u visited the Development Office with a petition of opposition.[44]

Opposition turned to heated contention in July of 1926 with the dramatic resignation of Chamber President Yoshida Hidejirō from the board of the Jinto, forcing the temporary resignation of the Jinto President Wakamatsu Usanjirō.[45] With the rift in the zaikai now public, Yoshida assumed leadership of the opposition, while Wakamatsu enlisted the support of major shareholders at the Jinto and Seoul Exchange, as well as government leaders to press the transfer. Rikimu Kurosamorimon gained Yoshida's support for his Coalition to Block the Transfer, and Chang Sŏk-u continued to speak publicly in opposition.[46] Meanwhile ten prominent Korean brokers including Yu Kun-sŏng and Inch'ŏn Brokers Association president Kim Kyu-myŏn joined ten Japanese brokers in their own association to oppose the transfer.[47] Furor over the transfer peaked in an demonstration disrupting the Jinto stockholders meeting. Rikimu and 18 comrades directed a barrage of questions about the proposal at President Wakamatsu, forcing the temporary suspension of the assembly. Stockholders leaving the building were confronted by an angry crowd in a street demonstration of "hundreds" of citizens from Seoul and Inch'ŏn, organized by Rikimu and Noguchi Bun'ichi.[48] Provincial Governor Yoneda hastily ordered an indefinite delay of the transfer, which in turn prompted a lawsuit from the Jinto owners.[49] Finally, the Brokers Association at both the Jinto and the Seoul Exchange threw their weight behind the opposition with three week boycotts.[50] The civic unrest and disruption at the Jinto forced the resignation of Wakamatsu and the board of directors at the Jinto on May 16, 1927.[51]

The fury of the opposition in Inch'ŏn prompted the administration to adjust the transfer plan, but did not thwart the government's determination to restructure the Jinto given their declining interest in rice exports and nagging problems of the prolonged rice market recession. Conciliatory but adamant statements by the government and the Jinto owners preceded legislation in July of 1928 mandating mergers in Japan, and soon in Korea.[52] What is remarkable in the controversy, however, is the organization of the opposition tapping a common interest in the Exchange among diverse groups at Inch'ŏn. The Jinsen Chamber of

Commerce and the Association of Public Officials orchestrated an effective, broad-based and articulate opposition, balancing the more radical effort of Rikimu. The Chamber under Yoshida's leadership fostered the efforts of the Assembly of Neighborhood Associations, the Assembly of Citizens, the Jinsen Promotion Association, and the Committee of Stockholders in Opposition.[53] The Public Officials Group assembled eight times already in 1926 to address the transfer problem, the Assembly of Neighborhood Association met seven times, and the Assembly of Citizens once. The stockholders and the citizens' groups formed a coalition in February 1927, assembling 47 times and sending six petitions to the Government-General in that year.[54] From March of 1929, the Jinsen Promotion Association took an active role in the opposition, with forty-three assemblies.

An alliance of the Committee of Stockholders in Opposition, and the Jinsen Promotion Association amassed a war chest of 17,000 yen in 1930, and brought the Assembly of Neighborhood Associations and a Youth Group into the alliance as well.[55] Reconsolidating their resources for the final campaign against the transfer, the opposition reorganized two months later under the umbrella of the Federation of Public Officials.[56] The roster of the Federation reflects distinction, subordination or relatively lower status, and cooperation of the chaegye in the zaikai-led opposition to the transfer. Two Koreans joined eight Japanese on the board of directors, including Yoshida Hidejirō and Chu Myŏng-gi. Four Koreans brokers found a place among sixteen Japanese on the Standing Committee of the Federation. Sim Ŭi-suk, Kim Pong-gi, Kim Yong-gyu and twenty-three other Koreans were listed with forty-one Japanese on the Federation's Action Committee.[57] The Federation convened some eighty-four times in 1931, published four policy papers or "opinions," and submitted twenty petitions to the Government-General.[58]

The government kept close watch on Inch'ŏn with reports of rising anger, and eventually moved ahead on a merger without transfer. The new Exchange Law and enforcement procedures were published in September of 1931,[59] and the new Chosen Exchange established on January 10 of 1932 with headquarters in Kogane-chō in Seoul, a branch in Inch'ŏn, and a paid-in capital of 2.4 million yen.[60] What distinguished the decade of controversy was procedure and organization. A discourse of petitions [chinjō], opinions [ikken], recommendations [kengi], and declarations [seimei] to the respective bureaus of the Government-General, of voting at assemblies of major stockholders at the Exchanges, and of representation before organized interest groups provided a format of control for the government and limited representation for zaikai and smaller merchants. Procedure was maintained not only by government authority, but also by a variety of organizations in the port, with the business associations of brokers or owners leading the respective camps.

Yoshida carried the banner of Jinto meaning "profit" or "interest [rieki], and "rights" or "authority" [kenri]. His petitions to the Governor-General highlighted a Jinto history of profit [rieki] for the government treasury, for the market, and for the port of Inch'ŏn.[61] Contention at the Jinto over interest and rights in system, capital, and market across the decade extended the initial colonial pattern of official and non-official sectors to a broader spectrum of official, private, and an emerging public sphere, with both camps claiming the high ground of the commonweal. An early exchange between Tennichi and Rikimu set the tenor of the controversy. Tennichi Tōjirō, president of the Exchange at Seoul in 1926 argued for the transfer to strengthen his institution of "stability and common prosperity where individual profit can be equated with communal benefit."[62] Chairing the Coalition to Halt the Transfer, Rikimu accused transfer advocates with "ignoring the opinions of the mass of Inch'ŏn citizens," and "maneuvering to obtain their own profit."[63] The conflict over public and private goods played out on various levels, but none more important than the primary level of space, site, and geography.

One benefit of the transfer would be better integration of the Inch'ŏn market within a wider colonial system, beginning with local grain markets reoriented to Inch'ŏn rather than Pusan or Kunsan, a linking of Seoul and Inch'ŏn as the commercial center of the peninsula, and finally a stronger tie between the peninsula's market center and the Japanese market at Osaka and Tokyo. The Jinto Brokers Association questioned the benefit of centralization at Seoul for local markets, but admitted the closer links of rural exchanges with Osaka under the proposed merger.[64] An argument for a "Keijin [Seoul and Inch'ŏn]" joint economic zone found more support in Seoul than among Inch'ŏnites wary of being absorbed by their huge neighbor. A Seoulite such as Tennichi Tōjirō early on set out stark restructuring options for the Jinto: a Jinto branch in Seoul; a merger; or a grain exchange in Seoul. Since most recognized the futility of the first option, the latter two options only aggravated fears of losing the Jinto to Seoul.[65] More than simply geography, there was a further system-wide push to align Korean exchanges with reforms in the home islands.[66]

A second issue of ownership and control left the government in an uneasy alliance with the major stockholders in the Seoul and Inch'ŏn exchanges. Governor General Saitō Makoto made it clear from the outset that government ownership of the now private exchanges was an option. The fact that legislation in Japan mandated government ownership, but was ultimately adjusted to permit privately held, joint-stock corporation ownership of the Chosen Exchange reflects the power of the Jinto and Chosen Exchange owners, and the unwillingness of the government to invest more government capital.[67] The Governor-General himself addressed the issue of accountability with stern warnings to both Exchanges to keep their discussions of the merger open to the public. Reporters for the *Donga Ilbo* singled out the credibility of the owners as the critical issue in the controversy: "people do not trust big capitalists to run exchanges in the public interest."[68] The colonial administration indirectly appeared to support the latter view with their insistence on broad oversight of the Exchanges, including approval of officers and constitution, and as final arbiter on the question of merger.[69]

Credibility of the exchange itself was a further issue in the debate, as critics denied the premise that exchanges could be identified with markets. A transfer and merger of the Jinto to the Seoul operation would consolidate two markets into one centralized, more credible, better funded, and more closely supervised market at Seoul. But Rikimu countered that it was only the merger of two corporations more interested in company profit than market benefit,[70] and the Association of Brokers at the Seoul Exchange cited the example of the Osaka Exchange where a merger only disrupted markets in both stocks and grains.[71] Some questioned whether the Exchanges really determined prices in a produce market such as grains, and therefore whether artificial price ceilings or fixed prices would be feasible.[72] Still others questioned the link between rice and stock options, but President Tennichi of the Exchange in Seoul asserted continuity.[73] A recession in Korean grain exports from 1926 made restructuring more difficult, and prompted criticism that the controversy itself had eroded credibility and prompted the recession.[74] Since precedent and continuity strengthened credibility, one strong argument for transfer opponents was the two decade tradition of the Exchange at Inch'ŏn.[75] Whether to allay fears of the Inch'ŏn citizens, or to strengthen the confidence of stock investors, traders, and brokers at the Exchanges, government officials joined the opposition in citing the significance of the long history of grain trading at Inch'ŏn.[76]

Issues and organizations in the debate reflect interest group development and contention among the mercantile interests at the port, divided now by investment rather than ethnicity, yet still organized within largely ethnically distinct groups such as the Jinto Brokers Association or the Inch'ŏn Brokers Association. Scholars of turn of the century China point to the development of a public sphere spurred by the political activities of chambers of commerce. Mary Rankin has suggested rather than looking to state and society, a more accurate assessment would distinguish the official, private, and less tightly organized but nonetheless emerging public sphere in the Chinese cities. Apart from emerging distinctions, the role of market within colonial civil society deserves further attention. A recent study of John Keane draws us beyond simply propertied civil society of bourgeoisie Europe, to look at the development of associated groups of citizens with a public interest, and how associations might mediate market interests. But the more difficult problem remains independence from the state, particularly in a colony such as Korea close to the home islands of Japan and strategically critical for expansion on the continent. The Federation of Public Officials, Jinsen Chamber, the Jinto Brokers Association and the Inch'ŏn Brokers Association brought formidable organizational resources to the campaign against the transfer and forced a compromise. Interests gained representation within channels, just as enterprise prospered only within circles. The controversy offers initial evidence of organization and ideologies among emerging interest groups necessary for social mobilization in civil society, but only within the boundaries established by the Government-General.

Conclusion

King Kojong's cabinet authorized the Merchants Association [Sinsang Hyŏphoe] of port brokers in 1897, joining former state officials [sin] and businessmen [sang] in a state-recognized commerce association. Falling short of the Enlightenment distinction between official and non-official sectors [kwanmin], the Merchants Association in the late Kingdom remained under the government direction but still permitted greater recognition for the status and function of brokers. The interpenetration of public and private sectors persisted under colonial rule, though now with clearer distinction in law and organization, and a more sophisticated institutional framework of corporations and chartered firms. Major chartered firms such as the Jinto and the successor Chosen Exchange mediated the commonweal within a joint-stock corporation with semi-official obligations. Law, business associations, and circles of enterprise including the chartered firms laid out a framework in which ideas of public, private, and official sectors gained definition through market transactions and adjustments.

Beyond fundamental issues of public and private, associated ideas of location and market function garnered attention in the transfer debate. Controversy over the role of Exchanges in Inch'ŏn and Seoul in organizing prices and supplies in the 1920s reflects the growth and complexity of markets. The fact that neither state nor chaegye, nor segments of the zaikai at Inch'ŏn were willing to sacrifice site and city for the promise of more efficient market dynamics at Seoul suggests new social priorities constraining the colonial market. What remained problematic was the leverage of organized interests against an alliance of the colonial state and the owners of the Exchanges. Adherence to government-mandated procedures, intense lobbying through petitions and visits to government ministries, and scapegoating not of the Government-General but only of Jinto owners distinguished the opposition campaign. Perhaps the significance of the transfer controversy can be found in both process and conclusion, where a divided zaikai gained a hearing and a compromise across the decade of contention.

An institutional framework in place by the 1920s fostered the consolidation and representation of interests crucial for the formation of at least commercial interest groups in civil society. The locally owned and moderately nationalist *Donga Ilbo* devoted an editorial to the transfer debate already in 1923. Arguing that Koreans in Inch'ŏn needed the Jinto to develop commerce, they cited the examples not of individual brokers, but rather of business associations.[77] The editorial included interviews with the presidents of the Inch'ŏn Brokers Association, of Chu Myŏng-gi's Inch'ŏn Rice Merchants Association, and also of Katō Heitarō's Jinsen Grain Association, tracing the history, membership, and functions of the associations. The subsequent prominence of association leaders in the opposition campaign against the transfer offers further evidence of their significance for representing interests within the borders mandated by the Government-General. Inch'ŏnites organized in associations on the base of circles of enterprise demanded a voice, together with the state and Jinto owners, in the reembedding of market in colonial society.

Restructuring of the exchanges sustained the port as a grain gateway and reinforced its links both to Seoul and to Japanese markets. A colonial transformation towards greater market autonomy continued, but not without new constraints of state and organized interest groups. Apart from the colonial system of markets, the colonial state role of referee, reformer, and initially reluctant arbiter in the controversy permitted some distance from the fray, but without diminishing its authority to intervene and press the final legislated solution. Moreover, a stronger role for the state in direction and oversight of the Chosen Exchange from 1932 was consistent with other interventions in the economy as the peninsula shifted to a wartime priorities of chemical and heavy industrial production.

With system strengthened and state defined, the decade of the transfer controversy chronicles the reformation of markets by colonial state and circles of enterprise. Korean brokers bridged a transition not from despotic state control of grain markets to free markets, but from despotic control to managed markets, mainly through the chartered firms and business associations, with a new interaction among priorities of self-regulation of the economy, self-preservation of society, and imperial state goals. As Governor-General Saitō Makoto reminded opposing camps early in the controversy, "competition between the Seoul Exchange and the Jinto is not in the public interest."[78]

Notes

1. *Osaka Asahi Shimbun* June 7, 1929, p. 7.

2. *Donga Ilbo* July 19, 1928, p. 8. The occasion was a press conference in which Seoul Exchange President Tennichi Tōjirō and Jinto President Arai Hatsutarō presented a formal statement (*seimei*) on the merger to avoid negative effects on the wider business community (*ippan zaikai*).

3. A report on the frustration of the Government-General, and the significance of the merger decision for markets on the peninsula, and particularly for other exchanges, can be found in *Osaka Asahi Shimbun*, March 14, 1982, p. 7.

4. *Jinsen Shōkō Kaigisho tōkei nempyō, 1937*, Table 62.

5. Interview of early 1930 printed in the *Chōsen Shimbun*, the *Chōsen Asahi Shimbun*, and the *Chōsen Shōkō Shimbun*. Reprinted in Inoue Shinichirō, ed., *Chōsen Torihikijokai* [The world of the Chosen Exchange] (Tokyo: Shōgyō Tsūshinsha, 1930), pp. 98-101.

6. Interview of early 1930 printed in the *Chōsen Shimbun*, the *Chōsen Shōkō Shimbun*, and the *Chōsen Maiinichi Shimbun*, and reprinted in Inoue, *Chōsen Torihikijokai*, pp. 148-153.

7. Nishiwaki was branch manager of the Inch'ŏn branch of the Daiichi Bank. Branches of the Daiichi in Korea were later reorganized as the Bank of Chosen. The Jinsen Grain Exchange [Kabushiki Kaisha Jinsen Beitō Torihikijo] was established on March 10, 1896. *Inch'ŏnsisa*, pp. 457-462; Jinsen Beitō Torihikijo, *Jinsen beitō torihikijo enkaku* [A history of the Inch'ŏn Rice and Soybean Exchange] (Jinsen: Jinsen Beitō Torihikijo, 1922). This volume will be cited as *Enkaku*.

8. TGKY 1921, p. 73; CGKKY, 1922, p. 215. Matsuo Ki, an Osaka investor, was reported to have purchased a majority of shares in 1912 bringing a much needed infusion of new capital. See Abe ed., *Chōsen kōrōsha meikan*, section on the "History of the Development of the Korean Economy," p. 190.

9. *Jinsenfushi*, pp. 1050-1052; *Inch'ŏnsisa*, p. 458.

10. *Enkaku*, pp. 25-34.

11. *Jinsenfushi*, p. 1064; *Jinsen shōkō annai*, p. 151. It also operated a major warehousing facility in the port with 14,500 square yards in use in 1930. *Jinsenkō*, p. 101. The source cited the area as 3,680 p'yŏng, which I have recalculated as square yards according to the formula of one p'yŏng equalling 3.95 square yards.

12. The Exchange permitted three types of contracts - one month, two month, and three month. It opened twice a day, morning and afternoon, with a set price each opening for one koku of rice or one koku of soybeans although transactions were permitted only in lots of 100 koku of rice, and 50 koku of soybeans. O Ch'ang-guk, *Chŭnggwŏn pisa* [The inside history of the Korean Exchange] (Seoul: Sinhŭng Printing, 1977), p. 17.

13. The Korean brokers included Yun Pyŏng-jun, Yi Sŏk-hyŏn, Yi Yong-gyu, Ch'oe Myŏng-yun, Kim U-kyŏng, Yi Hyo-gon, and Yun Pyŏng-ji. *Enkaku*, p. 36. Reports in the *Donga Ilbo* listed Yi Yung-gu as an officer of the Jinsen Brokers Association, February 17, 1922, and Yi Hyo-gŏn on April 20, 1922.

14. TGKY 1921, p. 73; CGKKY 1922, p. 215. Chang Tu-hyŏn and Yi Pyŏng-hak served as directors and were listed among the major shareholders in the firm five years later. CGKKY 1927, p.240; *Enkaku*, p. 35. A brief biography of Yi Pyŏng-hak can be found in Kōzō Makiyama, *Chōsen shinshi meiran* [A register of Korean gentlemen] (Keijō: Nihon Dempo Tsūshinsha, Keijō Jikyoku, 1911), p. 134.

15. CGKKY, 1928, p. 239; 1932, p. 364. Yi Pyŏng-hak appears on the board also of the Chosen Industrial Bank, and as a member of the Central Advisory Council [Chūsūin]. *Chōsen kōrōsha meikan*, p. 289.

16. The Jinto appears among the major stockholders of the Chosen Industrial Bank in CGKKY 1927, p. 5, and 1931, p. 4, and among major

stockholders in the Chosen Commercial Bank in CGKKY 1927, p. 7, and 1931, p. 6.

17. Officers of the Jinto Brokers Association [Jinsen Torihikijo Nakagai Kumiai] in 1922 included Kobayashi Tōemon, Uzu Katsu, Imai Kakujirō, and Nitta Yoshimin. *Donga Ilbo*, October 29, 1922, p. 4 (116). For a report of the contested election of Asano Taisaburō as president of the association in the same year, see *Donga Ilbo*, February 24, 1922, p. 4.

18. One measure of participation was in the annual awards for sales. In January of 1926, the Association recognized Nitta Yoshimin, Kobayashi Tōemon, and Rikimu Kurosamorimon as the leading brokerage operations, with subsequent award for another Japanese national, and then three Korean brokers. See *Donga Ilbo*, January 5, 1926, p. 1.

19. See for instance the following reports in the *Donga Ilbo*: May 26, 1921, p. 4; December 29, 1921, p. 4; January 17, 1922, p. 4; January 30, 1922, p. 4; December 30, 1922; December 24, 1923,p. 4.

20. *Donga Ilbo*, March 24, 1922, p. 4.

21. *Donga Ilbo*, July 15, 1926, p. 6. Kobayashi presented a petition on the handling fee to the Industry Section Chief of the Ministry of Commerce, as reported in the *Donga Ilbo* of October 17, 1926, p. 6.

22. *Donga Ilbo*, March 18, 1924, p. 4; April 2, 1924, p. 4; and February 21, 1925, p. 4.

23. *Donga Ilbo*, April 16, 1925, p. 4.

24. See editorials of early 1930 in the *Chōsen Shimbun* reprinted in Inoue ed., *Chōsen Torihikijokai*, pp. 29-30, 98-101.

25. The *Donga Ilbo* of May 1, 1928, p. 6, reported a meeting of the Jinto Brokers Association with their counterpart association at the Seoul Exchange about the merger of the two associations in a possible transfer to Seoul. It noted that Jinto Brokers who met separately as well were wary of a merger, but wary also of being left out in a merger.

26. Inoue, *Chōsen Torihikijokai*, pp. 15-17.

27. Inch'ŏn Chighalsa P'yŏnch'an Wiwŏnhoe, *Inch'ŏn kaehang paegnyŏnsa* [A one hundred year history from the opening of the port of Inch'ŏn] (Inch'ŏn: Kyŏnggi Ch'ulp'ansa, 1983), p. 222; Sin T'ae-bom, *Inch'ŏn hansegi* [One generation in Inch'ŏn] (Inch'ŏn: Hunmi Ch'ulp'ansa, 1983), p. 115. Lee Hyung-jin cited the larger number of authorized brokers in his "Ilche kangjŏmgi midu chŭnggwŏn sijang chŏngch'aek gwa Chosŏn ch'wiinso [The Chosen Exchange and policy of the grain and stock markets during the Japanese occupation]," M.A. thesis, History Dept., Yonsei University, 1992, p. 91.

28. *Chōsen Torihikijo nempō*, pertinent years. Yu Kun-sŏng is not listed after 1937. For the response of a prominent Korean broker to the closing of the grain operation at the Chosen Exchange, see the interview with Kang Ik-ha in *Donga Ilbo*, March 11, 1939, p. 6.

29. Chōsen Sōtōkufu Shokusankyoku Shōkōka Hensan, *Torihikijo ichiran* [An introduction to the Exchange] (Keijo: Chōsen Sōtōkufu, 1937), p. 8; *Jinsen Shōkō Kaigisho tōkei nempyō, 1937*, Table 67.

30. CGKKY 1935, pp. 388-389.

31. A biography of Kosugi is available in *Chōsen kōrōsha meikan*, pp. 76-77. Long involved with printing for the offices of the Government-General, Kosugi was listed as president and largest shareholder in the Chosen Printing Company [Chōsen Insatsu Kabushiki Kaisha] with a paid-in capital of 200,000 yen. DKB 1942, p. 85; TGKY 1942, p. 35. He also served as a director for the Chosen Book and Printing Company [Chōsen Shoseki Insatsu Kabushiki Kaisha] with a paid-in capital of 500,000 yen, and major shareholders such as the Chosen Industrial Bank, the Chosen Trust Bank, and the Chosen Commercial Bank. DKB 1942, p. 85; TGKY 1942, p. 41. Kosugi was also chair of the board and a major stockholder in the Chosen Stock and Finance Company [Chōsen Kinyū Kabushiki Kaisha], whose major shareholder was the Chosen Exchange. TGKY 1942, p. 41.

32. *Maeil Shinbo*, November 11, 1930, p. 8.

33. CGKKY 1932, p. 96. A brief history of the Chosen Grain Storage Company [Chōsen Beikoku Sōko Kabushiki Kaisha] is provided in *Chōsen kōrōsha meikan*, "Economic Development" Section, p. 68.

34. CGKKY 1932, p. 96; TGKY 1942, pp. 48-49.

35. CGKKY 1932, p. 96; DKB 1942, pp. 253, 256.

36. *Jinsen Shōkō Kaigisho tōkei nempyō, 1937*, Table 72.

37. Lee, "Ilcheha kangjŏmgi midu," p. 39-41; Inch'ŏn Sanggong Hoeŭiso, *Inch'ŏn Sanggong Hoeŭiso kusimnyŏnsa* [A ninety year history of the Inch'ŏn Chamber of Commerce and Industry], (Seoul: Samhwa, 1979), pp. 242-244.

38. Abe, *Chōsen kōrōsha meikan*, pp. 195-196. Initially of the Finance Ministry, and later a Jinto administrator Akiyama Mitsuo also joined the board at this time. See his biography in the biography section of Abe, pp. 90-91.

39. O Ch'ang-guk, *Chŭnggwŏn pisa*.

40. *Donga Ilbo*, November 22, 1922, p. 4. The meeting held at the Jinsen Grain Association included speeches by Kawai Tada, a Councillor of the chamber, and Tsujikawa Tōmicho of the Jinto Brokers Association.

41. *Chōsen kōrōsha meikan*, p. 196.

42. *Donga Ilbo*, April 2, 1923, p. 2. On the occasion of a discussion at the Jinto on the transfer proposal, officials of the Government-General established their position of authority, interest in consolidation, but reluctance.

43. *Donga Ilbo*, November 6, 1923, pp. 2-3. The petition to the Ministry of Development [Siksanbu] by the Coalition to Block the Transfer of the Jinsen Exchange to Seoul [Jinto Keijō iden bōshikai] was reported in the *Donga Ilbo* of November 10, 1923, p. 3.

44. The Jinto Association of Brokers published a position paper on the transfer, reported in *Donga Ilbo*, February 21, 1925, p.4. A task force was

then organized at the Association led by Kobayashi and Asano Taisaburō. *Donga Ilbo*, April 16, 1925, p. 4. A citizen protest against the opposition of the Jinsen Brokers Association was reported in the *Donga Ilbo* of April 26, 1925, p. 3. Petitions against the merger were reported in *Donga Ilbo*, April 26, 1925, pp. 2-3. Election of Chang as chair of the "Councilors [p'yŏngwiwŏnhoe]" was reported in *Donga Ilbo*, September 21, 1924, p. 4.

45. *Donga Ilbo*, July 8, 1926, p. 6; July 9, 1926, p. 6.

46. *Donga Ilbo*, July 11, 1926, p.6. Chang Sŏk-u joined Yi Dong-jin and two Japanese as lead speaker at an anti-transfer rally. *Donga Ilbo*, July 13, 1926, p. 6.

47. *Donga Ilbo*, July 14, 1926, p. 6.

48. The demonstrations are reported in the following issues of the *Donga Ilbo*: March 26, March 27, and March 31, 1927. Noguchi was a vice-president of the Jinsen Chamber of Commerce at the time. *Kusimnyŏnsa*, pp. 301-302. Yoshida Hidejirō and Noguchi were on the board of Karai Eitarō's Chosen Match Company. TGKY, 1921, p. 20. Noguchi, Chang Sŏk-u, and Yoshida were all on the board and major shareholders in the Seoul-based Jinsen Mutual Finance Company [Jinsen Muji Kabushiki Kaisha] under president Karai. CGKKY 1922, p. 51. Rikimu's disruption of the stockholders meeting apparently infuriated President Wakamatsu, but the more serious issue was the demonstration outside, forcing a order from the police to disperse the crowd. *Chōsen kōrōsha meikan*, p. 199.

49. *Donga Ilbo*, April 21, 1927, p. 6. The order of Keikki [Kyŏnggi] Province Governor Yoneda can be found in *Chōsen kōrōsha meikan*, p. 201.

50. *Donga Ilbo*, April 24, 1927, p. 6. The boycotts were initiated by the Brokers Association at the Seoul Exchange, and scheduled from April 24 until May 12.

51. *Chōsen kōrōsha meikan*, p. 201.

52. *Donga Ilbo*, March 14, 1928, p. 7; July 19, 1928, p. 8. The report of a press interview with Mr. Nagata, an official with the Ministry of Commerce and Industry in Tokyo, can be found in *Donga Ilbo*, July 28, 1928, p. 6.

53. Reports submitted by the Federation of Public Officials [Kōshokusha Rengōkai] Committee of Stockholders in Opposition [Hantai Kabunushi Dōmeikai], Jinsen Promotion Association[Jinsenfusei Shinkōkai], Assembly of Citizens [Fumin Taikai], and the Federation of Neighborhood Representatives [Chōri Sōtaikai] can be found in the Jinsen Chamber's *gōjunenshi*, pp. 97-107. Efforts of the Federation of Public Officials were reported in the *Donga Ilbo*, July 11, 1926, p. 6; January 9, 1931, p. 7; September 15, 1931, p. 8. Activities of the Committee of Stockholders in Opposition were reported in the *Donga Ilbo* of January 8, 1931, p. 7, and September 15, 1931, p. 8. A campaign to purchase shares of stockholders supporting the transfer was also reported in *Donga Ilbo*, June 27, 1929, p. 4.

54. *Gojunenshi*, p. 106.

55. See *Gojunenshi*, p. 109. The remarkably large warchest prepared by the opposition was reported in the *Donga Ilbo*, December 24, 1930, p. 7.

56. Reports of the Federation's activities, and the participation of still other groups such as the Assembly of Jinsen Citizens [Jinsen Fumin Taikai] can be found in *Donga Ilbo*, January 9, 1931, p.7; January 11, 1931, p. 7; September 15, 1931, p. 8.

57. *Gojunenshi*, pp. 113-114.

58. *Gojunenshi*, p. 112.

59. For a report of the press interview with Mr. Nagata, an official with the Ministry of commerce and Industry in Tokyo announcing the legislation stipulating the merger, see *Donga Ilbo* of July 28, 1928, p. 6. Details of the new Exchange Law [Torihikishorei] and enforcement procedures [shikō kensoku] are provided in *Donga Ilbo*, September 11, 1931, p. 8, and September 12, p. 8.

60. CGKKY 1932, pp. 363-364.

61. See petitions of May 13, 1929, February 23, 1930, and March 15, 1930, in *Gojunenshi*, pp. 98-106. See also petitions of early 1930 reprinted in *Chōsen Torihikijokai*, pp. 72-75.

62. *Donga Ilbo*, June 17, 1926, p. 6.

63. *Donga Ilbo*, July 11, 1926, p. 6.

64. *Donga Ilbo*, February 21, 1925, p. 4. See also a report in the *Osaka Asahi Shimbun* on the effect of the merger on local exchanges, March 14, 1928, p. 7.

65. *Donga Ilbo*, November 6, 1923, p. 2. Tennichi was identified as chair of the Keijo Grain Sales Association [Keijō Kokubutsushō Kumiai].

66. *Donga Ilbo*, August 12, 1923, p.2; March 23, 1924, p. 4; March 14, 1928, p. 7.

67. The interview with Governor-General Saitō was reported in the *Donga Ilbo*, August 23, 1923, p. 2. For other government statements about the questions of state versus private ownership of the Exchanges see *Donga Ilbo*, April 2, 1923, p. 2, and July 6, 1928, p. 6.

68. *Donga Ilbo*, April 23, 1924, p. 2.

69. *Donga Ilbo*, April 2, 1923, p. 2; August 23, 1923, p. 2; April 21, 1927,p. 6; January 9, 1931, p. 7.

70. *Donga Ilbo*, July 11, 1926, p. 6.

71. *Donga Ilbo*, June 17, 1926, p. 6.

72. The issue was discussed at the Jinsen Business Club [Jinsen Kurabu]. *Donga Ilbo*, February 25, 1925, p. 4.

73. *Donga Ilbo*, June 17, 1926, p. 4.

74. In a joint press conference of 1928, the presidents of the two Exchanges acknowledged that the recession would make the merger more difficult, and that the Exchanges would likely remain.

75. See for instance the statement of the Jinto Brokers Association in *Donga Ilbo*, February 21, 1925, p. 4.

76. See the interview with Governor-General Saitō Makoto in *Donga Ilbo*, March 23, 1924, p. 4.

77. *Donga Ilbo*, December 1, 1923, p. 3.

78. *Donga Ilbo*, March 23, 1924, p. 4.

8

Transformation

Plying their trade within a circle of locally owned and managed firms, business associations, and chartered colonial institutions, Koreans found a place in an international commerce in grains from the late nineteenth century. Traditions of ethnic continuity, close cooperation with political authorities, commerce and guild solidarity helped meld and maintain a Korean business community at Inch'ŏn. New patterns of law and contract, business-state ties, of corporations and chartered, semi-official firms in the colony brought the brokers into an interstate and intermarket colonial system. Accommodation on the one side, and precedents of enterprise and association on the other help account for the rise of a Korean chaegye distinct from the Japanese zaikai, subordinate to them in capital and technology, and cooperating with them at peak associations and chartered, semi-official firms.

Brokers prospered in the extension of international commerce to the peninsula which fostered the growing autonomy and legitimacy of markets, and more specifically, the ideas and organization of brokers. Issues of public versus private goods, of state and society, and of the autonomy of markets raised in the trade debate in the late kingdom returned with a vengeance in the transfer controversy of the 1920s at the Jinsen Grain Exchange or "Jinto." The latter struggle between official and private spheres presses us beyond market to group formation in the nascent civil society of the port city. A discourse of dissent, new forms of protest, and the consolidation of contending forces in the business community at Inch'ŏn offer evidence of private versus official interests and organizations, with efforts in the private sector to mobilize a "public" voice through associations of smaller merchants and the wider populace. The significance of the transformation from society to market lies both in the consolidation of the chaegye and in early forms of civil society.

Constraints imposed on dissent even among the well-established zaikai evident in the modulated forms of contention at the Jinto highlight limits on autonomous association in the colony, but also pose the anomaly of distinct interests without independent association. Rowe's insight of "negotiation" between state control and associational autonomy would suggest some latitude for establishing functional interests arising out of the mandate of the business community for productive enterprise necessary for the state's legitimacy. The Jinto transfer proposal encouraged by the colonial authorities divided the zaikai, with the Inch'ŏn chaegye joining the opposition to save the Exchange for their port. The ultimate compromise reflected state recognition of organized interests in both camps and room for diversity on issues in which the expertise of the business community was critical. We might extend Rowe's insight to suggest negotiation of associational autonomy and state control may well depend on interest group resources and expertise, as well as on the importance of their participation for wider state goals. One thing is clear: the colonial state desperately needed marketers to maintain the commerce in grains.

The transformation in Korea across seven decades from 1876 fostered new social structures such as professional associations of merchants. Markets gained greater scope and legitimacy through the institutionalizing of their credibility beyond personal or family or regional relationships, as well as through the extension of capital. The restructuring of trust in markets through law and contract, corporation and association, banks and Exchanges made possible the leap from spot sales to futures so critical in the expansion of the grain trade. Imperial expansion and authoritarian rule precluded a more consistent, integrated transformation of both authority and exchange, and severely constrained the transition in markets as evident even in tensions between the capitalist priorities of the zaikai and the imperial goals of the Government-General. The contradiction of market transformation without democratic reform limited the consolidation of colonial civil society even under the "cultural rule" of Admiral Saitō Makoto. Autonomous interests struggled to gain ground in the cauldron of fast changing ideas of exchange but tightly defined and brutally imposed norms of political authority.

Centralization consistent with Henderson's "vortex theory" distinguished both late kingdom and colony, but with what Mann terms "despotic power" in the former, and "infrastructural power" in the latter.

The fading of despotic rule following the Kabo Reforms of 1894 permitted an initial reshaping of state-business ties among the brokers prior to annexation, but the broader transformation towards greater legitimacy and credibility of market and marketers would only come with the economic institutions of the colony. Chartered, semi-official firms served as instruments of colonial state policy without burdening the state treasury. Semi-official status permitted more than economy, however, for the harnessing of private investment to public goals in the chartered firms also rooted state ties in the business community. The state in effect rooted itself in the zaikai and chaegye not solely by legislation stipulating state oversight in business association and chartered firm, but by serving as a coinvestor and codirector of the major economic institutions. Robinson and Gallagher cited the benefits and efficiencies of informal colonialism through economic hegemony as opposed to the huge investment of capital and administration necessary for formal colonial rule.[1] What we find in Korea is formal colonial rule in the polity but more informal rule in the market where the state allied with the Japanese zaikai in developing infrastructure and institution, and in that alliance the local chaegye gained at least limited economic opportunity despite political exclusion.[2] The state strategy of accommodation secured access to effective networks of information and enterprise within the business community, but also allowed the business community more of a voice in economic policy.

Cumings' thesis of the overdevelopment of infrastructure characterizes the investment of the Government-General allied with the Japanese zaikai in colonial projects with imperial goals. Exclusion of Koreans from middle and higher level administration in the projects until the Pacific War clearly resulted in an underdevelopment of local institutions, and institutions, not infrastructures, remain the central challenge of development. The building of infrastructures cannot be equated with institution-building, particularly in a colony with a large Japanese population under strong Japanese institutional controls. However impressive one may find the statistics on ports, roads, railways and postal communications, or on the activities of banks, Exchanges, and warehouses, such profiles are less significant than their actual operations, their personnel and clientele, and their effect on other organizations and ideas of exchange. A few institutions such as the Grain Exchange pioneered and fostered patterns of contract and law, business-state ties, and even professionalism in the business community that converged with earlier precedents of enterprise and association among the Korean brokers, and some of these institutions survived in some form long after liberation. Even in the few cases of relatively successful institutionalization such as business chambers, their histories reflect not only Korean precedents but societal dynamics that garner little attention in studies of colonial state direction in the economy.

Incorporation

A growing distinction from the state across kingdom and colony, from Japanese zaikai in the colony, and from emerging local interest groups of labor, intellectuals, and even agrarian producers all played a part in strengthening cohesion among the port chaegye. Japanese attempts at assimilation along the French colonial model made little headway in a colony deprived of political voice and constrained in market relations. Yanaihara eloquently contrasted the rhetoric of assimilation among colonial administrators with the reality of distinction and subordination, yet we cannot overlook the fact of limited accommodation evident in state policy and business practice, whether born of necessity or the unintended result of delayed assimilation efforts. What lay behind paternalism in the economy and authoritarianism in the polity was the belief that Koreans must first be "Japanized" and only then accepted as equals.[3] Serious attempts at acculturation in the waning years of colonial rule brought little change to patterns of distinction among the medium- and small-scale millers despite imposition of even stronger state controls in the wartime economy.

Fortified with a heritage of commercial practices, markets controls, and supply networks Korean brokers bartered and traded across an interlude of ethnic separation and foreign competition in the decades preceding annexation. The same years found the Korean monarchy deploying the brokers with semi-official tasks for collection of duties and with government-authorized market responsibilities in an effort to regain control of the grain trade. But the curious dynamic of distinction or separation from official sectors within the wider process of colonial incorporation can be traced to more than long-standing local patterns of organization and enterprise. If we look to Japanese business practices as a cause of distinction, we find the pace and timing of incorporation demanded rapid deployment of Japanese business networks on the peninsula and quick integration of the Korean grain markets. Events on and about the peninsula left the Meiji state and zaikai a free hand to put in place their own currency and banking system, transport networks, business associations, and even a Japanese grain exchange on the peninsula well before annexation. States and business associations, as well as enterprise separated Korean broker from Japanese trader through 1910, and a single alien state on the peninsula thereafter did little to reverse the separation of association and enterprise between Korean and Japanese business circles, despite decreeing the combined but unequal chambers from 1915.

But if the consolidation of a non-official sphere was gaining headway in kingdom and especially in colony, how did it affect interest and profession at the ports? Brokers in the waning years of the kingdom of Chosŏn appeared far more confident of ethnic distinction from the foreigners than they were of recognition from the Korean monarchy of their distinctive role or legitimate interests in profit. Language and ideas, enterprise and association provided a clear boundary between Korean brokers and Japanese traders. A long history of market controls by the monarchy, the ideological emphasis on the commonweal and disdain for private interests, and the efforts of the ruler to enlist the brokers as a frontline defense against Japanese economic encroachment discouraged distinction between a public "interest" and the private "interests" of the brokers. Semi-official commerce associations finally broke the earlier pattern of chartered and controlled guilds, but still did not provide the organizational resources brokers needed to forge their own interests in enterprise and market as distinct from a public interest. Yet we cannot ignore the importance of these hesitant, initial steps in the journey from guild to chamber. Aspirations for civil society separate from the state were apparent among intellectuals at the turn of the century, and the brokers were not far behind.

Mills, the Inch'ŏn Brokers' Association, and the Rice Sales Association under Chu Myŏng-gi provided an organizational base of distinction for the Korean brokers in the colony that was lacking in the kingdom. Enterprise and association gave the brokers a solid footing in cooperation and even limited competition with Japanese business circles, but the colonial context presented altogether different problems of interest formation for the fledgling interest group of Korean brokers, hustling to find a niche in the shadow of the Japanese traders. Korean intellectuals looked to entrepreneurs to sustain a broad national or ethnic interest, leaving brokers with the unenviable task of harmonizing their private interests with this undefined national interest, and that under an alien regime. Unlike dissident intellectuals, brokers at the ports could not afford options of isolation or exile. At the same time the colonial regime confronted the chaegye with a new challenge of somehow aligning their private interests with imperial priorities in market integration and expansion. And no doubt the most nagging problem of interests for the Korean brokers was the unequal competition with the Japanese. Sustained primarily by their own enterprise but also by business associations, the brokers moved warily among far better funded and organized Japanese traders where they had no choice but to risk their mills and agencies in the crucible of competition.

The rise of a Korean business community at Inch'ŏn gave notice of local interest formation critical for the development of a profession. Brokers even under alien rule had begun to crystallize their ideas of private profits consonant with the public interest and strengthen their bases of enterprise and association vis-à-vis other interest groups. Yet we can cite still other factors shaping the passage from chartered guild to more professional chamber and trade association among the brokers. The Merchants' Firm at Inch'ŏn was a far cry from the colonial Korean Brokers Association, yet these were more or less the same brokers in the same city in the same trade. We cited causes for the transition above, and here look only to the significance of the change. Problems of structure and attitude hampered the growth of professionalism among the brokers at the end of the kingdom. The absence of a legal framework of commercial law, or of substantive legal procedures in international markets to govern their trade at Inch'ŏn stymied professional organization. With neither a legal framework to define and govern their enterprise, nor an effective enforcement agency to insure contract in commercial transactions, the brokers stood alone in an unfamiliar world of international commerce at the ports. The reluctance of the monarchy to recognize the distinctive interests and contributions of the brokers further hampered their development as a profession. Given the context, I find precedents of organization all the more remarkable in the turbulent decades prior to annexation.

Colonization from 1910 brought a new challenge to the brokers of both professional development and adaptation to alien rule in polity and market. We can point to the joint mandate for grading and sorting grains, shared by Japanese Grain Association and the Korean Brokers' Association, as evidence of professional development in standardizing exchange, and of adjustment to Japanese dominance in the markets. We can look back to broker participation in both their own Association, and in the combined chamber as evidence of professionalism and adjustment in association beyond individual enterprise. Colonization challenged the brokers to develop expertise in both enterprise and association. The tasks were closely related for the mills and brokerages could not prosper without a secure niche in the grain trade supported by associations. Nor was this simply individual entrepreneurship where a role in sorting and grading would assure the brokers and millers a place in an expanding trade in grains, for Koreans had to adjust to a Japanese system of measurement and grading, and to the vagaries of demand and prices in Osaka and Tokyo. Incorporation demanded not just more professional organization but a reorientation to Japanese dynamics of supply and demand.

What we learn of market and society tells us as well of Korea's path of incorporation into a new interstate and intermarket system of international capitalism. One insight draws us back to the long tenure of the Chosŏn Dynasty, to the fading of the Chinese Empire, and to the rise of Japan as a regional power. Trade and diplomatic ties with Japan as "neighbor" can be traced for nearly two centuries prior to the opening, which coupled with the fact of similar Japanese efforts elsewhere indicate the shift was in process well before the Kanghwa Treaty (1876). Secondly, Hagen Koo has contrasted the economic integration of Latin American with the political integration of Korea and Taiwan under U.S. hegemony in the 1950s, but if we look back still earlier to Korea's initial integration into an international capitalist system, we find a blend of economic and political priorities.[4] Attention to market reminds us that Korea's incorporation was undertaken with economic as well as political goals, and that the Korean peninsula was far more important economically to Japan at the turn of the last century than to the U.S. by the middle of this century. The chronicle of transformation in Korea suggests also that long-term political goals of colonial control and integration could only be achieved within markets.

Incorporation of Korean society under Japanese economic and political rule fostered distinction among the brokers with their own enterprise, associations, and "interests" in profit and growth. Themes of *kwanmin* and chaegye etch out a profile of change spurred by integration into a new regional system, but do they tell us of transformation beyond Korea, or of the comparative utility of the Korean experience? Only a focus on local societal histories and on the interaction of colonizer and colonized can uncover dynamics of accommodation, assimilation, or extinction deeply affecting the ideas and organizations of the local markets. A similar focus on development histories including ideologies and organizations of other periphery states would strengthen our understanding of consolidation in world-systems and transformation in local societies. Moreover, two factors significant in the profile above of distinction, subordination, and cooperation must be recognized in any comparative analysis. The long tenure of the Chosŏn Dynasty (1392-1910) within the same stable borders across five centuries finds little parallel in East or West. Precedents of association and enterprise, and of bureaucratic oversight of commerce carry a remarkably long pedigree in Korea. In contrast, the Korean colonial experience was relatively brief compared to the duration of Western colonization in Southeast Asia, the Middle East, and Latin America. And even during the brief thirty-five year rule of Japan on the Korean peninsula, the role of the colony within the expanding empire changed dramatically in 1931 with the penetration of Manchuria, and then again with World War II ten years later. A longer colonial rule with more consistent priorities may well have permitted greater efforts at assimilation.

Embedded Ties

Subordination to the Japanese traders in the fading years of the Korean polity did not immediately advance local expertise in foreign standards and grading systems, nor in stable trade associations with professional mandates and adequate resources, and certainly not in the organization of large-scale, competitive firms. One problem for local merchants was the strategy of the monarchy in mobilizing the brokers to recover Korean sovereignty in the trade, rather than reorienting the brokers to more competitive forms of enterprise and association for management of open markets. Another problem was with the brokers themselves who reverted to earlier patterns of guild controls and monopolies rather than improving supplies and sales in competition with the Chinese and Japanese traders. Yet foreign economic and political penetration would have severely tested any more positive initiative of the monarchy or adjustment of brokers, and would quickly have undone any changes which did not align with priorities of expanding grain supplies for the markets of the home islands. And despite the rapid erosion of Korean sovereignty in the economy of the peninsula between 1876 and 1910, one can point to significant but inconsistent efforts towards more professional organization among the brokers such as Commerce Associations and the early Korean chambers.

A more positive picture of professional development can be gleaned from the early years of the colony, although clearly with precolonial roots. One finds brokers like Chu Myŏng-gi, Yi Hŭng-sŏn, and Yu Kun-sŏng moving between commerce and light industry with growing expertise in both areas. Similarly, one finds the brokers in the Inch'ŏn Brokers' Association adjusting and developing expertise to maintain a place in the market, and one cannot ignore the professionalism of the Korean brokers taking part in the combined chamber to gain a voice in the economic policies of the colonial state. Professionalism gained in a dependent situation is significant, but so too is the linking of professionalism and distinction in enterprise with cooperation. Millers like Chu, Yi and Yu could not have maintained such successful enterprise, nor gained the necessary expertise in procurement of machinery, large-scale consignment sales, and capital investment without ties to state-dominated finance and transport networks. Chu and Yi could develop their mills and secure a place in the market in part because of their status within the Jinsen Grain Association of Okuda. The Brokers' Association could enhance its expertise in Japanese methods of sorting and grading in large part because of its connection with the Jinsen Grain Association. A subordinate business circle can maintain distinction with its own set of enterprises and associations, but institutional isolation would quickly lead to extinction in the grain trade.

The comparative significance of the Korean experience lies neither in discrimination nor in economic collaboration, but rather in the simultaneous dynamic of separation and reintegration. Masters at their mills rather than compradors, the Korean brokers still had to cooperate to remain in a grain trade oriented to Japanese markets. Separation in enterprise and association between Japanese and Korean millers and brokers made possible the intersection of interests and activities termed here "cooperation," such as joint grain sorting responsibilities between Grain Association and Inch'ŏn Brokers Association, or lobbying against the Jinto transfer. Secondly, subordination of the Korean millers to major Japanese millers and traders further defined or "limited" cooperation of the smaller Korean millers with their larger Japanese counterparts. Full cooperation would suggest an interdependence and equality which was simply not to be found among the Korean brokers. We do find minority Korean participation in the direction of the combined chamber, and as noted above, and in at least four among the twenty-five seats on the Jinsen branch of the Chosen Exchange.

In colony as in kingdom, institutional cooperation between chaegye and zaikai played a major role in the grain trade. Trade associations give direction, continuity, and even definition to the basic interests of enterprise. A broker is interested in turning a profit today and tomorrow, but an association can focus on long-term development of markets which will insure continued profits for its member brokers. Cooperation between Japanese and Korean enterprises in the same professions may well result in mutual benefit, but given the discontinuities in scale and of ties with core consumer and capital markets between Japanese and Korean firms, close cooperation at the level of firms alone might well result in a Japanese takeover of the smaller Korean enterprise. Cooperation among trade associations permits maintenance of the interests of their separate memberships, even while pursuing joint tasks. A network of separate small and medium-scale Korean enterprises and associations made possible limited cooperation with larger Japanese firms which did not threaten the separate interests of the Inch'ŏn Brokers Association or the Rice Sales Association. Associations with some control over markets and members permit insulation from destructive competition among member firms and even larger firms of cooperating associations, without isolation. Similarly, limited cooperation among associations permits individual member firms some protection from the discrepancies in competitive power between larger and smaller firms.

I find limited cooperation significant not simply as a mode of survival, but as a road to professionalism for the chaegye. The thrust into international grain markets forced initial steps towards greater professionalism even in the last years of the kingdom. Moving quickly from monopoly control of markets to competition and cooperation with Chinese and Japanese traders, and then to subordination and cooperation with Japanese buyers prior to 1910, the brokers had begun the journey to more professional organization. Neither intellectuals nor the state offered the brokers any road map for this remarkable passage. Brokers did not join in these efforts on the basis of a clear collective design for expanding enterprise or regaining markets, but rather had to piece together enterprise and association to remain viable in a very competitive grain market at the ports dominated by the Japanese.

The Korean experience of change at the ports helps unravel the anomalies of interpenetration between state and society in a colonial context. Kohli's theme of distinction between state and private sector, and reintegration offers a path for explaining the colonial political economy rather than simply polity, and nudges us beyond sterile debates over "collaboration," "dependence," or "colonial hegemony."[5] States need entrepreneurs in any market economy, and the Japanese Government-General secure in its control of polity, banking and finance, welcomed private investment and expertise to expand trade. A profile of distinction and cooperation captures the colonial pattern of embedding ties between state and the private sector. When this insight turns attention back to what Mann terms the "infrastructural" power of the state in fostering effective coalitions for market growth, whether in semi-official firms or business associations, we learn of state, society, and the chaegye. But rather than assessing infrastructural power and policies, Kohli makes an unsuccessful attempt to draw out the colonial legacies for subsequent growth with weak parallels between the "developmental" states of post-war Japan or post-1960 South Korea with an admittedly brutal colonial administration dedicated to imperial goals. In contrast, attention to what he termed "competing legacies" would lead us beyond tenuous comparisons to a clearer understanding of more subtle continuities and discontinuities in the historical record.

The work of Peter Evans on effective linkages between a directive state and local economic elites leads beyond state autonomy and the consequent dangers of isolation from the central actors in the local market.[6] His recent thesis of autonomy and connection offers a useful foil for the study of indigenous Korean enterprise in the colony where isolation would lead only to extinction. But if we can assume capacity and relative autonomy for a strong colonial state, both features were problematic for the local brokers hard pressed to consolidate the resources necessary for effective competition and state recognition of their market role and expertise. Professionalism nurtured in association and enterprise was their institutional path to both economic viability and a limited role in shaping market policy. A focus on embedded ties between state and the chaegye contributes also to still broader comparative theses such as Woo's characterization of colonial rule as authoritarian corporatism.[7] Carefully designed corporatist ties between a dominant state and weak private sector with state authorized and even subsidized peak associations bring us back to association and enterprise within a distinct but nonetheless constrained sphere of private enterprise. I find greater comparative utility in corporatist continuities between colonial and post-1960 states in Korea than in strained parallels between alien and local developmental states.[8] One premise of embedded ties and of the effort to specify corporatist continuities is the dual focus on state and society. Addressing the imbalance of state-centric approaches, Migdal has recently written of "interactions of state and society that are mutually transforming."[9] Although mutuality between local state and society differs greatly from the interplay between a colonizing state and local society, efforts to specify the structures and results of the latter interaction will strengthen our understanding of colonial legacies.

Legacies

Expansion into Manchuria from 1931 turned the peninsula into a forward base for military expansion, but also for integration of the Manchurian frontier with the markets of core and colony. The years leading up to the Pacific War witnessed further expansion in the rice trade, and consolidation of the business communities at the ports under tighter state controls as rice exports grew to forty-five million tons in 1934 and peaked at fifty-five million tons in 1937. Patterns of distinction persisted but dependence deepened as the state extended control over local markets. Constraints on machinery supplies and controls on energy consumption led to consolidation of the mills by the 1940s.[10] Liberation from colonial rule in 1945 severed links between Japanese buyers for markets in Osaka and Tokyo, and the Korean suppliers at the port cities of Inch'ŏn and Pusan. The First Republic of Korea (1948-1960), established on the southern section of a peninsula now divided by ideology and polity, allied with the Western capitalist powers and survived a brutal war with the Socialist regime to the north (1950-1953).

Isolated from Japanese markets and ravaged by war, grain exports were beyond the capacity of the First Republic preoccupied with feeding the population and rebuilding a shattered industrial base, and the Republic would remain a net importer of grains as it expanded into an export base for light manufactures. The shift from agricultural exporter to importer left the mills under close state supervision, with the Inch'ŏn mills surviving mainly as government contractors for cleaning and storage of aid-supported grain imports. In time technological improvements and rural electrification programs would permit more efficient milling closer to grain production sites further eroding the role of the mills at the port cities. A few entrepreneurs like Sin Tŏg-gyun of the Dongbang Corporation continued as millers into the First Republic even as they diversified into other areas of industrial investment, but most millers had transferred their capital and expertise into other areas.[11] We do not find an extensive legacy of enterprise from the colonial brokers and millers, but rather a legacy of entrepreneurial experience and association.

Chambers were quickly reorganized at the port cities and Seoul following liberation from colonial rule and served as the central forum for a business lobby throughout the First Republic. I would point to the chambers as a significant institutional continuity among the port chaegye who had made the journey from guild to combined chamber, and finally to the Korean chambers of the First Republic. Economic controls of the Rhee state again threatened the distinction between state and civil society in the immediate postcolonial years. Colonial state ownership of utilities and railroads reverted to the Rhee government, as did all Japanese-owned industrial and commercial properties. Even as the government sold off the properties to selected local entrepreneurs, the base of enterprise among the business community remained frail in contrast to the extensive properties of the government. Associations represented one of the best hopes for maintaining identity and cohesion among business elites in the face of strong state controls and ownership in the economy.

Chambers established a format for cooperation in the business community, and provided a forum for discussions of government economic policy. The discussions quickly returned to unresolved issues of state direction and control over private enterprise, and the balance between public interest and private interests. The *kwanmin* theme of "officials and citizens" continued in the recommendations of the Chamber of Commerce & Industry in Seoul in the First Republic, though now with greater emphasis on participation of private enterprise in the formation of government policy.[12] Far from protesting state intervention, the chamber campaigned for more efficient direction and more extensive support. Economic stability, support for private enterprise, and "rational, comprehensive" direction remained prominent themes throughout the early Republics.[13] Local state recognition of a "private" or autonomous sector within a war or reconstruction economy proved difficult but necessary, if for no other reason than to gain legitimacy as a democratic alternative on the peninsula and placate Western aid donors.[14]

Structured reciprocity between business association and state bureaucracy permitted state supervision on the one hand, and some advisory role for business in state economic policy on the other, but clearly the state was the senior partner.[15] A feature editorial in the Chamber's *Sanŏp Kyŏngje* of June, 1949 gave notice of a prominent state role with a remarkable argument for "planned capitalism" under state leadership as a temporary expedient to foster an autonomous national economy. The author took pains to distance his advocacy of government planning to support private enterprise from government control of the private sector. But Chamber President Chŏn Yong-sun signalled a more adversarial role for private enterprise in the same journal a year later with criticism of government expenditure coupled with a decline in foreign aid. The Rhee government finally pressured the Chamber to remove Chŏn two years later, and with Chŏn's departure, the Chamber quickly softened its criticism but continued to campaign for private enterprise. The Chamber often faulted the state for weak support of private capital and advocated confidence-building measures to stimulate private investment.[16] They supported stabilization and liberalization of controls on finance and access to foreign capital in efforts to stimulate local investment.[17] The Chamber also raised a familiar colonial theme of efficiency: ever more rational government planning.[18] Nonetheless, frequent, irregular government interventions continued to pester private enterprise, and apart from a few major entrepreneurs in sugar, flour, and textile production, business groups found it difficult to gain added leverage with the government due to their weak base of enterprise. The business community could not muster an autonomous voice in the political economy of the First Republic.

Three continuities in ties between state and business community can be drawn across late kingdom, colony, and early Republic. The principle of impersonal contract and the formal structure of law appeared problematic across the all three periods. Difficulties of legal separation from the state and autonomy for the business community were apparent in the late years of the kingdom. A colonial administration imposed clear laws defining the role of the business community, but now with close state controls to insure alignment with imperial markets, and without substantive political voice. A local administration in the First Republic intervened in the procedures of the chamber as necessary to insure chamber alignment with the priorities of the Rhee state. Personal relations and extra-legal or illegal favors played a major role in the disbursement of state-owned properties to Korean entrepreneurs.[19]

A dominant state role in the economy also runs as a motif from the late nineteenth century through the First Republic and beyond in South Korea. State intervention has hampered development of cohesion and clear common interests among the business community. States in each of the three periods did little to maintain clear distinctions between public and private interests. The monarchy hesitated in defining and trying to mobilize the population in pursuit of a national or public good during the years of fading sovereignty. Japanese authorities imposed an alien definition of the imperial good during the colonial period. Definitions of the public good under the Rhee regime in the First Republic often coincided closely with the survival of his Liberal Party, fostering strong skepticism among the populace. Interest associations among Korean business circles suggest a third motif across the three periods, with varying degrees of distinction from the polity, dependence on government or foreign economic powers, and participation in international markets.

Limited continuities persisted despite dramatic discontinuities in state authority, and in ties with foreign markets and polities. Attention to both organization and ideas permits a structural focus on enterprise and association without losing sight of the ideological developments which give direction to these structures. Problems of civil society in colony and Republic will continue to gain attention as we move beyond polity to society in the study of Korea's modern history. Closer attention to labor, intellectuals, religious groups, and landowners would fill out the sketch we have begun here of society at the turn of the century.

Comparative Colonialism

The chronicle of the port brokers draw us across colonies beyond Korea, and across time within Korea. A transition from cultural empire to colonial system in Korea suggests an imperialism quite unlike that found in dependencies of the West. Efforts to distinguish Japanese colonialism from Western patterns of expansion and control reveal differences in goals, strategies, and character of colonial rule. Edwin Winckler distinguished between goals of "external political incorporation" into an interstate system negotiated largely by state elites across nations, and "internal political incorporation" into patterns of local rule negotiated between elites and masses within a particular nation.[20] He concluded that external political incorporation took priority over internal incorporation in the colony of Taiwan, citing the persistence of the Japanese as the significant political elite in the colony, and at best only partial political incorporation of the local elite into the home islands. The fact of weak Japanese links to the markets and traders in Taiwan prior to annexation support his argument. Tom Gold pointed to the absence of strong Japanese ties with local classes prior to annexation in Taiwan where unlike Western colonizers, the Japanese had no long-standing mercantile interests to protect.[21]

Interstate priorities, and the absence of extensive, long-standing Japanese mercantile interests on the peninsula likewise characterize incorporation of Korea. Although we can identify political and economic collaborators already within the early colony, they did not command the resources nor respect to effectively reorient the local population towards imperial goals. It was not only a long history of domestic autonomy on the peninsula, but also the absence of a well-established pro-Japanese elite that doomed early efforts at political integration of the largely rural population. And quite apart from supporters or opponents on the peninsula, imperial commitment to Japanese security across a regional interstate system beyond Korea overrode concerns for political assimilation of the colonized, and provided a rationale for control rather than assimilation. But the priority on external incorporation did not deter efforts at economic integration of the grain markets, nor did the absence of Japanese-affiliated local mercantile interest on the peninsula prevent the rise of local brokers in the grain trade. On the contrary, rapid Japanese economic expansion at the ports brought consumer needs from the home islands to the Korean countryside as Japanese traders conveyed a demand for local grains that they alone could not meet, and opened opportunities for local mercantile interests without previous ties to the Japanese.

Apart from goals, the Japanese strategy of penetration likewise permitted a role for the earlier circles of brokers at the ports, but not for local political elites. Extensive immigration to the peninsula, a large administration, and comprehensive Japanese control of finance, business, and trade networks resulted in far more extensive penetration of the colony than was common in cases of Western imperialism.[22] Samuel Ho reflected:

> Unlike other colonial powers that relied heavily on native administrations, the colonial governments and Japanese corporations imported large amounts of human capital from Japan -- competent and loyal personnel to place in higher and lower echelons of the colonial establishment, to manage both the government and the economy.[23]

But if the strategy left little opportunity for Korean leadership at government bureau or major enterprise, it did not push local brokers or millers out of the grain trade. The grain trade was particularly important for linking the breadth of the local economy to markets in Japan. Cal Clark has pointed to economic integration of Taiwan into the Japanese home islands as evidence of Taiwan's status as "periphery" but not "enclave."[24] Similarly, extensive penetration of the Korean agrarian economy, and the linkage of subsequent industrialization projects in the colony to the home islands did not replicate enclave patterns found in colonies of Western imperial powers. People, proximity, and products determined the extent of integration. We noted above extensive Japanese immigration for commercial purposes, as well as regional proximity, but the items of trade likewise deeply affected the lives of the rural Korean peasantry.   As apart from traders of luxury items or specialized agricultural goods, local brokers and millers worked in the commerce and trade of grains planted, tilled, and harvested by the vast majority of the Korean population. Indeed, the Japanese interest in Korean grains, in contrast to their priority on sugar in Taiwan, bought the colonizers even deeper into the lifeblood of the Korean economy than in Taiwan.

Japanese accommodation of rural production networks offers another point of contrast to Western styles of reorganization into new networks of production and distribution dominated by the colonizers.[25] Rather than reorganizing land and cultivation into large-scale, colonial plantations, the Japanese appeared content to simply draw off the products of a local network. Certainly there were investments to increase grain production through irrigation and fertilizers, and we could point to large-scale Japanese investment inland in Korea, although even these agricultural estates maintained patterns of tenant farming.   On the whole, the colonizers accommodated even when they owned and operated estates as long as the local network did not hinder integration of the local economy with demand in the home islands. But accommodation in the former "hermit kingdom" of Korea did not permit insulation of the brokers and millers in the grain trade, and much less isolation. Chinese merchants on Java could sustain control and expand their role in the grain trade with the Dutch due to the small numbers of Dutch commercial settlers, and to the difficulty of language, transportation, rural settlement for the Europeans.   With the Dutch largely confined to management of international trade and shipping, Chinese networks of brokerage and milling remained relatively insulated from competition. Taiwanese grain brokers and millers likewise faced little competition from the Japanese through the first few decades in the colony as the sugar industry absorbed most of the Japanese investment and manpower. Again, the Japanese in the early grain trade in Taiwan were largely limited to international trade and transport. Korean brokers and millers in rice and soybeans, however, faced the full brunt of Japanese immigration, investment, and association on the peninsula, surviving the competition only by finding their own niche of enterprise and association.

Turning from goals and strategy to the character of Japan's colonialism in Korea, features such as centralized, rapid, and brief come immediately to mind. Gann argued that "Japanese rule, with its centralizing tradition, its weakening parliamentary restraints, and its commitments to etatisme -- the priority of the state over the individual citizen -- in some respects followed the French rather than the British pattern."[26] Fieldhouse questioned the easy distinction between British accommodation and French assimilation, but did point out a conventional belief among the French in direct bureaucratic rule and assimilation to French culture.[27] Roberts looked to French colonial rule in Indochina and concluded that "reduced to fundamentals, the French system is simply subordination."[28] Subordination represented one continuity between French and Japanese colonialism. The Japanese colonial scholar Yanaihara Tadao echoed the latter conclusion with his critique of "paternalistic protection and bureaucratic oppression" in Korea where assimilation amounted to little more than subordination and "Japanific-ation."[29] Our study of business circles in the grain trade suggests a blend of accommodation and assimilation significant for both colonial studies and for patterns of business/state relations in Korea's political economy.

The fact that subordination did not lead to elimination raises complex issues of process and result in the colonial interaction. Assimilation among the brokers to Japanese business practices such as standardization of grading, contracts, and deliveries provided an opening for cooperation in capitalist patterns of trade. Accommodation of Korean business associations with precolonial roots permitted continuity among brokers hustling to adjust in Japanese-dominated markets. Consolidation of ethnic chambers into joint chambers of commerce by decree of 1915 established legal precedent for unequal integration without eliminating, assimilating, or equal accommodation of local brokers. Apart from a process important for comparative studies of colonialism, results were significant for later patterns of business-state ties in Korea. Linking colonial experience to subsequent development, Barbara Ingham has recently called for closer attention to "who lost and who won, which social groups, states and regions were able to capture markets and take advantage of economic opportunities."[30]

Notes

1. Ronald Robinson, "Non-European Foundations of European Imperialism: A Sketch for a Theory of Collaboration," in Roger Owen and Bob Sutcliffe, eds., *Studies in the Theory of Imperialism* (London: Longman, 1972), pp. 117-142; Ronald Robinson and John Gallagher, "The Partition of Africa," in F. H. Hinsley, ed. *New Cambridge Modern History*, vol. 11 (Cambridge: Cambridge University Press, 1962), pp. 73-127, and "The Imperialism of Free Trade," *Economic History Review* (2nd series) VI (1953), pp. 1-15.

2. Stewart Lone has recently argued that the Japanese government in 1905 indeed hoped to establish informal control on the peninsula and avoid the expense of formal annexation. See Stewart Lone, "The Japanese Annexation of Korea 1910: The Failure of East Asian Co-Prosperity," *Modern Asian Studies* vol. 25, part I (February 1991): 143-174. The author cited civilian efforts to develop an expansion policy for a new Japanese order in East Asia with a strategy of "discreet civilian control" not unlike that of the British colonial administrator Cromer in Egypt. Lone concluded the policy failed because Resident-General Itō Hirobumi and the civilian cabinet in the home islands could not deliver on promises of commercial "co-prosperity," and seriously underestimated the extent of Korean resentment to Japanese rule. The premise of civilian direction of a "Korea policy" in the home islands deserves closer scrutiny. The cabinet's deferral to military advice on the Korean issue was evidence of the priority given to Korea in a wider military strategy of security and expansion. The historical record indicates a strong military hand in decisions on the peninsula at least from the turn of the century. See my "Imperial Expansion and Nationalist Resistance: Japan in Korea, 1876-1910," Ph.D. diss., Harvard University, 1983, and also "Comparative Colonial Response: Korea and Taiwan, 1895-1919," *Korean Studies* 10 (1986), pp. 54-68.

3. Yanaihara Tadao, "Problems of Japanese Administration in Korea," *Pacific Affairs* (June 1938), vol. 11, no. 2: 196-207.

4. Hagen Koo, "The Interplay of State, Social Class, and World System in East Asian Development: the Cases of South Korea and Taiwan," in Frederic Deyo, ed., *The Political Economy of the New Asian Industrialism* (New York: Cornell University Press, 1987), pp. 165-181.

5. "Where Do High Growth Political Economies Come From?"

6. See the following works of Peter Evans: *Embedded Autonomy: States and Industrial Transformation* (Princeton NJ: Princeton University Press, 1995);

"Predatory, Developmental, and Other Apparatuses: A Comparative Political Economy Perspective on the Third World State," pp. 84-111 in A. Douglas Kincaid and Alejandro Portes, eds., *Comparative National Development: Society and Economy in the New Global Order* (Chapel Hill NC: The University of North Carolina Press, 1994); "The State as Problem and Solution: Predation, Embedded Autonomy, and Structural Change," pp. 139-181 in Stephan Haggard and Robert R. Kaufman, eds., *The Politics of Economic Adjustment: International Constraints, Distributive Conflicts, and the State* (Princeton NJ: Princeton University Press, 1992).

7. Woo Jung-en, *Race to the Swift* (New York: Columbia University Press, 1991), p. 39,

8. I have examined the comparative utility of the corporatist thesis in an Asian context in a study titled *Textiles and Industrial Transition in Japan* (Ithaca, New York: Cornell University Press, 1995), and in "Bridging State and Society, East and West," Research Paper B-10, Institure of International Relations, Sophia University, August 1994.

9. Joel S. Migdal, "The State in Society: An Approach to Struggles for Domination," in Joel S. Migdal, Atul Kohli, and Vivienne Shue, eds., *State Power and Social Forces: Domination and Transformation in the Third World* (New York: Cambridge University, 1994), p. 23; see also the concluding chapter in the same volume by Atul Kohli and Vivienne Shue, "State Power and Social Forces: On Political Contention and Accommodation in the Third World," pp. 293-326.

10. Chosŏn Unhaeng Chosabu, *Chosŏn kyŏngje yŏnbo 1948* [The Korean economic annual, 1948] (Seoul: Chosŏn Unhaeng, 1948), pp. I-237, 238; I-113.

11. See Yi Sang-jo, *Han'guk midu sijangron* [A study of Korean markets for rice and soybeans] (Seoul: Taesŏng Munhwasa, 1977). A list of mills in Pusan in 1954 can be found in Pusan Sanggong Hoeŭiso, *Pusan -- Sanggong myŏngram 1954* [Pusan -- directory of commerce and industry, 1954] (Pusan: Pusan Sanggong Hoeŭiso, 1954), pp. 1-9. Sin Tŏg-gyun is registered as representative directory of the Pusan Hapdong Grain Company [Pusan Hapdong Koksan Chusik Hoesa] in the Chamber's directory. We also find Mr. Sin listed as president of the Kyŏngsang Namdo Grain Cooperative [Kyŏngsang Namdo Kongmul Hyŏphoe], as representative of the Kyŏngnam Food Grains Market [Kyŏngnam Yangsik Sijang], and as vice-president of the Pusan Chamber of Commerce and Industry. For a brief biography of Sin, see Ch'oe Hae-gun, *Pusan ŭi maek*, pp. 249-252.

12. Recommendations [*kŏnŭi*] dated according to month/day/year presented on June 29, 1954, June 17, 1955, and September 20, 1955. See Sŏ Pyŏng-gyu, ed., *Sanggyo Hoeŭiso kusimnyŏnsa* [A ninety year history of the Chambers of Commerce and Industry] (Seoul: Taehan Sanggong Hoeŭiso: 1976).

13. Recommendations presented on April 3, 1957, February 26, 1958, and April 21, 1961, and cited in *Kusimnyŏnsa*.

14. McNamara, "Reincorporation and the American State in South Korea: the Textile Industry in the 1950s," *Sociological Perspectives*, vol. 35, no. 2, (fall 1992): 329-342.

15. McNamara, "State and Concentration in Korea's First Republic, 1948-60," in *Modern Asian Studies*, vol. 26, no. 4 (1992): 701-718.

16. Recommendations of February 2, 1955, and June 17, 1955 cited in *Kusimnyŏnsa*.

17. Recommendations of September 20, 1955, April 3, 1957, February 26, 1958, and August 28, 1959 in *Kusimnyŏnsa*.

18. Recommendations of April 3, 1957, February 26, 1958, and April 21, 1961 in *Kusimynŏnsa*.

19. Kim Kyong-dong, "Political Factors in the Formation of the Entrepreneurial Elite in South Korea," *Asian Survey* 16, 5 (May 1976): 465-477; Chang Yun-shik, "The Personalist Ethic and the Market in Korea," *Comparative Studies in Society and History* 33, 1 (Jan. 1991): 106-129.

20. Edwin A. Winckler, "Mass Political Incorporation, 1500-2000," in Edwin A. Winckler and Susan Greenhalgh, eds., *Contending Approaches to the Political Economy of Taiwan* (Armonk, NY: M. E. Sharpe, Inc., 1988), pp. 41-66.

21. Thomas B. Gold, "Colonial Origins of Taiwanese Capitalism," in Winckler and Greenhalgh, eds., *Contending Approaches*, p. 103.

22. Lewis H. Gann, "Western and Japanese Colonialism: Some Preliminary Comparisons," in Ramon H. Myers and Mark R. Peattie, eds., *The Japanese Colonial Empire, 1895-1945* (Princeton: Princeton University Press, 1984), p. 513; Angus Maddison, "Dutch Colonialism in Indonesia: Comparative Perspective," in Anne Booth, W. J. O'Malley, and Anna Weidemann, eds., *Indonesian Economic History in the Dutch Colonial Era* (New Haven: Yale University Southeast Asia Studies, 1990), pp. 322-335. See also Murayama Yoshitada, "The Pattern of Japanese Economic Penetration of the Prewar Netherlands East Indies," in Shiraishi Saya and Takashi Shiraishi, eds., *The Japanese in Colonial Southeast Asia* (Ithaca: Southeast Asia Program, Cornell University, 1993), pp. 89-112; and in the same volume Shiraishi Saya and Takashi Shiraishi, "The Japanese in Colonial Southeast Asia: An Overview," pp. 5-20.

23. Samuel Pao-San Ho, "Colonialism and Development: Korea, Taiwan, and Kwantung," in Myers and Peattie, eds., *The Japanese Colonial Empire*, p. 386.

24. Cal Clark, *Taiwan's Development: Implications for Contending Political Economy Paradigms* (New York: Greenwood Press, 1989), p. 60.

25. Gold, "Colonial Origins," p. 105; Bruce Cumings, *The Origins of the Korean War: Liberation and the Emergence of Separate Regimes, 1945-1947*

186

(Princeton: Princeton University Press, 1981), p. 48.

26. Lewis H. Gann, "Western and Japanese Colonialism," p. 519.

27. D. K. Fieldhouse, *Colonialism, 1870-1945: An Introduction* (New York: St. Martin's Press, 1981), p. 36.

28. Stephen A. Roberts, *The History of French Colonial Policy, 1870-1925* (London: Frank Cass and Co., 1929), p. 636. Roberts added that "France, like Japan, viewed the mother-country as a machine, and the colonies as feeders."

29. Yanaihara, "The Problems of Japanese Administration in Korea," pp. 204, 207.

30. Barbara Ingham, "Colonialism and Peripheral Development," in Barbara Ingham and Colin Simmons, eds., *Development Studies and Colonial Policy* (London: Frank Cass, 1987), p. 135.

Glossary

Adachi Takajirö	足立瀧三郎
Akimoto Masatsugu	秋本正次
Akiyama Mitsuo	秋山滿夫
Aoki Heigaku	青木柄學
Arai Hatsutarö	荒井初太郎
Arai Kengo	荒井健五
Arima Junji	有馬順二
Asano Taisaburö	淺野太三郎
budan seiji	武斷政治
chaegye	財界
Chang Sôk-u	張錫佑
Ch'angûi taejang	倡義 大將
chinjö [chinjông]	陳情
Cho Chun-ho	趙俊鎬
Cho Pyông-sik	趙秉式
Chông Ch'i-guk	丁致國
Chông Yông-hwa	鄭永化
chôngmiso [seimaisho]	精米所
Chöri Sötaikai	町里 總大會
Chösen Beikoku Shijö	朝鮮 米穀 市長 會社
Chösen Beikoku Söko	朝鮮 米穀 倉庫 會社
Chösen Chochiku Ginkö	朝鮮 財蓄 銀行
Chösen Ginkö	朝鮮 銀行
Chösen Kögyö Shinkö	朝鮮 鑛業 振興 會社
Chösen Makuneseito Kaihatsu	朝鮮Makuneseito 開發
Chösen Ringyö Kaihatsu	朝鮮 林業 開發 會社
Chösen Shokuryö Eidan	朝鮮食料營團
Chösen Shintaku Ginkö	朝鮮 信託 銀行
Chösen Shokusan Ginkö	朝鮮 殖産 銀行

Chösen Sötokufu	朝鮮 總督
Chu Myông-gi	朱命基
Chu Pong-gi	朱奉基
Chu Sông-kûn	朱性根
döka	同化
Donga Ilbo	東亞 日報
Fukami Torashi	深見寅郎
Furuno Yoshiko	古野義行
Gotö Tsurahei	後藤連平
Ha Sang-hun	河相勳
Hakcha yusaeng	學者儒生
Hana-chö	花町
hankan hanmin	半官半民
Harada Kinnoyu	原田金之祐
Hayashi Shigeki	林茂樹
Hirai Nosaburö	平井能三郎
Hirano Sözörö	平野宗三郎
Hirayama Matsutarö	平山松太郎
Hong Chae-bôm	洪在範
hyögiin [p'yôngûiwôn]	評議員
Hwa / i	華 / 異
Hwangsong Sinmun	皇城 新聞
Hwaso Yi Hang-no	華西　李恒老
idan	異端
iik	理益
Ikeda	池田
ikensho	義見書
Imai Kakujirö	今井覺次郎
Imai Keitarö	今井京太郎
Imai Shözö	今井省三
Imamura Junjirö	今材順次郎

Inch'ôn Chosônin
  Sangôp Hoeûiso   仁川 朝鮮人 商業 會議所
Inch'ônhang Sinsang   仁川港 紳商 協會
  Hyôphoe
Inch'ôn Kaekchu Tanhap 仁川 客主 團合
Inch'ôn Mulsan Kaekchu
  Chohap   仁川 物産 客主 組合
ippan zaikai   一般材界
Ishigaki Kôjirö   石垣孝治
Ishizuka Takashi   石川登盛
Jinsen Beitö Torihikijo 仁川 米豆 取引所
Jinsenfusei Shinkökai   仁川府勢 振興會
Jinsen Beitö Torihikijo 仁川 米豆 取引所
Jinsenfusei Shinkökai   仁川府勢 振興會
Jinsen Kokubutsu Kyökai 仁川 穀物 協會
Jinsen Nihonjin Shögyö
  Kaigisho   仁川 日本人 商業 會議所
Jinsen Seimei Kumiai   仁川 精米 組合
Jinsen Shökögyö Kaigisho
  [Jinshö]   仁川 商工業 會議所
Jinsenko Shöhö Kaigisho 仁川港 商法 會議所
Jinsen Söko K.K.   仁川 倉庫 株式 會社
Jinto Keijö Iten Böshikai 仁取 京城 移轉 防止會
jitsugyöka [sangôpga] 商業家
jömu torishimariyaku   常務取締役
  [sangmu ch'wich'eryôk]
Kada Tomobu   賀田以武
kaehwa   開化
kaemong   開夢
Kaigan-chö   海岸町
Kang Ik-ha   康益夏
Kanghwa   江華

kansa [kamsa]	監事
Kapsin	甲申
Karai Eitarö	加來榮太郎
Karai Jifu	加來次夫
Katö Heitarö	加藤平太郎
Katö Keizaburö	加藤敬三郎
Kawai Tada	川井田
Keijinto Hantai	
Kabunushi Dömeikai	京仁取 反對株主同盟會
Keijö	京城
kengi [kônûi]	建義
ketsugi	決議
Ki Sam-yôn	奇參衍
Kim Chong-ik	金鍾翊
Kim In-o	金仁梧
Kim Kwang-jun	金光準
Kim Kyu-myôn	金奎晃
Kim Pong-gi	金鳳基
Kim Pong-hun	金奉勳
Kim P'yông-su	金平洙
Kim Pong-gi	金鳳基
Kim Pong-hun	金奉勳
Kim P'yông-su	金平洙
Kim Yong-gyu	金容奎
Kitajima Gorö	北島三郎
Kobayashi Keiji	小林敬治
Kobayashi Töemon	小林藤右衛門
Kogane-chö	黄金町
Kojö Kandö	古城管堂
Kojö Sugadö	古城菅堂
Kojong	高宗
koku [sôk]	石
Komura Mikisan	小林幹三

Kokusha Rengōkai	公職者 聯合會
Kōno Takenosuke	河野竹之助
Kōno Yoshinarika	河野矛古成一
Kosugi Kinhachi	小杉謹八
Kugimoto Tōjirō	釘本藤次郎
kugga	國家
kunja	君子
kunsin	君臣
Kurahara Arata	倉原新
kwallyo yusaeng	官僚儒生
Kwangsŏngt'ae	光成泰
kwanmin [kanmin]	官民
Kwŏnŏpsa	勸業社
Manmin Kongdonghoe	萬民共同會
Matsui Fusajirō	松井房治郎
Matsumoto Yōgorō	松本要五郎
Matsuo Ki	松尾其
Meiji	明治
Minato-chō	港田
Ming	明
minshū	民衆
Misang Chohap	米商組合
Murano Eihachi	杉野榮八
Myŏnam Ch'oe Ik-hyŏn	勉庵 崔盆鉉
Naisen ittai	內鮮一體
Nitta Yoshimin	新田義民
Noda Hiroshi	野田搏
Noguchi Bunichi	野口文一
Noriyama Iwao	模山巖
Ochiai	落合
Ogawara Tadashi	小笠原儀雄
Okuda Teijirō	奥田貞次郎
Ōta Shinobu	太田忍

Pak Ûn-sik	朴殷植
Pak Yông-hyo	朴泳孝
paeksông	百姓
pobusang	褓負商
puja	父子
Qing	清
Rikimu Kajirö	力武嘉次郎
Rikimu Kurosaemorimon	力武黑左衛門
Sai Gensuke	讚井源輔
Saitö Kyütarö	齊藤久太郎
Sakoma Fusatarö	迫間房太郎
sa / kong	私 / 公
sadae	事大
sangôpgye [shögyökai]	商業界
seimei	聲明
Senbei taisaku	鮮米對策
sengmin	生民
senmu torishimariyaku [chônmu ch'wich'eryôk]	專務取締役
Shin Tatsuma	進辰馬
Sim Nûng-dôk	沈能德
Sim Ûi-suk	沈宜淑
Sinsang Hoesa	紳商會社
so	疏
Sô Chae-p'il [Philip Jaisohn]	徐載弼
Sô Sang-bin	徐相彬
sohwa	小華
soilbon	小日本
Son Hong-jun	孫弘俊
Sôngjae Ki Sam-yôn	省齊 奇參衍

Sôyu Kyônmun	西遊見聞
Sugimura	杉村逸樓
Sung	宋
Tachikawa Rokurô	立川六郎
taedo	大道
Taehan Maeil Shinbo	大韓每日申報
taeûi	大義
Tagawa Tsunejirö	田川常次郎
Takano Kenji	桑野健治
Tanaka Saburôshin	田中三郎進
Tanaka Sano	田中三郎
Tanaka Sashichirö	田中佐七郎
Tanaka Tomokichi	田中友吉
Ten'nichi Köichi	天日光一
Ten'nichi Töjirö	天日當次郎
Tokugawa	德川
tokushu kaisha	特殊 會社
Tonghak	東學
t'onghwa t'ongsaek	通貨通色
Tongnip Sinmun	獨立新聞
Töyö Takushoku K.K.	東洋拓植會社
Tsujikawa F.	迁川不屈志
Tsujikawa Tomichö	迁川富重
Ûiam Yu In-sôk	毅菴 柳麟錫
ûmbun kiwan	淫奔 奇玩
ûmsa	淫事
Uzu Katsu	堆活
wang	王
Wakamatsu Tosanjirö	苦松免三郎
Wakamatsu Usanjirö	苦松
Watanabe Sadaichirö	渡邊定一郎
wijong ch'ôksa	衛正斥邪
Yamamoto Gensaku	山本源作

Yamamoto Tametaru	山本爲善
Yamanuchi Matsudaira	山內松平
Yanagi-chö	柳町
yanghwa	洋禍
Yazaki Sugizö	矢崎杉造
yeûi	禮義
Yi Ô-hûng	李於興
Yi Pyông-hak	李炳學
Yoshida Hidejirö	吉田秀次郎
Yoshimura Moriyü	吉村雄
Yoshimura Shinzö	吉村信三
Yoshino Yoshikö	吉野義行
Yu Ki-yông	劉其英
Yu Kil-chun	兪吉濬
Yu Kun-sông	劉君星
Yu Rae-hang	柳來恒
yugûijôn	六矣廛
Yun Ch'i-ho	尹致昊
yurim	儒林
yusaeng yangban	儒生 兩班
yusin	儒臣

Bibliography: Asian Language

Abe Kaoru. *Chōsen kōrōsha meikan* [A list of eminent figures in Korea]. Keijo: Minshū Jironsha, 1935.

An Byŏng-t'ae. *Chōsen shakai no kōzo to Nihon teikokushugi* [Japanese imperialism and the structure of Korean society]. Tokyo: Ryūkei Shosha, 1977.

An Pyŏng-jik, Yi Tae-gŭn, Nakamura Satoru, and Kajimura Hideki, eds. *Kŭndae Chosŏn ŭi kyŏngje kujo* [The economic structure of modern Korea]. Seoul: Piryu Publishing, 1989.

Chang Che-hŭp. *Chōsenjin shakai daishōten jiten* [A reference for the larger commercial enterprises in Korean society]. Keijo: Seikaisha, 1928.

Cho Ki-jun. *Han'guk kiŏpgasa* [A history of Korean entrepreneurs]. Seoul: Pagyŏngsa, 1974.

_____. *Han'guk chabonjuŭi sŏngnipsa ron* [A study of the development of Korean capitalism]. Seoul: Taewangsa, 1973.

_____. "Kaehang gwa woeguk sangsa [Port openings and foreign commercial firms]." *Kyŏnghyŏp*, no. 11-12 (1971): 41-42.

Ch'oe Ch'ang-gyu, ed. *Hanmal aeguk myŏngsangso munjip* [Anthology of patriotic memorials at the close of the Chosŏn Dynasty]. Seoul: Sŏmundang, 1975.

Ch'oe Hae-gun. *Pusan ŭi maek* [The pulse of Pusan]. Pusan: Donga Chŏnsa Insoesa, 1990.

Ch'oe Ho-jin. *Kindai Chōsen keizaishi* [An economic history of modern Korea]. Tokyo: Tokyo Shuppan Henkyū, 1942.

Ch'oe Ik-hyŏn. *Myŏnamjip* [Collection of Myŏnam, Ch'oe Ik-hyŏn]. Tr. by Ju-hi Kim. Seoul: Munhwa Ch'ujin Wiwŏnhoe, 1977.

Ch'oe Tang. "Kaehanghu sasang ŭi hwaldong [Efforts of private merchants after the port openings]." Seoul: M.A. thesis, Sunggyungwan University, 1982.

Chōsen Bōeki Kyōkai. *Chōsen bōekishi* [A history of trade in Korea]. Keijo: Chōsen Bōeki Kyōkai, 1943.

_____. *Chōsen bōeki nempō* [Annual of Korean trade]. Keijo: Chōsen Bōeki Kyōkai, annual.

Chōsen Sōtokufu, *Chōsen Sōtokufu tōkei nempō* [Statistical annual of the Chōsen Government General]. Keijo: Government General, annual. Cited as CSTN.

_____. *Chōsen no shijō* [Markets in Korea]. Keijo: Chōsen Insatsu Kabushiki Kaisha, 1929.

196

_____. *Chōsen ni okeru naichijin* [Japanese nationals in Korea]. Keijo: Chōsen Sōtokufu, 1923.

Chōsen Sōtokufu Tetsudō Kyoku. *Chōsen tetsudōshi* [A history of railroads in Korea]. Keijo: Chōsen Sōtokufu, 1923.

Chōsen Takushoku Ginkō [Chosen Industrial Bank]. "Chōsen ni okeru dochaku shihon no kenkyū [A study of indigenous capital in Korea]." *Shokugin Chōsa Geppo* no. 59 (1943): 1-9.

_____. "Chōsen shikin mondai no shin dankai [A new phase in the problem of Korean capital]." *Shokugin Chōsa Geppo* no. 76 (May 1941): 35-43.

_____. "Chōsen tōka naichi shihon go kore ni yoru jigyō [The enterprise of Japanese capital invested in Korea]." *Shokugin Chōsa Geppo* no. 65 (June 1940): 12-43.

_____. "Chōsen no kōgyō go kōjō [The industries and plants of Korea]." *Shokugin Chōsa Geppo* no. 58 (Dec. 1939): 53-94.

Chōsen Torihikijo. *Chōsen Torihikijo nempō* [Annual of the Chosen Exchange]. Keijo: Chōsen Insatsujo, annual.

Chosŏn Ŭnhaeng Chosabu. *Chosŏn kyŏngje yŏnbo 1948* [Korean Economic Annual, 1948]. Seoul: Chosŏn Ŭnhaeng Chosabu, 1948.

Daiichi Ginkō. *Daiichi Ginkō gojūnen shōshi* [A brief history of fifty years of the Daiichi Bank]. Edited by Hasei Chiyomatsu. Tokyo: Tokyo Insatsu, 1926.

Fuzanfu. *Fuzan no sangyō* [Industry in Pusan]. Fuzan: Kyōdō Insatsusha, 1940.

Han Ŭ-gŭn. *Han'guk kaehanggi ŭi sangŏp yŏn'gu* [A study of commerce in the period of port openings in Korea]. Seoul: Ilchogak, 1974.

Han'guk Muyŏk Hyŏphoe [Korean Trade Association]. *Han'guk muyŏksa* [A history of trade in Korea]. Seoul: Han'guk Muyŏk Hyŏphoe, 1972.

Han'guk Sahoesa Yŏn'guhoe, ed. *Ilcheha ŭi sahoe undong gwa nongch'on sahoe* [Rural society and social movements in colonial Korea]. Seoul: Han'guk Sahoesa Yŏn'guhoe, 1990.

Hatada Takashi. "Kindai ni okeru Chōsenjin no Nihonkan [Modern Korean views of Japan]." *Shisō* 520 (1967): 59-73.

Hŏ Su-yŏn. "Ilcheha Chosŏnin hoesa mit Chosŏnin chungyŏk ŭi punsŏk [An analysis of Korean firms and Korean executives under Japanese colonial rule]. Pp. 354-387 in An Pyŏng-jik, Yi Tae-gŭn, Nakamura Satoru, and Kajimura Hideki, eds. *Kŭndae Chosŏn ŭi kyŏngje kujo* [The economic structure of modern Korea]. Seoul: Piryu Publishing, 1989.

Hong Sun-gwŏn. "Kaehangi kaekchu ŭi yut'ong sihai e kwanhan yŏn'gu [A study of the brokers' dominance in commodity circulation in the period of port openings]." *Han'guk Hakpo* no. 39 (Summer 1985): 83-117.

Hwang Sŏn-min. *Pobusang ŭi kyŏngyŏng hwaldong yŏn'gu* [A study of the economic management activities of the peddlers]. Seoul: Pogyŏng Munhwasa, 1989.

Hwang Myŏng-su. *Kiŏpgasa yŏn'gu* [Studies in entrepreneurship]. Seoul: Ch'ŏndae Publishing, 1983.

Hwangsŏng Staff. *Hwangsŏng Sinmun* [The Hwangsŏng Newspaper]. Seoul: Hwangsŏng Sinmun.

Inch'ŏn Chighalsa P'yŏnch'an Wiwŏnhoe. *Inch'ŏn kaehang paegnyŏnsa* [A one hundred year history from the opening of the port of Inch'ŏn]. Inch'ŏn: Kyŏnggi Ch'ulp'ansa, 1983.

Inch'ŏn Sanggong Hoeŭiso. *Inch'ŏn Sanggong Hoeŭiso kusimnyŏnsa* [A ninety year history of the Inch'ŏn Chamber of Commerce and Industry], edited by Kim Dong-sun. Seoul: Samhwa, 1979.

Inch'ŏnsisa P'yŏnch'an Wiwŏnhoe, ed. *Inch'ŏnsisa* [A history of the city of Inch'ŏn]. Inch'ŏn: Kyŏngil Publishing, 1973.

Itō Chōjirō. *Kankoku oyobi Kyūshūdan* [An account of travels in Kyūshū and Korea]. Kobe: Sueyama Miji, 1905.

Jinsen Beitō Torihikijo. *Jinsen Beitō Torihikijo enkaku* [A history of the Jinsen Grain Exchange]. Edited by Akiyama Funio. Jinsen: Tsukiji Printing, 1922.

Jinsen Nijūgonen Kinenkai. *Jinsen kaikō nijūgo nenshi* [A twenty-five year history from the opening of the port of Inch'ŏn]. Osaka: Shiobarakin, 1922.

Jinsen Shōgyō Kaigisho [Jinsen Chamber of Commerce]. *Jinsen Shōgyō Kaigisho tōkei nempyō, 1926-1927* [Statistical annual of the Jinsen Chamber of Commerce, 1926-1927]. Keijo: Chikazawa Shōten, 1928.

_____. *Jinsen ni okeru seisan kōgyō* [Manufacturing industry in Inch'ŏn]. Jinsen: Jinsen Shōgyō Kaigisho, 1928.

_____. *Jinsen shōkō annai* [A guide to commerce and industry in Inch'ŏn]. Jinsen: Jinsen Shōgyō Kaigisho, 1921.

Jinsen Shōkō Kaigisho [Jinsen Chamber of Commerce and Industry]. *Jinsen Shōkō Kaigisho tōkei nempyō, 1937* [Statistical annual of the Jinsen Chamber of Commerce and Industry, 1937]. Jinsen: Tsukiji Publishing, 1938.

_____. *Jinsen Shōkō Kaigisho gojūnenshi* [A fifty year history of the Jinsen Chamber of Commerce and Industry]. Edited by Okamoto Yasumasa. Keijo: Sawada Saichi, 1934.

_____. *Jinsenkō* [The port of Inch'ŏn]. Jinsen: Jinsen Shōkō Kaigisho, 1931.

Jinsenfu. *Jinsenfushi* [A history of the city of Inch'ŏn]. Edited by Sawada Sakaichi. Keijo: Chikazawa Shōten, 1933.

Kajikawa Hanzaburō. *Jitsugyōji Chōsen* [The actual situation in Korea]. Keijo: Keijo Insatsujo, 1911.

Kajimura Hideki, ed. *Ilcheha Han'guk sahoe kusŏngch'eron sŏsŏl* [An introduction to theories of social structure in Korea under Japanese rule]. Seoul: Ch'ŏnga, 1986.

Kang Che-ŏn [Kan Chi-an]. *Chōsen kindaishi kenkyū* [Studies of modern

198

Korean history]. Tokyo: Hyōronsha, 1970.

_____. *Chōsen no kaika shisō* [Enlightenment thought in Korea]. Tokyo: Iwanami Shoten, 1980.

Kang Man-gil. "Kaehwagi ŭi sanggongŏp munje [Commerce and industry in the enlightenment period]." Pp. 265-304 in his *Chosŏn sidae sanggongŏpsa yŏn'gu* [Studies of commerce and industry in the Chosŏn Dynasty]. Seoul: Hangilsa, 1984.

_____. *Chosŏn hugi sangŏp chabon ŭi paldal* [The development of commercial capital in the later Chosŏn Dynasty]. Seoul: Korea University Press, 1974.

Karasawa Takeko. "Bōkoku rei jiken [Grain embargo incidents]." *Chōsen Kenkyūkai Ronbunshū* (June, 1969): 64-93.

Keijō Nihonjin Shōgyō Kaigisho. *Shōgyō Kaigisho nempō 1911* [Annual of the Chamber of Commerce, 1911]. Keijo: Keijō Nihonjin Shōgyō Kaigisho, 1912.

Keijō Shōkō Kaigijo. *Chōsen kaishahyō 1939* [List of firms in Korea, 1939]. Keijo: Gyōsei Gakkai Insatsujo, 1939.

_____. *Chōsen kaishahyō 1935* [A list of companies in Korea, 1935]. Keijo: Keijō Shōkō Kaigisho, 1935.

Kim Chu-yŏng. *Kaekchu* [Brokers]. Seoul: Ch'angjak gwa Pip'yŏngsa, 1981.

Kim Chun-po. *Han'guk chabon juŭisa yŏn'gu* [Studies in the history of Korean capitalism], vol. 3. Seoul: Ilchogak, 1977.

Kim Ho-sŏng. *Hanmal ŭibyŏng undongsa yŏn'gu* [A study of the Righteous Army Movement at the end of the Chosŏn Dynasty]. Seoul: Koryŏwŏn, 1987.

Kim Jun. "1920-1930 nyŏndae nodong undongesŏ ŭi minjok munje wa kyegŭp munje [Problems of class and nation in the labor movement of the 1920s]. Pp. 50-67 in Han'guk Sahoesa Yŏn'guhoe, ed. *Ilcheha ŭi sahoe undong gwa nongch'on sahoe* [Rural society and social movements in colonial Korea]. Seoul: Han'guk Sahoesa Yŏn'guhoe, 1990.

Kim Kwang-un. "Ilcheha Chosŏn tojŏng nodongja kyegŭp ŭi hyŏngsŏng kwajŏng [The process of class formation among labor at the rice mills in Pusan during the period of Japanese colonial rule]. Seoul: M.A. thesis, Hanyang University, 1989.

Kim Kyŏng-t'ae. "Kapsin Kabogi ŭi sanggwŏn koebok munje [The problem of the recovery of commercial rights in the Kapsin and Kabo periods (1884-1895)]." *Han'guksa Yŏn'gu* nos. 50-51 (December 1985): 202-218.

Kim Pyŏng-ha. *Han'guk kyŏngje kyŏngyŏngsa yŏn'gu* [A history of ideas of management in the Korean economy]. Seoul: Kaemyŏng Taehakkyo Ch'ulp'ansa, 1989.

Kim Sŏng-su. *Ilcheha Han'guk kyŏngjesaron* [An economic history of colonial Korea]. Seoul: Kyŏngjinsa, 1985.

Kim Ŭi-hwan. "Hanmal ŭibyŏng undong ŭi punsŏk: Yi Kang-nyŏn ŭibyŏng pudae rŭl chungsim ŭro [An analysis of the late Chosŏn Dynasty Righteous

Army movement: the Righteous Army unit of Yi Kwang-nyŏn]. Pp. 575-599 in his *Han'guk kŭndaesa yŏn'gu nonjip* [A collection of studies on modern Korean history]. Seoul: Sŏngjin Munhwasa, 1972.

_____. *Ŭibyŏng undongsa* [A history of the campaigns of the Righteous Armies]. Seoul: Pagyŏngsa, 1974.

Kim Yŏng-guk. "Hanmal minjok undong ŭi kyebokjŏk yŏn'gu [A study of the roots of national movements in the late Chosŏn Dynasty]." *Han'guk Chŏngch'ihak Hoebo* no. 3 (1969): 87-106.

Kim Yong-sŏp. "Hanmal Ilcheha ŭi chijuje: Kanghwa Kimshiga ŭi ch'sugi rŭl t'onghaesŏ pon chiju kyŏngyŏng [System of landownership at the end of the Chosŏn Dynasty: landlord management as evident in the harvest records of the Kanghwa Kim family]." *Donga Munhwa* no. 11 (1972): 1-86.

_____. *Chosŏn hugi nongŏpsa yŏn'gu* [Studies in the agrarian history of the late Chosŏn Dynasty]. Seoul: Ilchogak, 1971.

_____. "Kwangmu nyŏngan ŭi yangjŏn saŏp e kwanhan il yŏn'gu [A study of efforts at a farmland survey, 1899-1904)." *Asea Yŏn'gu* vol. 11, no. 3 (1968): 81-210.

Kobayashi Hideo. "Nihon no kinhonisei ikō to Chōsen [Korea and Japan's shift to the gold standard]." Pp. 167-196 in Hatada Takashi Sensei Koki Kinenkai, ed., *Chōsen rekishi ronshū* [Collection of articles on Korean history], vol. 2. Tokyo: Ryūkei Shosha, 1979.

Ko Il. *Inch'ŏn kŭmsŏk* [Inch'ŏn, then and now]. Inch'ŏn: Sŏnmin Ch'ulp'ansa, 1955.

Koh Seung-jae. *Han'guk kyŏngyŏngsa yŏn'gu* [Studies in the history of business management in Korea]. Seoul: Samwha, 1975.

_____. *Han'guk kŭmyungsa yŏn'gu* [Studies in the history of Korean finance]. Seoul: Ilchogak, 1970.

Koryŏdae Dong'a Munje Yŏn'guso, compil. *Ku Han'guk woegyo munsŏ* [Diplomatic documents of the late Chosŏn Dynasty]. Seoul: Korea University Press, 1965. Cited as KHWM.

Kukhoe Tosŏgwan, Ipbŏb Chosaguk. *Kuhanmal choyak hwich'an* [A collection of treaties of the late Chosŏn Dynasty]. Edited by Chŏng Hae-sik. Seoul: Kukhoe Tosŏgwan, 1964.

Kuksa P'yŏnch'an Wiwŏnhoe, ed. *Han'guksa* [A history of Korea]. Seoul: T'amgudang, 1978.

Kŭm Jang-t'ae. "Cho Chŏng-am gwa Chosŏn ŭi sŏnbi chŏngsim [Cho Chŏng-am and the spirit of the Confucian scholar in the Chosŏn Dynasty]." *Han'guk Hakpo* no. 10 (1978): 180-194.

Lee Byung-cheun [Yi Pyŏng-ch'an]. "Kaehanggi woeguk sangin ŭi ch'imip gwa Han'guk sangin ŭi taeŭng [The entry of foreign traders to Korea's treaty ports, and the response of Korean merchants]." Seoul: Ph.D. diss., Seoul National University, 1985.

Lee Byung-chull. "Yi Pyŏng-ch'ŏl." Pp. 278-377 in Wŏllo Kiŏpin, ed.,

Chaegye hoego [Memories of the business world], vol. I. Seoul: Han'guk Ilbosa, 1981.

Lee Hyung-jin. "Ilcheha t'ugi wa sut'al ŭi hyŏnjang - midu, chŭnggwŏn sijang [The reality of speculation and exploitation under Japanese colonial rule - the grain and stock market]." *Yŏksa Pip'yŏng* no. 18 (fall 1992): 93-107.

_____. "Ilche kangjŏmgi midu chŭnggwŏn sijang chŏngch'aek gwa Chosŏn ch'wiinso [The Chosen Exchange and policy of the grain and stock markets during the Japanese occupation]." Seoul: M.A. thesis, Yonsei University, 1992.

Lee Kwang-rin. *Han'guksa kangchwa, V: kŭndaepyŏn* [Lectures on Korean history: volume V, the modern period]. Seoul: Ilchogak, 1981.

Lew Young-ick. "Kabo kyŏngjang ŭl wiyohan Ilbon ŭi tae Han chŏngch'aek: Kabo kyŏngjang t'ayullon e taehan sujŏng jŏk pip'an [Japan's Korea policy regarding the Kabo reforms: a critical revision regarding the thesis of heteronomous Kabo reforms]." *Yŏksa Hakpo* no. 65 (March 1975): 53-74.

Makiyama Kōzō. *Chōsen shinshi meiran* [A register of Korean gentlemen]. Keijo: Nihon Dempo Tsūshinsha, Keijo Jikyoku, 1911.

Miyajima Hiroshi. "Chōsen kango kaikaku igo no shōgyōteki nogyō [Commercial agriculture in Korea after the Kabo Reforms]." *Shirin* vol. 57, no. 6 (Nov. 1974): 38-77.

Naigai Shōhin Shimbunsha. *Chōsen shōgyō sōran* [A comprehensive review of Korean commerce]. Keijo: Masafumisha, 1915.

Naikaku Tōkei Kyoku [Statistical Office of the Cabinet]. *Nihon teikoku tōkei nenkan* [Statistical annual of the Empire of Japan, annual]. Tokyo: Naikaku Tōkei Kyoku, annual. Cited as NTTN.

Nikkan Tsūshō Kyōkai [Japan-Korea Trade Association]. *Nikkan Tsūshō Kyōkai Hokoku* [Report of the Japan-Korea Trade Association]. Seoul: 1895-1897.

Nongŏp Hyŏptong Chohap [National Agricultural Cooperative Federation, NACF]. *Nonghyŏp isimnyŏnsa* [A twenty year history of the NACF]. Seoul: NACF, 1982.

Nōrinsho Nōmukyoku [Agricultural Bureau of the Ministry of Agriculture and Forestry]. *Kokubutsu yoram 1939* [Grain Annual 1939]. Tokyo: Nōrinsho, 1939.

O Ch'ang-guk. *Chŭnggwŏn pisa* [The inside history of the Korean Exchange]. Seoul: Sinhŭng Printing, 1977.

O Sŏng. *Chosŏn hugi sangin yŏn'gu* [A study of merchants in the late Chosŏn Dynasty]. Seoul: Ilchogak, 1989.

Pak Sŏng-su. *Tongnip undongsa yŏn'gu* [Studies of the history of the independence movement]. Seoul: Ch'angjak gwa Pip'yŏngsa, 1980.

Pak Su-gyŏng. "Kaehanggi Inch'ŏnhang kaekchu e kwanhan yŏn'gu: 1883-1894 [A study of the kaekchu at the port of Inch'ŏn in the early years: 1883-1894]." Seoul: M.A. thesis, Ewha University, 1983.

Pak Su-i. *Yicho muyŏk chŏngch'aek nongo* [A study of trade policy in the Chosŏn Dynasty]. Seoul: Minjung Sŏgwan, 1974.

Pak Sung-un. "Kuhanmal ŭibyŏng chŏnjeng gwa Yugyojŏk aeguk sasang [The Righteous Army struggle and Confucian ideas of patriotism in the late Chosŏn Dynasty]." *Taedong Bunka Yŏn'gu* nos. 6-7 (Dec. 1970): 163-196.

Pak Ŭn-sik. *Pak Ŭn-sik* [Pak Ŭn-sik], edited by Yi Man-yŏl. Seoul: Han'gilsa, 1980.

_____. *Chŏnsŏ* [Complete works of Pak Ŭn-sik]. Seoul: Somundang, 1975.

Pak Wŏn-p'yo. *Kaehang kujunyŏn* [Ninety years from the opening of the port]. Pusan: Taehwa Inswoeso, 1976.

Pak Wŏn-sŏn. *Pobusang* [Peddlers]. Seoul: Han'guk Yŏn'guso, 1965.

Pusan Chikhalsisa P'yŏnch'an Wiwŏnhoe, ed. *Pusansisa* [A history of the city of Pusan]. Pusan: Cheil Printing, 1989.

Pusan Sanggong Hoeŭiso. *Pusan sangŭisa* [A business history of Pusan]. Pusan: Pusan Sanggong Hoeŭiso, 1989.

_____. *Pusan - Sanggong myŏngram 1954* [Pusan - directory of commerce and industry, 1954]. Pusan: Pusan Sanggong Hoeŭiso, 1954.

Russian Finance Ministry. *Kuhanmal ŭi sahoe wa kyŏngje* [Society and economy at the end of the Chosŏn Dynasty], tr. by Kim Pyŏng-rin. Seoul: Yup'ung, (1900) 1983.

Sawamura Tōhei. "Richō makki menseihin yunyū bōeki no hatten [Developments in the cotton import trade at the end of the Chosŏn Dynasty]. *Shakai Keizaishi Gaku* vol. 19, nos. 2 & 3 (1953): 57-80.

Shikata Hiroshi. "Chōsen ni okeru kindai shihonshugi no seiritsu [The development of modern capitalism in Korea]." *Chōsen Shakai Keizaishi Kenkyū* no. 6 (1933): 1-233. Republished in volume two of his *Chōsen shakai keizaishi kenkyū* [Studies of the socio-economic history of Korea]. Tokyo: Kokusho Kankōkai, 1977.

Shin Yong-ha. *Han'guk kŭndae sahoe sasangsa yŏn'gu* [Studies of the history of ideas in modern Korean society]. Seoul: Iljisa, 1987.

_____. *Tongnip hyŏphoe yŏn'gu: Tongnip Sinmun* [Studies of the Independence Club: the Independent]. Seoul: Ilchogak, 1976.

Sin T'ae-bŏm. *Inch'ŏn hansegi* [One generation in Inch'ŏn]. Inch'ŏn: Hunmi Ch'ulp'ansa, 1983.

Sŏ Kwang-un. *Han'guk kŭmyung paegnyŏn* [A century of finance in Korea]. Seoul: Ch'angyosa, 1972.

Sŏ Pyŏng-gyu, ed. *Sanggyo Hoeŭiso kusimnyŏnsa* [A ninety year history of the Chambers of Commerce and Industry], two vols. Seoul: Taehan Sanggong Hoeŭiso, 1976.

Tabohashi Kiyoshi. "Kindai Chōsen ni okeru seijiteki kaikaku [Political reform in modern Korea]." *Kindai Chōsen Kenkyū* no. 1 (1940): 1-302.

_____. *Kindai Nissen kankei no kenkyū* [Studies of modern Japanese-Korean relations]. Reprint. Tokyo: Harashobō, 1974.

Taehaksa. *Han'guk hyŏndae sup'ilchip charyo ch'ongsŏ* [A compendium of materials on modern Korean essays]. Seoul: Taehaksa, 1987. Cited as HHS.

Takao Shinemon, ed. *Genzan hattenshi* [A history of the development of Wŏnsan]. Osaka: Keimunsha, 1916.

Takashima Masaaki. *Chōsen ni okeru shokuminchi kinyūshi no kenkyū* [Studies in the financial history of colonial lands: Korea]. Tokyo: Ohara Shinseisha, 1978.

Tanaka Ichinosuke. *Zen Chōsen shōkō kaigisho hattatsushi* [A history of the growth of chambers of commerce and industry in Korea]. Fuzan: Kawai Ryūkichi, 1935.

Teikoku Kōshinjo. *Teikoku ginkō kaisha yōroku* [A list of banks and corporations in the empire], Chōsen and Manchuria Section. Tokyo: Teikoku Kōshinjo, annual. Cited as TGKY.

Tōa Keizai Jihōsha. *Chōsen ginkō kaisha kumiai yōroku* [A list of banks, corporations, and partnerships in Korea], ed. by Nakamura Sukeryō. Tokyo: Tōa Keizai Jihōsha. Cited as CGKKY.

Tōkanfu [Japanese Residency General in Korea]. *Kankoku shūyaku ruisan* [A collection of Korean agreements]. Tokyo: Hideyōsha, 1908.

Tongnip Undongsa P'yŏnch'an Wiwŏnhoe, ed. *Tongnip undongsa I: ŭibyŏng hangjaengsa* [History of the independence movement: resistance of the Righteous Armies]. Seoul: Tongnip Undongsa P'yŏnch'an Wiwŏnhoe, 1970.

_____. *Tongnip undongsa charyojip: ŭibyŏng hangjaengsa charyojip* [Collection of documents on the history of the Independence Movement: documents on the history of the resistance of the Righteous Armies]. Seoul: Tongnip Undongsa P'yŏnch'an Wiwŏnhoe, 1970.

Tōyō Keizai Shinpōsha. *Dairiku kaisha benran, 1942* [Handbook of companies on the continent, 1942]. Edited by Sawano Akahishi. Tokyo: Tōyō Keizai Shinpōsha, 1942.

Yamada Shōji. "Meiji zenki no Nik-Kan bōeki [Japanese- Korean trade in early Meiji]." Pp. 60-82 in Ienaga Saburō Kyoju Tokyo Kyoiku Daigaku Taikan Kinen Ronshū Kankō Iinkai, ed., *Kindai Nihon no kokka to shisō* [The nation and ideas of modern Japan]. Tokyo: Sanseido, 1979.

Yi Chae-ch'im, ed. *Sanggong hoeŭiso paegnyŏnsa* [A one hundred year history of the chambers of commerce and industry]. Seoul: Taehan Sanggong Hoeŭiso, 1984.

Yi Hang-no. *Hwasŏjip* [Collected works of Hwasŏ Yi Hang-no], edited by Kim Chu-hi. Seoul: Taeyang Sŏjŏk, 1973.

Yi Hun-byŏn. *Pobusang kwanggye saryo* [Research materials on the peddlers]. Seoul: Pogyŏng Munhwasa, 1988.

Yi Hŏn-ch'an. "Kaehanggi sijang kujo gwa pyŏnhwa e kwanhan yŏn'gu [A

study of the structure and change of markets at the time of port openings]."
Seoul: Ph.D. diss., Seoul National University, 1990.

_____. "Han'guk kaehangjang ŭi sangp'um yut'ong gwa sijanggwŏn [Commodity circulation and the commodity area of Korea's open ports]." *Kyŏngjesahak* no. 9 (Dec. 1985): 119-294.

Yi Hong-sik, ed. *Kuksa taesajŏn* [Encyclopedia of Korean history]. Seoul: Paekmansa, 1962.

Yi Hun-byŏn. *Pobusang kwanggye saryo* [Research materials on the peddlers]. Seoul: Pogyŏng Munhwasa, 1988.

Yi I-hwa. "Ch'ŏksa wijŏng ŭi pipanjŏk kŏmt'o: Hwasŏ Yi Hang-no ŭi soron ŭl chungsimŭro [A critical study of the 'ban heterodoxy, protect orthodoxy' argument: the ideas of Hwasŏ Yi Hang-no]." *Han'guksa Yŏn'gu* vol. 18 (Oct. 1977): 111-140.

Yi Pyŏng-ch'ŏn. "Kaehanggi woeguk sangin ŭi naechi sanggwŏn ch'imip [Penetration of interior commercial rights by foreign merchants in the treaty port era]." *Kyŏngjesahak* no. 9 (December 1985): 295-331.

_____. "Kaehanggi woeguk sangin ŭi ch'imip gwa Han'guk sangin ŭi taeŭng [Penetration of foreign traders and the response of Korean merchants in the treaty port era]." Seoul: Ph.D. diss., Seoul National University, 1985.

Yi Sang-jo. *Han'guk midu sijanron* [A study of Korean markets for grains]. Seoul: Taesŏng Munhwasa, 1977.

Yoshino Makoto. "Yicho makki ni okeru beikoku yushutsu no hatten to bōkokurei [Rice embargoes and the development of rice exports at the end of the Chosŏn Dynasty]." *Chōsenshi Kenkyūkai Ronbunshū* (March 1973): 101-132.

_____. "Riki makki ni okeru menseihin yunyu no hatten [Developments in the import of cotton goods at the end of the Chosŏn Dynasty]." Pp. 133-166 in Hatada Takashi Sensei Koki Kinenkai, ed., *Chōsen rekishi ronshū* [Collection of studies on Korean history] vol. 2. Tokyo: Ryūkei Shosha, 1979.

Yu In-sŏk. *Ŭiam munjip* [Anthology of Ŭiam Yu In-sŏk]. Seoul: Somundang, 1972.

Yu Kil-chun. *Sŏyu kyŏnmun* [Observations on the West]. Tr. by Kim T'ae-chun. Seoul: Pagyŏngsa, 1976.

Yu Kwang-yŏl. *Hang'il sŏnŏn, ch'angŭi munjip* [A collection of anti-Japanese proclamations and righteous documents]. Seoul: Sŏmundang, 1975.

Yun Ch'i-ho. *Yun Ch'i-ho ilki* [The diary of Yun Ch'i-ho]. Seoul: Kuksa P'yŏnch'an Wiwŏnhoe, 1976.

Yun Chin-su. "Ilcheha Pusansi ŭi tosi kujo [The urban organization of the city of Pusan under Japanese rule]." Seoul: Ph.D. diss., Kyung Hee University, 1990.

Yun Pyŏng-sŏl. "Hang-il ŭibyŏng [Anti-Japanese resistance of the Righteous Armies]." Pp. 341-460 in Kuksa P'yŏnch'an Wiwŏnhoe, ed., *Han'guksa*

[A history of Korea], vol. 19. Seoul: T'amgudang, 1978.

Zenshō Eisuke. *Chōsenjin no shōgyō* [The commerce of the Koreans]. Keijo:
Chōsen Sōtokufu, 1925.

Bibliography: Western Language

Ahn, Doo-Soon. "Contribution of Different Types of Trading Agents for Korean Trade." *Asian Economies* No. 43 (December 1982), pp. 7-21, and No. 44 (March 1983): 28-42.

Andrews, Bruce. "The Political Economy of World Capitalism: Theory and Practice." *International Organization* 36, 1 (Winter 1982): 135-163.

Arrighi, Giovanni. "Peripheralization of Southern Africa, I: Changes in Production Processes." *Review* III (1981): 161-191.

Baker, Edward J. "The Role of Legal Reforms in the Japanese Annexation and Rule of Korea, 1905-1919." Pp. 17-42 in David McCann et al., eds, *Studies on Korea in Transition*. Honolulu: Center for Korean Studies, 1979.

Balandier, G. "The Colonial Situation: A Theoretical Approach." Pp. 34-61 in Immanuel Wallerstein, ed., *Social Change: The Colonial Situation*. New York: John Wiley, 1966.

Balibar, Etienne. "The Basic Concepts of Historical Materialism." Pp. 199-325 in Louis Althusser and Etienne Balibar, eds., *Reading Capital*. Tr. by Ben Brewster. London: NLB, 1970.

Ban, Sung Hwan. "Agricultural Growth in Korea, 1918-1971." Pp. 90-116 in Yujiro Hayami, Vernon W. Ruttan, and Herman M. Southworth, eds., *Agricultural Growth in Japan, Taiwan, Korea, and the Philippines*. Honolulu: University Press of Hawaii, 1979.

Bergere, Marie-Claire. *The Golden Age of the Chinese Bourgeoisie, 1911-1937*. Cambridge: Cambridge University Press, 1989.

Betts, Raymond F. *The False Dawn: European Imperialism in the Nineteenth Century*. Minneapolis: University of Minnesota Press, 1975.

Bishop, Isabella Bird. *Korea and Her Neighbors*. Seoul: Yonsei University Press, 1970.

Black, Anthony. "Civil Society." P. 77 in David Miller, ed., *The Blackwell Encyclopedia of Political Thought*. New York: Basil Blackwell, 1987.

_____. *Guilds and Civil Society in European Political Thought from the Twelfth Century to the Present*. London: Methuen & Co., 1984.

Booth, William James. "On the Idea of the Moral Economy." *American Political Science Review*, vol. 88, no. 3 (Sept. 1994): 653-667.

Brandt, Loren. "Chinese Agriculture and the International Economy, 1870-1930s: A Reassessment." *Explorations in Economic History* 22 (1985): 168-193.

Bratton, Michael. "Beyond the State: Civil Society and Associational Life in Africa." *World Politics* 41, 3 (Apr. 1989): 407-429.

Brenner, Robert. "The Origins of Capitalist Development: a Critique of Neo-Smithian Marxism." *New Left Review* No. 104 (July-August 1977): 25-93.

Brudnoy, David. "Japan's Experiment in Korea." *Monumenta Nipponica* 25 (1970): 155-195.

Callaghy, Thomas. "Toward State Capability and Embedded Liberalism in the Third World: Lessons for Adjustment." Pp. 115-38 in Joan Nelson, ed., *Fragile Coalitions: The Politics of Economic Adjustment*. Overseas Development Council US- Thjird World Policy Perspectives No. 12. New Brunswick, NJ: Transaction Books, 1989.

Chandra, Vipan. "Review of Key-Hiuk Kim, *The Last Phase of the East Asian World Order: Korea, Japan, and the Chinese Empire, 1860-1882*; Martina Deuchler, *Confucian Gentlemen and Barbarian Envoys: The Opening of Korea, 1875-1885*." *Journal of Korean Studies* vol. 6 (1988-1989): 234-244.

_____. *Imperialism, Resistance, and Reform in late Nineteenth-Century Korea*. Berkeley: Center for Korean Studies, Institute of East Asian Studies, University of California Berkeley, 1988.

_____. "Nationalism and Popular Participation in Government in Late Nineteenth Century Korea: the Contribution of the Independence Club (1896-1898)." Ph.D. diss., Harvard University, 1977.

_____. "The Concept of Popular Sovereignty: The Case of Sŏ Chae-p'il and Yun Ch'i-ho." *Korea Journal* vol. 21, no. 4 (April 1981): 4-13.

Chang, Chin-sok. "A Study of the *Maeil Sinbo*." *Journal of Social Sciences and Humanities* no. 52 (1980): 59-114.

Chang Yun-shik. "The Personalist Ethic and the Market in Korea." *Comparative Studies in Society and History* 33, 1 (Jan. 1991): 106-129.

Chase-Dunn, Christopher. *Global Formation: Structures of the World-Economy*. Cambridge MA: Basil Blackwell, 1989.

_____. "The Korean Trajectory in the World-System." Pp. 270-304 in Kyong-dong Kim, ed., *Dependency Issues in Korean Development*. Seoul: Seoul National University Press, 1987.

Chen, Edward I-te. "The Attempt to Integrate the Empire: Legal Perspectives." Pp. 240-274 in Ramon H. Myers and Mark R. Peattie, eds., *The Japanese Colonial Empire, 1895-1945*. Princeton: Princeton University Press, 1984.

Cho Ki-jun. "The Impact of the Opening of Korea on its Commerce and Industry." *Korea Journal* 16, 2 (1973): 27-44.

Chŏng, To-Yŏng. "Korea's Foreign Trade under Japanese Rule." *Journal of Social Sciences and Humanities* no. 27 (December 1967): 19-44.

Chun, Hae-jong. "Sino-Korean Tributary Relations during the Ch'ing Period." Pp. 90-111 in John K. Fairbank, ed., *The Chinese World Order*.

Cambridge: Harvard University Press, 1969.

_____. "An Historical Survey of the Sino-Korean Tributary Relationship." *Journal of Social Sciences and Humanities* (Seoul) vol. 12 (1966): 1-31.

Chung, Chai-sik. *A Korean Confucian Encounter with the Modern World: Yi Hang-no and the West.* Berkeley: Institute of East Asian Studies, University of California,Berkeley, 1995.

_____. "In Defense of the Traditional Order: *ch'ŏksa wijŏng* (Ban Heterodoxy, Protect Orthodoxy)." *Philosophy East and West* 30 (July 1980): 355-374.

_____. "On the Quest for Confucian Reformation." *Journal of Social Sciences and Humanities* (June 1979): 1-38.

_____. "Christianity as Heterodoxy: An Aspect of General Cultural Orientation in Traditional Korea." Pp. 57-86 in Yung-hwan Jo, ed., *Korea's Response to the West.* Kalamazoo: Korea Research Publications, 1971.

Chung, Henry. *Treaties and Conventions between Corea and Other Powers.* New York: Nichols, 1919.

Chung, Young-iob. "The Traditional Economy of Korea." *The Journal of Modern Korean Studies*, vol. 1 (April 1984): 21-52.

_____. "Korean Investment under Japanese Rule." *Korea Journal* vol. 17, no. 3 (March 1977): 4-21.

Clark, Cal. *Taiwan's Development: Implications for Contending Political Economy Paradigms.* Contributions in Economics and Economic History, No. 100. New York: Greenwood Press, 1989.

Clark, Donald C. "Yun Ch'i-ho (1864-1945): Portrait of a Korean Intellectual in an Era of Transition." Pp. 36-76 in James B. Palais and Margery D. Lang, eds., *Occasional Papers on Korea, No. 4.* Seattle: Joint Committee on Korean Studies of the American Council of Learned Societies and the Social Science Research Council, 1975.

Cohen, Jean L., and Andrew Arato. *Civil Society and Political Theory.* Cambridge, MA: The MIT Press, 1992.

Connolly, William E. "Interests." Pp. 243-244 in David Miller, ed., *The Blackwell Encyclopedia of Political Thought.* New York: Basil Blackwell, 1987.

Conroy, Hilary. *The Japanese Seizure of Korea, 1868-1910.* Philadelphia: University of Pennsylvania Press, 1960.

Cook, Harold F. *Korea's 1884 Incident.* Seoul: Korea Branch of the Royal Asiatic Society, 1972.

Cumings, Bruce. World System and Authoritarian Regimes in Korea, 1848-1984." Pp. 249-269 in Edwin A. Winckler and Susan Greenhalgh, eds., *Contending Approaches to the Political Economy of Taiwan.* Armonk NY: M. E. Sharpe, 1988.

_____. "The Legacy of Japanese Colonialism in Korea." Pp. 478-496 in Ramon H. Myers and Mark R. Peattie, eds., *The Japanese Colonial Empire, 1895-1945.* Princeton: Princeton University Press, 1984.

208

_____. "The Origins and Development of the Northeast Asian Political Economy: Industrial Sectors, Product Cycles, and Political Consequences." *International Organization* vol. 38 (Winter 1984): 1-40.

_____. *The Origins of the Korean War: Liberation and the Emergence of Separate Regimes, 1945-1947*. Princeton: Princeton University Press, 1981.

De Tocqueville, Alexis. *Democracy in America*. The Henry Reeve Text, revised by Francis Bowen, and edited by Phillips Bradley. New York: Vintage Books, 1945.

Deuchler, Martina. "Reject the False and Uphold the Straight: Attitudes Toward Heterodox Thought in Early Yi Korea." Pp. 375-410 in Wm. Theodore de Bary and JaHyun Kim Haboush, eds., *The Rise of Neo-Confucianism in Korea*. New York: Columbia University Press, 1985.

_____. *Confucian Gentlemen and Barbarian Envoys: The Opening of Korea, 1875-1885*. Seattle: University of Washington Press, 1977.

_____. "The Opening of Korean Ports." *Korea Journal* vol. 9, no. 1 (January 1969): 11-20.

Dong, Wonmo. "Japanese Colonial Policy and Practice in Korea, 1905-1945: A Study in Assimilation." Ph.D. diss., Georgetown University, 1965.

Duus, Peter. "The Reaction of Japanese Big Business to a State-Controlled Economy in the 1930s." *Scienze Economiche E Commerciali* vol. 31, no. 9 (September 1984): 119-131.

_____. "The Economic Dimensions of Meiji Imperialism: The Case of Korea." Pp. 128-171 in Ramon H. Myers and Mark R. Peattie, eds., *The Japanese Colonial Empire, 1895-1945*. Princeton: Princeton University Press, 1984.

Eckert, Carter Joel. *Offspring of Empire. The Koch'ang Kims and the Colonial Origins of Korean Capitalism, 1876-1945*. Seattle: University of Washington Press, 1992.

_____. "The South Korean Bourgeoisie: A Class in Search of Hegemony." *Journal of Korean Studies* 7 (1990-1991): 115 - 148.

_____. "The Colonial Origins of Korean Capitalism: The Koch'ang Kims and the Kyongsong Spinning and Weaving Company, 1876-1945." Ph.D. diss., University of Washington, 1986.

Elisonas, Jurgis. "The Inseparable Trinity: Japan's Relations with China and Korea." Pp. 235-300 in John Whitney Hall, ed., *The Cambridge History of Japan*. Vol 4, "Early Modern Japan." Cambridge: Cambridge University Press, 1991.

Evans, Peter. *Embedded Autonomy: States and Industrial Transformation*. Princeton NJ: Princeton University Press, 1995

_____. "Predatory, Developmental, and Other Apparatuses: A Comparative Political Economy Perspective on the Third World State." Pp. 84-111 in A. Douglas Kincaid and Alejandro Portes, eds., *Comparative National Development: Society and Economy in the New Global Order*. Chapel Hill

NC: The University of North Carolina Press, 1994

_____. "The State as Problem and Solution: Predation, Embedded Autonomy, and Structural Change." Pp. 139-181 in Stephan Haggard and Robert R. Kaufman, eds., *The Politics of Economic Adjustment: International Constraints, Distributive Conflicts, and the State*. Princeton NJ: Princeton University Press, 1992.

_____. *Dependent Development: The Alliance of Multinational, State and Local Capital in Brazil*. Princeton: Princeton University Press, 1979.

Fairbank, John K., Edwin O. Reischauer, and Albert M. Craig. *East Asia: The Modern Transformation*. Boston: Houghton Mifflin Company, 1965.

Fewsmith, Joseph. *Party, State, and Local Elites in Republican China. Merchant Organizations and Politics in Shanghai, 1890-1930*. Honolulu: University of Hawaii Press, 1985.

Fieldhouse, D. K. *Colonialism, 1870-1945: An Introduction*. New York: St. Martin's Press, 1981.

Fletcher, William Miles. *The Japanese Business Community and National Trade Policy, 1920-1942*. Chapel Hill: The University of North Carolina Press, 1989.

Foreign Economic Administration, Enemy Branch. *Japanese Economic Penetration into Korea as of 1940 as Shown by an Analysis of Corporations Operating in Korea*. Washington DC: State Department, October 23, 1945.

Foster-Carter, Aidan. "The Modes of Production Controversy." *New Left Review* no. 107 (Jan.-Feb. 1978): 47-79.

Frank, Andre Gunder. *Dependent Accumulation and Underdevelopment*. London: Macmillan, 1978.

Fujita, Teiichirō. "Local Trade Associations (*dōgyō kumiai*) in Prewar Japan." Pp. 87-113 in Hiroaki Yamazaki and Matao Miyamoto, eds., *Trade Associations in Business History*. Tokyo: University of Tokyo Press, 1988.

Furnivall, J. S. *Colonial Policy and Practice. A Comparative Study of Burma and Netherlands India*. New York: New York University Press, 1956.

Gann, Lewis H. "Western and Japanese Colonialism: Some Preliminary Comparisons." Pp. 497-525 in Ramon H. Myers and Mark R. Peattie, eds., *The Japanese Colonial Empire, 1895-1945*. Princeton: Princeton University Press, 1984.

Gifford, Daniel L. "Korean Guilds and Other Associations." *Korean Repository* (Feb. 1895): 41-49.

Gold, Thomas B. "Colonial Origins of Taiwanese Capitalism." Pp. 101-117 in Edwin A. Winckler and Susan Greenhalgh, eds., *Contending Approaches to the Political Economy of Taiwan*. Armonk, NY: M. E. Sharpe, Inc., 1988.

Goldfrank, Walter L. "Silk and Steel: Italy and Japan between the Two World Wars." Pp. 297-315 in Richard Tomasson, ed., *Comparative Social*

Research, vol. 4. Greenwich Connecticut: JAI Press, 1981.

Government General of Chosen. *Annual Report on Reforms and Progress in Korea.* Keijo: Government General of Chosen, annual.

_____. *Laws and Regulations relating to the Customs of Chosen and Japan Proper.* Tokyo: Tōa Insatsu, 1912.

Grajdanzev, Andrew J. *Modern Korea.* New York: John Day, 1944.

Granovetter, Mark. "Economic Action and Social Structure: The Problem of Embeddedness." *American Journal of Sociology*, volume 91, no. 3 (Nov. 1985): 481-510.

Habermas, Jurgen. *The Structural Transformation of the Public Sphere.* An Inquiry into a Category of Bourgeois Society. Tr. Thomas Burger. Cambridge MA: The MIT Press, 1989.

_____. "The Public Sphere: An Encyclopedia Article." Originally appeared 1964. *New German Critique* 1, 3 (1974): 49-55.

Haboush, JaHyun Kim. "The Confucianization of Korean Society." Pp. 84-110 in Gilbert Rozman, ed., *The East Asian Region: Confucian Heritage and its Modern Adaptation.* Princeton: Princeton University Press, 1991.

Haggard, Stephan, David Kang, and Chung-in Moon. "Japanese Colonialism and Korean Development: A Critique." Research Report of the Graduate School of International Relations and Pacific Studies, # 95-04, 1995.

_____, Chung-In Moon, and Byung-kook Kim. "The Transition to Export-led Growth in South Korea: 1954-1966." *The Journal of Asian Studies* 50, no. 4 (November 1991): 850-873.

_____, and Chung-In Moon. "Institutions and Economic Policy: Theory and a Korean Case Study." *World Politics* vol. 42, no. 2 (January 1990): 210-237.

_____. *Pathways from the Periphery: The Politics of Growth in the Newly Industrializing Countries.* Ithaca NY: Cornell University Press, 1990.

_____, and Chung-In Moon. "The South Korean State in the International Economy: Liberal, Dependent, or Mercantile." Pp. 131-189 in Gerald Ruggie, ed., *The Antinomies of Interdependence: National Welfare and the International Division of Labor.* New York: Columbia University, 1983.

Hahn, Sang-bok. "The Korean Marketing System for Marine Products: An Approach from the Perspective of Economic Anthropology." *Social Science Journal* (Unesco, Korea) vol. 5, no. 1 (1978): 100-126.

Hall, Thomas D. *Social Change in the Southwest, 1350-1880.* Lawrence, Kansas: University Press of Kansas, 1989.

_____. "Incorporation in the World-system: Toward a Critique." *American Sociological Review*, vol. 51 (June 1986): 390-402.

Hamashita, Takeshi. "Tributary Trade System and Modern Asia." *Memoirs of the Research Department of the Tōyō Bunko* 46 (1988): 7-26.

Han, Woo-Keun. *The History of Korea.* Tr. by Kyung-shik Lee, and edited by Grafton K. Mintz. Honolulu: University Press of Hawaii, 1974.

Hao, Yen-P'ing. *The Commercial Revolution in Nineteenth-Century China. The Rise of Sino-Western Mercantile Capitalism.* Berkeley: University of California Press, 1986.

_____. *The Comprador in Nineteenth Century China: Bridge between East and West.* Cambridge: Harvard University Press, 1970.

Hatada, Takashi. *A History of Korea.* Tr. and edited by Warren W. Smith and Benjamin H. Hazard. Santa Barbara: Clio Press, 1969.

Hazard, Benjamin H. "Korea and Japan: Premodern Relations (to 1875)." Pp. 276-279 in Kodansha Publishing, *Kodansha Encyclopedia of Japan*, vol. 4. Tokyo: Kodansha, 1983.

Heidenheimer, Arnold J. and Frank C. Langdon. *Business Associations and the Financing of Political Parties: A Comparative Study of the Evolution of Practices in Germany, Norway and Japan.* The Hague: Martinus Nijhoff, 1968.

Hirschmeier, Johannes and Tsunehiko Yui. *The Development of Japanese Business.* Cambridge: Harvard University Press, 1975.

_____. "Shibusawa Eiichi: Industrial Pioneer." Pp. 209-247 in William W. Lockwood, ed., *The State and Economic Enterprise in Japan.* Princeton: Princeton University Press, 1965.

Ho, Samuel Pao-San. "Colonialism and Development: Korea, Taiwan, and Kwantung." Pp. 347-398 in Ramon H. Myers and Mark R. Peattie, eds., *The Japanese Colonial Empire, 1895-1945.* Princeton: Princeton University Press, 1984.

Ho, Yhi-min. "On Taiwan's Agricultural Transformation under Colonialism: A Critique." *Journal of Economic History* vol. 31, no. 3 (Sept. 1971): 672-681.

Hopkins, Terence K. and Immanuel Wallerstein. "Structural Transformations of the World-Economy." Pp. 121-142 in Terence K. Hopkins, Immanuel Wallerstein et al., eds., *World-Systems Analysis: Theory and Methodology.* Beverly Hills: Sage Publications, 1982.

_____. "Sociology and the Substantive View of the Economy." Pp. 271-306 in Karl Polanyi, Conrad M. Arensbert, and Harry W. Pearson, eds. *Trade and Market in the Early Empires.* Economies in History and Theory. Glencoe, Illinois: The Free Press, 1957.

Huang, Philip C. C. *The Peasant Economy and Social Change in North China.* Stanford: Stanford University Press, 1985.

Hulbert, Homer. *Hulbert's History of Korea.* Orig. publ. 1905. Edited by Clarence Norwood Weems. New York: Hilary House Publishers, 1962.

Hunter, Janet. "Japanese Government Policy, Business Opinion, and the Seoul-Pusan Railway, 1894-1906." *Modern Asian Studies* 11 (1977): 573-579.

Hwang, In K. *The Korean Reform Movement of the 1880's.* Cambridge: Schenkman, 1978.

Independent Staff. *Independent.* Seoul: 1896-1898.

Ingham, Barbara. "Colonialism and Peripheral Development." Pp. 125 -137 in Barbara Ingham and Colin Simmons, eds., *Development Studies and Colonial Policy*. London: Frank Cass, 1987.

International Monetary Fund. *Directions of Trade Statistics Yearbook, 1994*. Washington DC: IMF Publications, 1994.

Ishida, Takeshi. "The Development of Interest Groups and the Pattern of Political Modernization in Japan." Pp. 293-396 in Robert E. Ward, ed., *Political Development in Modern Japan*. Princeton: Princeton University Press, 1968.

Jaisohn, Philip. "Korean Finance." *Korean Repository* III (1986): 166-168.

Johnson, Chalmers. "Political Institutions and Economic Performance: The Government-Business Relationship in Japan, South Korea and Taiwan." Pp. 136-164 in Frederic C. Deyo, ed., *The Political Economy of the New Asian Industrialism*. Ithaca: Cornell University Press, 1987.

Jones, George Herbert. "Chemulpo." *Korean Repository* IV (1897): 374-384.

Ka, Chih-Ming. "Land Tenure, Development and Dependency in Colonial Taiwan (1895-1945)." Ph.D. diss., Sociology, State University of New York at Binghamton, 1987.

Kahn, Alfred C. "Cartels and Trade Associations." Pp. 320-325 in David L. Sills, ed., *International Encyclopedia of the Social Sciences*, vol. 2. New York: Macmillan and the Free Press, 1968.

Kajima, Morinosuke. *The Diplomacy of Japan 1894-1922*, vol. I. Tokyo: Kajima Institute of International Peace, 1976.

Kamesaka, Tsunesaburo. *Who's Who in Japan, 1939-1940, with Manchouko and China*. Tokyo: The Who's Who in Japan Publishing Office, 1939.

Kawashima, Fijia. "Yi Dynasty." Pp. 324-325 in Kodansha Publishing, *Kodansha Encyclopedia of Japan*, vol. 8. Tokyo: Kodansha, 1983.

Keane, John. "Introduction." Pp. 1-31 in John Keane, ed., *Civil Society and the State -- New European Perspectives*. London: Verso, 1988.

_____. "Despotism and Democracy: The Origins and Development of the Distinction Between Civil Society and the State 1750-1850." Pp. 35-71 in John Keane, ed., *Civil Society and the State - New European Perspectives*. London: Verso, 1988.

Kelly, M. Patricia. "Broadening the Scope: Gender and the Study of International Development." Pp. 143-168 in A. Douglas Kincaid and Alejandro Portes, eds., *Comparative National Development: Society and Economy in the New Global Order*. Chapel Hill: The University of North Carolina Press, 1994.

Kim, C. I. Eugene and Han-kyo Kim. *Korea and the Politics of Imperialism, 1876-1910*. Berkeley: University of California Press, 1967.

Kim, Eun Mee. "From Dominance to Symbiosis: State and Chaebol in the Korean Economy, 1960-1985." Ph.D. diss., Brown University, 1987.

Kim, Hyung-chang. "Yu Kil-chun: A Korean Crusader for Reform." *Korea*

Journal 12 (Dec. 1972): 36-42.

_____. *Letters in Exile: The Life and Times of Yun Ch'i-ho*. Covington, Georgia: Rhoades Printing, 1980.

Kim, Key-hiuk. *The Last Phase of the East Asian World Order*. Berkeley: University of California Press, 1980.

Kim, Kyong-dong. "Political Factors in the Formation of the Entrepreneurial Elite in South Korea." *Asian Survey* 16, 5 (May 1976): 465-477.

Kim, Pyŏng-ha. "Economic Thought of Yu Kil-chun." *Korea Journal* 18 (July 1978) 30-48, and (Aug. 1978): 42-51.

Kim, Ui-hwan. "Japanese in Pusan [Fusan] after the Opening of the Port." *Journal of Social Sciences and Humanities*, no. 40 (Dec. 1974): 87-102.

Kim, Young-ho. "Yu Kil Chun's Idea of Enlightenment." *Journal of Social Sciences and Humanities* 33 (Dec. 1979): 37-60.

Koh, Byung-ik. "The Attitude of Korea Toward Japan." Pp. 43-52 in Marshall R. Phil, ed., *Listening to Korea*. New York: Praeger, 1965.

Koh, Sung-jae, *Stages of Industrial Development in Asia. A Comparative History of the Cotton Industry in Japan, India, China and Korea*. Philadelphia: University of Pennsylvania Press, 1966.

Kohli, Atul. "Where Do High Growth Political Economies Come From? The Japanese Lineage of Korea's 'Developmental State.'" *World Development* vol. 22, no. 9 (September 1994): 1269-1293

Koo, Hagen. "Strong State and Contentious Society." Pp. 231-249 in Hagen Koo, ed., *State and Society in Contemporary Korea*. Ithaca: Cornell University Press, 1993.

_____. "The Interplay of State, Social Class, and World System in East Asian Development: the Cases of South Korea and Taiwan." Pp. 165-181 in Frederic Deyo, ed., *The Political Economy of the New Asian Industrialism*. New York: Cornell University Press, 1987.

Korea, Chief Commissioner of Customs. *Korea: Tables of Foreign Trade and Shipping for the Year 1908*. Seoul: Customs Office, 1908.

Korea, Department of Finance. *State of the Progress of the Reorganization of Finances in Korea, 1905-1907*. Keijo: Department of Finance, 1907.

Korea, Imperial Maritime Customs, Chief Commissioner of Customs. *Report on the Trade of Korea for the Year 1906*. Seoul: Imperial Maritime Customs, 1906.

Korea Branch of the Royal Asiatic Society. "Tables of the McCune-Reischauer System for the Romanization of Korean." *Transactions of the Korea Branch of the Royal Asiatic Society* 38 (Oct. 1961): 121-128.

Korean Development Bank. *Korean Industry in the World, 1994*. Seoul: KDB, 1994.

Korean Repository Staff. "The Trade of Korea for 1895." *Korean Repository* (March, 1896)

_____. "The Budget for 1896." *Korean Repository* (March 18966): 31-32.

214

_____. "Mr. Consul-General Jordan's Trade Report for 1897." *Korean Repository* (Oct. 1898): 381-387.

Korea Review Staff. "The New Century: Chemulpo." *Korea Review* I, 1 (Jan. 1901): 11-16.

_____. "Korean Domestic Trade." *Korea Review* vol. 5 (November 1905): 403-411.

_____. "The Korean Customs Service." *Korea Review* vol. 5, no. 10 (Oct. 1905): 367-380.

_____. "Export Duties." *Korea Review* vol. 6, no. 7 (July 1906): 260-261.

Lasek, Elizabeth. "Imperialism in China: A Methodological Critique." *Bulletin of Concerned Scholars* 15, 1 (1983): 50-64.

Lee, Chong-sik. *The Politics of Korean Nationalism.* Berkeley: University of California Press, 1963.

Lee, Hoon K. *Land Utilization and Rural Economy in Korea.* New York: Greenwood, [1936] 1969.

Lee, Hyon-jong. "On Political, Journalistic and Social Organizations in the Days of the Han Empire (1897-1910)." *Journal of Social Sciences and Humanities* 27 (1967) 62-69, 28 (1968) 31-41, 29 (1968): 110-117.

Lee, Ki-baik. *A New History of Korea.* Tr. by Edward Wagner with Edward J. Shultz. Cambridge MA: Harvard University Press, 1984.

Lee, Kwang-rin. "The Enlightenment Thinking of Sŏ Che-p'il." *Social Science Journal* vol. 7 (1980): 48-91.

_____. "Korea's Response to Social Darwinism." *Korea Journal* vol. 18, no. 4 (April 1978) 36-47; vol. 18, no. 5 (May 1978): 42-49.

_____. "'I-Yen' and the Ideas of Enlightenment in Korea." *Journal of Social Sciences and Humanities* 31 (Dec. 1969): 1-10.

Lee, Yong-ha. "The Spiritual Aspect of Korea-Japan Relations: A Historical Review of Complications Arising from the Consciousness of Peripheral Culture." *Social Science Journal* (Seoul) 3 (1975): 20-45.

Lee, Yoon Ki. "The Sŏnbi Spirit and its Manifestation in the Political Domain." *Korea Journal* (April 1989): 12-17.

Lew, Young-ick. "The Conservative Character of the 1894 Tonghak Peasant Uprising: A Reappraisal with Emphasis on Chŏn Pong-jun's Background and Motivation." *Journal of Korean Studies* vol. 7 (1990): 149-180.

_____. "Korean-Japanese Politics behind the Kabo-Ulmi Reform Movement, 1894-1896." *Journal of Korean Studies* (Seattle) 3 (1981) 39-81.

_____. "An Analysis of the Reform Documents of the Kabo Reform Movement, 1894." *Journal of Social Sciences and Humanities* 40 (Dec. 1974): 29-86.

Lim, Hyun-chin and Woon-seon Paek. "State Autonomy in Modern Korea: Instrumental Possibilities and Structural Limits." *Korea Journal* (November 1987): 19-32.

Lindblom, Charles E. *Politics and Markets.* New York: Basic Books, 1977.

Lockwood, William W. "The State and Economic Enterprise in Modern Japan, 1868-1939." Pp. 537-602 in Simon Kuznets, Wilbert E. Moore, and Joseph J. Spengler, eds., *Economic Growth: Brazil, India, Japan*. Durham: Duke University Press, 1955.

Lone, Stewart. "The Japanese Annexation of Korea 1910: The Failure of East Asian Co-Prosperity." *Modern Asian Studies* vol. 25, part I (February 1991): 143-174.

Maddison, Angus. "Dutch Colonialism in Indonesia: Comparative Perspective." Pp. 322-335 in Anne Booth, W. J. O'Malley, and Anna Weidemann, eds., *Indonesian Economic History in the Dutch Colonial Era*. New Haven: Yale University Southeast Asia Studies, 1990.

Mancall, Mark. *China at the Center: 300 Years of Foreign Policy*. New York: The Free Press, 1984.

_____. "The Ch'ing Tribute System: An Interpretive Essay." Pp. 63-89 in John King Fairbank, ed., *The Chinese World Order: Traditional China's Foreign Relations*. Cambridge MA: Harvard, 1968.

Masuda, Koh, ed. *New Japanese-English Dictionary*. Tokyo: Kenkyūsha, 1974.

McCune, George M. "Korean Relations with China and Japan, 1800-1864." Ph.D. diss., University of California, Berkeley, 1941.

McNamara, Dennis L. *Textiles and Industrial Transition in Japan*. Ithaca, New York: Cornell University Press, 1995.

_____. "Bridging State and Society, East and West." Research Paper B-10, Institure of International Relations, Sophia University, August 1994.

_____. "State and Concentration in Korea's First Republic." *Modern Asian Studies*, vol. 26, no. 4 (1992): 701-718.

_____. "Reincorporation and the American State in South Korea: the Textile Industry in the 1950s." *Sociological Perspectives*, special issue on Studies in the New International Political Economy, vol. 35, no. 2, (fall 1992): 329-342.

_____. "*Kwanmin* in Colony and Republic: Theme and Variation in Korean Capitalism." Presented for seminar on "Colonial Korea" at the Regional Seminar on Korean Studies at the University of California, Berkeley on April 29, 1991.

_____. *Colonial Origins of Korean Enterprise, 1910-1945*. Cambridge: Cambridge University Press, 1990.

_____. Review of Vipan Chandra's *Imperialism, Resistance and Reform in Late Nineteenth-Century Korea*. *Korean Studies* no. 14 (1990): 195-197.

_____. "The Keishō and the Korean Business Elite." *Journal of Asian Studies* vol. 48, no. 2 (May 1989): 310-323.

_____. "Toward a Theory of Korean Capitalism: A Study of the Colonial Business Elite." Pp. 713-725 in Academy of Korean Studies, ed., *Korean Studies, Its Tasks and Perspectives*, vol. 2. Seoul: Academy of Korean

Studies, 1988.

_____. "Entrepreneurship in Colonial Korea: Kim Youn-su." *Modern Asian Studies* vol. 22, no. 1 (1988): 165-177.

_____. "Survival Strategies: Korean Solidarity in a Hostile World." Pp. 55-66 in Ronald A. Morse, ed., *Wild Asters. Explorations in Korean Thought, Culture and Society.* New York: University Press of America, 1987.

_____. "Korea and Brazil at the Turn of the Century: Trade, Elites and Foreign Ties." Pp. 496-511 in Kyong-dong Kim, ed., *Dependency Issues in Korean Development: Comparative Perspectives.* Seoul: Seoul National University Press, 1987.

_____. "Comparative Colonial Response: Korea and Taiwan, 1895-1919." *Korean Studies* 10 (1986): 54-68.

_____. "A Frontier Ideology: Meiji Japan and the Korean Frontier." *Journal of International Studies* (Tokyo: Sophia University) 12 (Jan. 1984): 43-64.

_____. "Imperial Expansion and Nationalist Resistance: Japan in Korea, 1876-1910." Ph.D. diss., Harvard University, 1983.

McRaith, James Frederick. "The Marketing of Rice in the Republic of Korea." Ph.D. diss., Columbia University, 1960.

Mann, Michael. "The Autonomous Power of the State: Its Origins, Mechanisms and Results." *The European Journal of Sociology.* 25, 2 (1984): 185-213.

Mann, Susan. *Local Merchants and the Chinese Bureaucracy, 1750-1950.* Stanford: Stanford University Press, 1987.

_____. "Brokers as Entrepreneurs in Presocialist China." *Comparative Studies in Society and History* vol. 26, no. 4 (Oct. 1984): 614-636.

Marshall, Byron. *Capitalism and Nationalism in Prewar Japan. The Ideology of the Business Elite, 1868-1941.* Stanford: Stanford University Press, 1967.

Maunier, Rene. *The Sociology of Colonies. An Introduction to the Study of Race Contact.* Tr. and edited by E. O. Lorimer, 2 vols. London: Routledge and Kegan Paul, 1949.

Miyamoto Matao. "The Development of Business Associations in Prewar Japan." Pp. 1-45 in Hiroaki Yamazaki and Matao Miyamoto, eds., *Trade Associations in Business History.* Tokyo: University of Tokyo Press, 1988.

Mizoguchi, Toshiyuki, and Yamamoto Yūzō. "Capital Formation in Taiwan and Korea." Pp. 399-419 in Ramon H. Myers and Mark R. Peattie, eds., *The Japanese Colonial Empire, 1895-1945.* Princeton: Princeton University Press, 1984.

_____. "Foreign Trade in Taiwan and Korea under Japanese Rule." *Hitosubashi Journal of Economics* 14 (February 1974): 37-53.

Moon, Pal Yong. "The Evolution of Rice Policy in Korea." *Food Research Institute Studies* 14, 4 (1975): 381-402.

Morse, Hosea Ballou. *The Gilds of China.* Taipei: Ch'eng-Wen Publishing

Company, 1966.

Moskowitz, Karl. "Current Assets: The Employees of Japanese Banks in Colonial Korea." Ph.D. diss., Harvard University, 1979.

_____. "The Creation of the Oriental Development Company: Japanese Illusion Meets Korean Reality." In James B. Palais, ed., *Occasional Papers on Korea*, no. 1 73-109. Seattle: Joint Committee on Korean Studies of the American Council of Learned Societies and the Social Science Research Council, 1974.

Murayama, Yoshitada. "The Pattern of Japanese Economic Penetration of the Prewar Netherlands East Indies." Pp. 89-112 in Saya Shiraishi and Takashi Shiraishi, eds., *The Japanese in Colonial Southeast Asia*. Ithaca: Southeast Asia Program, Cornell University, 1993.

Murphey, Rhoads. "The Treaty Ports and China's Modernization." Pp. 17-71 in Mark Elvin and G. William Skinner, eds., *The Chinese City Between Two Worlds*. Stanford: Stanford University Press, 1974.

Myers, Ramon H., and Yamada Saburō. "Agricultural Development in the Empire." Pp. 399-419 in Ramon H. Myers and Mark R. Peattie, eds., *The Japanese Colonial Empire, 1895-1945*. Princeton: Princeton University Press, 1984.

Naquin, Susan, and Evelyn S. Rawski. *Chinese Society in the Eighteenth Century*. New Haven: Yale University Press, 1987.

Nelson, M. F. *Korea and the Old Orders in East Asia*. Baton Rouge: Louisiana State University Press, 1945.

Nemeth, Roger J. and David A. Smith. "The Political Economy of Contrasting Urban Hierarchies in South Korea and the Philippines." Pp. 183-206 in Michael Timberlake, ed., *Urbanization in the World-Economy*. New York: Academic Press, 1985.

Nishio, Harry Kaneharu. "Political Authority Structure and the Development of Entrepreneurship in Japan (1603-1890)." Ph.D. diss., University of California, Berkeley, Sociology, 1966.

Oh, Bongwan Bonnie. "Introduction" and "Meiji Imperialism: Phenomenally Rapid." Pp. 121-130 in Harry Wray and Hilary Conroy, eds., *Japan Examined: Perspectives on Modern Japanese History*. Honolulu: University of Hawaii Press, 1983.

_____. "The Kabo Kaengjang of 1894 in Korea and the Policy of Mutsu Munemitsu." *Journal of Social Sciences and Humanities* 44 (Dec. 1976): 85-103.

Oh, S. E. "Dr. Philip Jaisohn's Reform Movement 1896-1898: A Critical Appraisal of the Independence Club." Ph.D. diss., The American University, 1971.

O'Neill, P. G. *Japanese Names. A Comprehensive Index by Characters and Readings*. New York: Weatherhill, 1972.

Pak, Wŏn-sŏn. "The Market in Korea: A Historical Survey." *Korea Journal*

(June 1989): 4-21.

_____. "Korean Factors: Types of Kaekchu." *Journal of Social Sciences and Humanities* 35 (Dec. 1971): 64-84.

_____. *Kaekchu* [Brokers]. Seoul: Yonsei University Press, 1968.

_____. "The Merchant System Peculiar to Korea." *Journal of Social Sciences and Humanities* 26 (June 1967): 100-113.

Palais, James B. "Political Leadership in the Yi Dynasty." Pp. 3-40 in Daesook Suh and Chae-jin Lee, eds., *Political Leadership in Korea*. Seattle: University of Washington Press, 1976.

_____. *Politics and Policy in Traditional Korea*. Cambridge: Harvard University Press, 1975.

Palat, Ravi. "The Incorporation and Peripheralization of South Asia, 1600-1950." *Review* [Fernand Braudel Center] 10, 1 (Summer 1986): 171-208.

Palmer, Spencer J., ed. *Korean-American Relations, Documents Pertaining to the Far Eastern Diplomacy of the United States*. Berkeley: University of California Press, 1963.

Park, Il-Keun. ed. *Anglo-American and Chinese Diplomatic Materials Relating to Korea*. Volume I: 1866-1886; Volume II: 1887-1897. Seoul: Shin Mun Dang Publishing, 1982. Cited as ACDM.

Perez-Diaz, Victor. *The Return of Civil Society: The Emergence of Democratic Spain*. Cambridge MA: Harvard University Press, 1991.

Perdue, Peter C. "The Qing State and the Gansu Grain Market, 1739-1864." Pp. 100-125 in Thomas G. Rawski and Lillian M. Li, eds., *Chinese History in Economic Perspective*. Berkeley: University of California Press, 1992.

Polanyi, Karl. *The Livelihood of Man*. Edited by Harry W. Pearson. New York: Academic Press, 1977.

_____. "The Economy as Instituted Process." Pp. 243-270 in Karl Polanyi, Conrad M. Arensbert, and Harry W. Pearson, eds. *Trade and Market in the Early Empires*. Economies in History and Theory. Glencoe, Illinois: The Free Press, 1957.

_____. *The Great Transformation*. Beacon Hill, Boston: Beacon Press, (1944) 1957.

Ranis, Gustav. "The Community-Centered Entrepreneur in Japanese Development." *Explorations in Entrepreneurial History* 8, 2 (December 1955): 80-97.

Rankin, Mary Backus. "Some Observations on a Chinese Public Sphere." *Modern China*, vol. 19, no. 2 (April 1993): 158-182.

_____. *Elite Activism and Political Transformation in China: Zhejiang Province, 1865-1911*. Stanford: Stanford University Press, 1986.

Roberts, Stephen A. *The History of French Colonial Policy, 1870-1925*. London: Frank Cass and Co., 1929.

Robinson, Michael. "Perceptions of Confucianism in Twentieth-Century Korea." Pp. 204-225 in Gilbert Rozman, ed., *The East Asian Region:*

Confucian Heritage and Its Modern Adaptation. Princeton: Princeton University Press, 1991.

_____. *Cultural Nationalism in Colonial Korea, 1920-1925*. Seattle: University of Washington Press, 1988.

Robinson, Ronald. "Non-European Foundations of European Imperialism: A Sketch for a Theory of Collaboration." Pp. 117-142 in Roger Owen and Bob Sutcliffe, eds., *Studies in the Theory of Imperialism*. London: Longman, 1972.

_____, and John Gallagher. "The Partition of Africa." Pp. 73-127 in F. H. Hinsley, ed. *New Cambridge Modern History*, vol. 11. Cambridge: Cambridge University Press, 1962.

_____, and John Gallagher. "The Imperialism of Free Trade." *Economic History Review* (2nd series) VI (1953): 1-15.

Ro, Chung-Hyun. "A Study on Administrative Reorganization in Yi [Chosŏn] Dynasty Korea, 1894-1910." *Journal of Social Sciences and Humanities* No. 28 (June 1968): 51-103.

Rowe, William T. "The Problem of 'Civil Society' in Late Imperial China." *Modern China*, vol. 19, no. 2 (April 993): 139-157.

_____. "The Public Sphere in Modern China." *Modern China*, vol. 16, no. 3 (July 1990): 309-329.

Ruggie, John Gerard. "International Regimes, Transactions, and Change: Embedded Liberalism in the Postwar Economic Order." *International Organization* 36, 2, (Spring, 1982): 379-415.

Sarfatti Larson, Magali. *The Rise of Professionalism, A Sociological Analysis*. Berkeley: University of California Press, 1977.

Schoppa, R. Keith. *Chinese Elites and Political Change*. Zhejiang Province in the Early Twentieth Century. Cambridge MA: Harvard University Press, 1982.

Sheldon, Charles David. *The Rise of the Merchant Class in Tokugawa Japan, 1600-1868*. Locust Valley, New York: J. J. Augustin, 1958.

Shin, Gi-wook. "Social Change and Peasant Protest in Colonial Korea." Ph.D. diss., University of Washington, 1991.

Shin, Susan. "The Tonghak Movement: From Enlightenment to Revolution." *Korean Studies Forum* 5 (Winter-spring 1979): 1-79.

_____. "Tonghak Thought: the Roots of Revolution." *Korea Journal* 19, 9 (Sept. 1979): 11-20.

Shin, Yong-ha. "Pak Un-sik's Idea of National Salvation by Industry." *Journal of Social Sciences and Humanities* no. 50 (December 1979): 17-53.

_____. "Landlordism in the Late Yi Dynasty." Part I, *Korea Journal* vol. 18, no. 6 (1978) 25-32, and Part II, *Korea Journal* vol. 18, no. 7 (1978): 22-29.

_____. "The Opening of Korea and Changes in Social Thought." *Korea Journal* vol. 16, no. 2 (Feb. 1976): 4-9.

Shiraishi, Saya and Takashi Shiraishi. "The Japanese in Colonial Southeast Asia: An Overview." Pp. 5-20 in Saya Shiraishi and Takashi Shiraishi, eds., *The Japanese in Colonial Southeast Asia*. Ithaca: Southeast Asia Program, Cornell University, 1993.

Sisa Yŏngŏsa. *New World Korean-English Dictionary*. Seoul: Sisa Yŏngŏsa Publishers, 1979.

Skocpol, Theda. "Wallerstein's World Capitalist System: A Theoretical and Historical Critique." *American Journal of Sociology* vol. 82, no. 5 (1977): 1075-1090.

Smith, Neil Skene. "The Rice Trade." Pp. 117-137 in his *Tokugawa Japan, Materials on Japanese Social and Economic History*, vol. I. Washington DC: University Publications of America, 1979.

Smith, Tony. *The Pattern of Imperialism. The United States, Great Britain, and the Late-industrializing World since 1815*. Cambridge: Cambridge University Press, 1981.

So, Alvin Y. *The South China Silk District: Local Historical Transformation and World-system Theory*. New York: State University of New York Press, 1986.

_____. "The Process of Incorporation into the Capitalist World-System: the Case of China in the Nineteenth Century." *Review* vol. 8, no. 1 (Summer 1984): 91-116.

Sokolovsky, Joan. "Logic, Space, and Time: The Boundaries of the Capitalist World-Economy." Pp. 41-52 in Michael Timberlake, ed., *Urbanization in the World-Economy*. New York: Academic Press, 1985.

Stepan, Alfred. *Rethinking Military Politics*. Brazil and the Southern Cone. Princeton: Princeton University Press, 1988.

_____. *The State and Society: Peru in Comparative Perspective*. Princeton, NJ: Princeton University Press, 1978.

Sugihara, Kaoru. "Patterns of Inter-Asian Trade, 1898-1913." *Osaka City University Economic Review* No. 16 (1980): 55-76.

Sugiyama, Shinya. *Japan's Industrialization in the World Economy, 1859-1899*. London: Athlone Press, 1988.

Suh, Jae Jean. "Capitalist Class Formation and the Limits of Class Power in Korea." Ph.D. diss., University of Hawaii, 1988.

Suh, Sang-chul. *Growth and Structural Change in the Korean Economy, 1910-1940*. Cambridge MA: Harvard University Press, 1978.

Tagawa, Kōzō. "An Example of the Granary Workers in the Latter Half of the Yi Period." *Memoirs of the Tōyō Bunko* 37 (1979): 133-158.

Tiedemann, Arthur E. "Big Business and Politics in Prewar Japan." Pp. 267-316 in James William Morley, ed., *Dilemmas of Growth in Prewar Japan*. Princeton: Princeton University Press, 1971.

Toby, Ronald, P. *State and Diplomacy in Early Modern Japan. Asia in the Development of the Tokugawa Bakufu*. Princeton: Princeton University

Press, 1984.

Vleming jnr, J. L. "The Chinese Business Community in Netherlands India." Pp. 90-260 in M. R. Fernando and David Bulbeck, eds., *Chinese Economic Activity in Netherlands India.* Selected Translations from the Dutch. Singapore: ASEAN Economic Research Unit, Institute of Southeast Asian Studies, 1992.

Vinacke, Harold M. "Chinese Guilds." Pp. 219-221 in Edwin R. A. Seligman and Alvin Johnson, eds., *Encyclopedia of the Social Sciences.* New York: Macmillan, 1932.

Wade, Robert. *Governing the Market: Economic Theory and the Role of Government in East Asian Industrialization.* Princeton: Princeton University Press, 1990.

Wallerstein, Immanuel. *The Modern World-System III. The Second Era of Great Expansion of the Capitalist World-Economy, 1730-1840s.* New York: Academic Press, 1989.

_____, and William G. Martin. "Peripheralization of Southern Africa, II: Changes in Household Structure and Labor-Force Formation." *Review* (Ferhand Braudel Center) III (1979): 193-207.

_____. "The Rise and Future Demise of the World Capitalist System: Concepts for Comparative Analysis." Pp. 1-36 in Immanuel Wallerstein, ed., *The Capitalist World-Economy.* Cambridge: Cambridge University Press, 1979.

_____. "Class-Formation in the Capitalist World-Economy." *Politics and Society* vol. 5, no. 3 (1975): 367-376.

_____, ed. *Social Change. The Colonial Situation.* New York: John Wiley, 1966.

Washbrook, David. "South Asia, the World System, and World Capitalism." *Journal of Asian Studies* vol. 49, no. 3 (Aug. 1990): 479-508.

Weber, Max. *General Economic History..* New York: Collier, 1961.

Weems, Benjamin. *Reform, Rebellion and the Heavenly Way.* Tucson: University of Arizona Press, 1964.

Weems, Clarence N. "Reformist Thought of the Independence Program (1896-1898)." Pp. 163-218 in Yung-hwan Jo, ed., *Korea's Response to the West.* Kalamazoo, Michigan: The Korean Research and Publications, Inc, 1971.

Wells, Kenneth M. "Yun Ch'i-ho and the Quest for National Integrity: the Formation of a Christian Approach to Korean Nationalism at the end of the Chosŏn Dynasty." *Korea Journal* vol. 22, no. 1 (January 1982): 42-59.

Wickizier, V. D., and M. K. Bennett. *The Rice Economy of Monsoon Asia.* Stanford: Food Research Institute, Stanford University, 1941.

Wilkinson, W. H. "The Corean Government." *Korean Repository* 4 (1897), p. 12.

Williams, Jack F. "Sugar: The Sweetner in Taiwan's Development." Pp. 219-252 in Ronald G. Knapp, ed., *China's Island Frontier: Studies in the*

Historical Geography of Taiwan. Honolulu: University Press of Hawaii, 1980.

Winckler, Edwin A. "Mass Political Incorporation, 1500-2000." Pp. 41-66 in Edwin A. Winckler and Susan Greenhalgh, eds., *Contending Approaches to the Political Economy of Taiwan*. Armonk, NY: M. E. Sharpe, Inc., 1988.

Wolf, Eric R. *Europe and the People Without History*. Berkeley, CA: University of California Press, 1982.

Woo, Jung-en. *Race to the Swift: State and Finance in Korean Industrialization*. New York: Columbia University Press, 1991.

World Bank. *The East Asian Miracle: Economic Growth and Public Policy*. New York: Oxford University Press, 1993.

Worsley, Peter. "One World or Three? A Critique of the World-system Theory of Immanuel Wallerstein." Pp. 504-525 in David Held et al., eds. *States and Societies*. New York: New York University Press, 1983.

Wuthnow, Robert. *Communities of Discourse: Ideology and Social Structure in the Reformation, the Enlightenment, and European Socialism*. Cambridge: Harvard University Press, 1989.

Yanaga, Chitoshi. *Big Business in Japanese Politics*. New Haven: Yale University Press, 1968.

Yanaihara, Tadao. "The Problems of Japanese Administration in Korea." *Pacific Affairs* 11, 2 (June 1938): 198-207.

Yoo Se Hee. "The Korean Communist Movement and the Peasantry under Japanese Rule." Ph.D. diss., Columbia University, 1974.

Index

About the Book and Author

Exploring the interaction among system, state, and society, this book illuminates the social and economic history of late nineteenth- and early twentieth-century colonial Korea. Dennis McNamara argues that transformation within and trade abroad, led by rice exports, spurred Korea's shift from isolation to inclusion in a modern regional system. In his chronicle of the bustling grain export center of Inch'ŏn, the author draws an engaging portrait of leading Korean brokers and their efforts to maintain autonomy while cooperating with Japanese millers.

McNamara contends that Korean precedents of enterprise and guild association, couple with Japanese colonial patterns of accommodation, deeply affected the emergence of a modern Korean business community. By focusing especially on the role of rice brokers and millers as important agents of change, this study advances our understanding of the formation of the Korean business community and offers valuable insights in to the trade history of one of the world's leading export nations.

Dennis L. McNamara is Y. H. Park Professor of Sociology and Korean Studies and chair of the Sociology Department at Georgetown University.